50 FLIPPEN BRILLIANT SOUTH AFRICANS

Alexander Parker
& Tim Richman
with cartoons from the archive of
Zapiro

50 FLIPPEN BRILLIANT SOUTH AFRICANS

Alexander Parker
& Tim Richman
with cartoons from the archive of
Zapiro

Published by Mercury
an imprint of Burnet Media

•

Burnet Media is the publisher of Mercury and Two Dogs books
PO Box 53557, Kenilworth, 7745, South Africa
info@burnetmedia.co.za,
www.burnetmedia.co.za

•

First published 2012
1 3 5 7 9 8 6 4 2

•

Publication © 2012 Burnet Media
All text © 2012 Alexander Parker & Tim Richman
Illustrations © Zapiro, except where noted

•

Lyrics from *Biko* by Peter Gabriel © 1980 Peter Gabriel,
published by Real World Music Ltd / EMI Music Publishing
Lyrics from *Impi* by Johnny Clegg and Juluka © 1981 Johnny Clegg and Juluka,
published by Rhythm Safari

•

The cartoons and caricatures herein are replications
or adaptations of works by Zapiro that have appeared in a variety
of publications over the years. They are all products of the
specific circumstances of the time.

•

Distributed by Jacana Media www.jacana.co.za
Printed and bound by Ultra Litho, Johannesburg

•

ISBN 9780987043719

About the authors

Alexander Parker is a journalist and author whose work has appeared in the *Sunday Times*, *Business Day*, *Stuff Magazine*, *The Witness*, *The Financial Mail*, *FHM* and *Top Car*, among others. He was the launch deputy editor of *Top Gear* magazine, a producer and presenter of SABC3's *Car Quest*, and is currently motoring editor at *Business Day*. He is the author of the forerunner to this book, *50 People Who Stuffed Up South Africa*, as well as *25 Cars To Drive Before You Die*.

Tim Richman is an author and editor, and a publisher of South African books. He has written for a number of local and international publications, including *GQ*, *Men's Health* and *Vogue Living*. He is the co-author of the best-selling *Is It Just Me Or Is Everything Kak?* series and a number of other titles.

About the cartoonist

Zapiro – also known as Jonathan Shapiro – is the editorial cartoonist for the *Mail & Guardian*, the *Sunday Times* and *The Times*. Born in Cape Town, he studied architecture and became active in the UDF in 1983. He was detained by the security police shortly before taking up a Fulbright Scholarship at the School of Visual Arts in New York in 1988. He has published 17 cartoon collections, the most recent of which is *But Will It Stand Up In Court?*, as well as a large-format hardcover, *The Mandela Files*. He has received numerous international and South African awards and holds two honorary doctorates.

Acknowledgments

From Alexander Parker: As I emphasise in the Introduction to come, writing this book was a collaborative process, with collaborator-in-chief being Jonathan Shapiro, a.k.a. Zapiro. His counsel has been invaluable and there is little point adding to a general chorus of approval for his body of work other than to say it brings this book to life magnificently. Many thanks obviously go to him, and to Eleanora Bresler, his assistant. I cannot express enough how grateful I am to Tim Richman, whose patience, forbearance, talent and sheer bloody hard work has to be seen to be believed. For introducing me to history as it ought to be known, I will always be grateful to my much-missed friend and mentor David Rattray and to Nicky Rattray of Fugitive's Drift Lodge. Thanks also go to: the many readers of *50 People Who Stuffed Up South Africa* who have got hold of me on Twitter (@thealexparker) and have helped me stay the course; Talk Radio 702's Stephen Grootes, for lending me his encyclopaedic political brain; Peter Bruce, my boss, for allowing me to do this, and for letting me come home to *Business Day*; Dylan Muhlenberg and Miles Keylock, both highly talented men of the South African magazine industry, for their contributions; Stuart Hendricks, for everything; my friends Nick and Lianda Holleman, Cathryn Pearman and Toby Shapshak, for their help at a difficult time, and Pierre Steyn for understanding. I could not have done this without the ever-present advice and help of my parents, Jim and Jeannie, my daughter's carer Gertrude Mpila and my partner Bronwyn Nortje. My daughter Olweyn, now only four, will one day read this and understand just how much she helped me too, by being the light of my life and an ever-present source of joy.

From Tim Richman: On top of everyone Alex mentions, many thanks for their contributions, feedback and counsel go to Rob Ambler-Smith, Brett Aubin, Jon Burnett, Ed Durrant, Larry Pharo and Chris Warncke; the men at SASASU; Kelly Burke, Tim Noakes and Ryan Sandes; Brian Warner and Heidi Jee; Brian Richman; Robert Rowand; Sean Fraser and Ania Rokita; Shay Heydenrych, Bridget Impey and all at Jacana; and Francesca Beighton. A particularly large thank you to my beautiful wife, Jules, who was more than just inspiring and supportive; she was very often the critical voice of insight. And, of course, to Alex, for bringing excitement and brilliance to my work life – long may the collaboration continue.

To Ben and Lily

Contents

Introduction

IT CAN'T HAVE BEEN EVEN DAYS after the publication of *50 People Who Stuffed Up South Africa* that people were telling me to start writing this book. I was only too happy to oblige, even if I'm not completely convinced they were serious. And I am only too happy to have done it because it's been nothing less than an epic adventure.

It may be obvious in hindsight, but it is far easier to be rude about someone when you don't care whether offence is taken than it is to heap praise (while avoiding the saccharine). And so, while writing a book is never easy, I must concede that *50 Flippen Brilliant South Africans* has had an exponentially harder birth than its forebear did. It has taken longer, my publisher and I have argued more, and choosing the candidates has been a more complex process. But it was, ultimately, brilliant fun.

As I type, the ratings agency Moody's has downgraded South Africa, the government has cancelled valuable trade treaties with our most important partners and capital is in flight after the Marikana massacre and its ensuing shambles. And all the while the Zuma administration vacillates as Rome burns. Times are truly worrying. Researching the people in here has, though, reminded me that we are a tough, resourceful, belligerent, talented, passionate and wonderful nation. It has also taught me, as seems to be the way in life, that the more you know, the more you realise you don't know. The importance and the diversity of what South Africans have achieved really blows the mind, and that has meant that this book has undergone far more of a consultative process than the previous one – to ensure that, whether we're discussing struggle politics or Zulu fighting tactics or astronomical history or surfing in J-Bay or zef culture, every entry here has the depth and credibility it deserves. One wonderful revelation that came from writing this book is the realisation that people are so willing to give up their time for a positive venture like this; the amount of encouragement we have received – before even signing off the proofs – has been eye-opening. And because no-one ever really reads the Acknowledgments I would like to emphasise again how thankful I am to all those who added their expertise to proceedings, including several of the entrants themselves, and particularly the 51st brilliant South African in these pages, Zapiro.

Another realisation I have had in the making of this book is that South Africa produces far more truly brilliant people than we do the plonkers who made the first one. Inevitably a compilation of excellent South Africans will be controversial and may even be cause for anger, so I would like to emphasise how much time and thought went into this selection, and how frequently it was revised. How could we leave out Oliver Tambo and Natalie du Toit and Hugh Masekela and Mike Horn and Phillip Tobias and and and? Good questions. And if you feel strongly about those or any other omissions, or some of the more controversial inclusions, do please direct all emails on the matter, particularly the outraged ones, to my publisher at info@burnetmedia.co.za.*

So, I have taken far more advice in the making of this book, I have had to work harder generally – as it turns out, that's not always a bad thing – and I've been far more inspired for it. What that work has established is that this country is worth fighting for and, despite the litany of appalling governments we've had to suffer in our history, that we'll always struggle on gamely. We have overcome colonialism and apartheid and, I have no doubt, we will overcome kleptocracy and the looting taking place now. Let's just hope it doesn't require the sacrifice that some of the folk in these pages have had to make.

Here they are, then: 50 flippen brilliant South Africans. Some lovable, some lucky, some unpleasant and yet talented. I hope you approve.

Alexander Parker
October 2012

---

* For those keeping track, we've counted Ian Player & Magqubu Ntombela and Walter & Albertina Sisulu as four people, but Eric Merrifield & Aubrey Krüger as one. It makes sense, promise.

Christiaan Barnard

8 November 1922 – 2 September 2001

Pioneering heart surgeon; celebrity doctor; author; South African playboy; internationally renowned philanderer

MANY, MANY YEARS BEFORE DR PHIL AND HIS IRKSOME ILK, there was Christiaan Neethling Barnard, the rock star with a scalpel – the man who performed the first successful heart transplant on a human being, at Groote Schuur Hospital in December 1967 and who became, as a result, one of the most famous people in the world. While there will always be the party-poopers who remind us that the patient, Louis Washkansky, only survived for another eighteen days, and that Barnard got the jump on a number of other surgeons only with the good grace of the medical gods, there's no denying that he became a global sensation. And a rather photogenic one he was, too. The operation led to a lifetime spent in the international spotlight, one of affairs and high-end womanising and not a small amount of *skandaal* and controversy.

Take a small-town boy from a humble upbringing in Beaufort West and thrust him into the global spotlight, and there will always be the potential for trouble. "On Saturday I was a surgeon in South Africa, very little known, and on Monday I was world-renowned," they say he said. Either way, it was true.

The problems began because Barnard was a good-looking guy, a dashing medical hero who became almost instantly feted the world over. "Maybe that was one of the reasons for a lot of my trouble," he once mused. "I never acted like a big professor. I liked girls and dancing."

One of the girls he liked, once he had the opportunity, was Sophia

Loren. Another was the sultry Italian actress-cum-sex-symbol Gina Lollobrigida. Probably as a result of a highly publicised affair with the latter, Barnard's first marriage of 21 years, to nurse Aletta Louw, mother of his two children, collapsed. This, in today's terms, wouldn't be unlike a doctor from Groote Schuur having a hot and heavy affair with, say, Halle Berry or Heidi Klum. It was, to say the least, notable; Barnard's medical renown had quickly morphed into high-society celebrity.

After another alleged affair, this time with French actress Françoise Hardy, Barnard went on to marry Johannesburg socialite Barbara Zoellner. She was 19, he was 48. True love? Perhaps. A possibly apocryphal tale recounted in *People* magazine has it that when Barnard told fellow surgeon Denton Cooley he intended to marry a teenager he was advised that "when men of our age marry a young woman, it may prove fatal!" The story goes that Barnard responded by telling Cooley, "Well, if she dies, I'll get a younger one…"

That marriage also bore two children and also failed, this time after twelve years. Barnard, now in his mid-sixties, then met and married Karin Stezkorn, a young model – yet another marriage that produced a set of two siblings and ended in divorce.

So then, far from being a saint, *onse* Dr Barnard had a wandering eye and was oh-so-fallibly human. But – and while he made a good pitch for entry in these pages on his philandering alone – he's here because he was a seriously good heart doctor, not to mention bold and pioneering.

Back in those days people would just die. Got a heart issue? Too bad. In the modern world, heart transplants are almost routine, and can extend the lives of sufferers for years – more than 3,500 such procedures are performed around the world every year, and 75 percent of today's transplant recipients survive for more than five years. For this, Chris Barnard has to take a healthy dose of credit.

It is true – and, of course, entirely unsurprising – that there were other doctors around the world who were working towards the first human-to-human heart transplant. By 1964 already, a Dr James Hardy had inserted a chimpanzee's heart into a human in Mississippi. Unsurprisingly that experiment, and others with sheep hearts, didn't end well, but progress

> "Chris's depth of knowledge of cardiac surgery and his ability to induce his team to deliver their best efforts resulted in the achievement of the highest standards and excellent results. His staff had to accept his rigid, non-compromising leadership but... his patients and their relatives never had reason to complain because our results were excellent. I had many problems with Chris, but his contribution to cardiac surgery is far greater than that for which he is remembered."
>
> *– Marius Barnard, writing in his memoir Defining Moments*

was being made. (Amazingly, Barnard would himself transplant a chimpanzee heart into a human *after* the Washkansky transplant. The patient would have died anyway, but it was controversial nonetheless.) Importantly, the realisation that the procedure itself was not that complicated meant that, eventually, someone just had to do the thing. As with many ground-breaking discoveries, inventions and procedures throughout history, that someone could have been a number of different people – but it turned out to be Barnard, who was perhaps just a little more game than the rest.

In late 1967, he realised that in Washkansky, he had an ideal candidate: still relatively young at just 55, and suffering from untreatable cardiac failure. His prognosis was very clear: he would die within weeks, possibly days.

Barnard later wrote that for Washkansky the decision to go ahead with such an experimental procedure would not have been difficult: "For a dying man it is not a difficult decision, because he knows he is at the end. If a lion chases you to the bank of a river filled with crocodiles, you will leap into the water convinced you have a chance to swim to the other side. But you would not accept such odds if there was no lion."

Indeed so. Barnard's next good move was to find the right donor. Of course, whenever a life is saved by transplantation, there is the equal and opposite emotion for another family somewhere. Donors aren't elderly or sick. They're usually young and in the flush of life, which is how –

after an earlier donor's heart had become unusable before the operation could begin – fate found 24-year-old Denise Darvall, out shopping for cake on Main Road in Observatory, Cape Town, when she was hit by a drunk driver, rendering her brain dead.

That the operation went incredibly smoothly is testimony both to the skills of those involved and the spirit of adventure in an almost amateur-seeming give-it-a-bash era. For one, it was a Saturday night so not all the attending physicians were in the most appropriate state of mental wellbeing. Marius Barnard, Chris's brother and a critical member of the team, was "well wined and dined", in his own words, having been celebrating his wedding anniversary with friends when he was called to surgery. Another essential doctor, tasked with Washkansky's post-operative care, was also summoned from a party and was said to have been so hammered that he passed out in the viewing gallery and missed the whole procedure. For good measure, the anaesthetist was Dr Cecil Moss, ex-Springbok wing; imagine you were going in for pioneering heart surgery today and Chester Williams was the guy in charge of putting you to sleep…

"Dit werk." (It works.)

– Chris Barnard's reaction once Louis Washkansky's new heart had started beating spontaneously

Afterwards, most of the team involved seemed naively unaware of the magnitude of their achievements. Local and international media went absolutely bonkers; after all, doctors had just replaced a man's heart, the very organ that defines life and humanity. It was the greatest medical procedure ever performed. But Groote Schuur hadn't even arranged a press conference.

Sadly, that post-operative care was the problem, as was always predicted. Washkansky died of pneumonia less than three weeks later, his body weakened by the immunosuppressant drugs he was taking. But

Barnard and his team had crossed a barrier, and had extended the life of a man by transplanting a heart. It was – and it still is – quite astonishing.

And Barnard carried on. He performed a further ten transplants from 1967 to 1973 even as many surgeons gave up on the procedure due to the poor survival rates. In the two-and-a-half years after Washkansky, approximately 150 heart transplants were performed all over the world, from India to Venezuela, Turkey to Texas. Most patients died within days, if not hours. Only 21 of these operations were deemed vaguely successful. The Groote Schuur team was one of the few that produced good results; Barnard's second patient lived for a year and a half and his sixth, Dirk van Zyl, survived for 23 years after his operation in 1971. Later, the introduction of the immunosuppressant drug cyclosporine, which prevents rejection with far fewer side effects than other drugs, helped to make heart (and other organ) transplants the successful medical procedures they have now become.* In 1975 Barnard devised the so-called heterotopic transplant, in which the failing heart is left inside the body and given a chance to recover while the donor heart works away, which itself can be removed eventually if the original heart recovers. He performed another 49 of these operations until his retirement in 1983 at the age of 61.

He eventually packed it in due to the chronic arthritis that had dogged him through his adult life, meaning he could no longer perform surgery. But he could write books – two autobiographies, four thrillers and three health- and heart-related self-help books – even as he kept his eye on the skirts and kept making the news for this, that and the other.

There is no doubt, in the end review, that Chris Barnard was a complex, troubled and fascinating creature. He had a monumental ego, was a difficult boss and fell out with everyone, including his family. He was a great charmer and outspoken against apartheid at a time when

---

* Cyclosporine has its own interesting story. It was discovered in Basel, Switzerland, in the early 1970s, having been isolated from a fungus, *Tolypocladium inflatum*, from a soil sample from Norway. When people talk about great medical cures and advancements possibly existing undiscovered in wild rain forests or exotic environments, this is the type of thing they're talking about.

> "He was widely seen as a medical maverick, somewhere between God and Frankenstein, hailed or reviled for his apparent power over this most mystical of human organs."
>
> *– Extract from Chris Barnard's obituary in The Times*

other high-profile South Africans were not. (Though he would say later that he should have been more outspoken.) He was obsessed with his looks and staying young, he sought the limelight and the ladies – and he was eventually hounded and criticised by an unrelenting press for that and everything else. But he was a meticulous surgeon who produced excellent results. And, don't forget, he changed the world.

So, a truly great South African was Dr Barnard, so long as we all agree that even the greatest people are flawed.

Steve Biko

18 December 1946 – 12 September 1977

Icon of the Black Consciousness Movement; political martyr; leader of men; socialiser; drinker; talker; friend; inspirational human being

THE WONDERFUL THING ABOUT BANTU STEPHEN BIKO was that he scared the crap out of the apartheid government. He did this by proving the very lie that justified their position in power: that white people, by virtue of the colour of their skin, were superior to black people. And in doing so he became a hero to blacks and whites alike.

Steve Biko spent less than a decade on the South African political landscape. He first rose to prominence as the co-founder and inaugural president of the all-black South African Students' Organisation (SASO) in 1969; he gained a meaningful following as the voice of the Black Consciousness Movement in the early 1970s; and he was killed in 1977, aged 30. (By contrast, Nelson Mandela's political career only really got going at that age.) But in the years given to him, Biko completely reinvigorated the anti-apartheid movement, particularly among students and the young, and he lived to see the first real shots of a new and fiery revolution in the form of the 1976 Soweto riots. What he could not see was that the flames of this revolution, fanned by his vicious murder in detention, would eventually burn down the apartheid edifice that he fought so passionately against.

Born in King William's Town in the Eastern Cape, Biko developed what he would refer to as "authority problems" at a relatively early age. His father died when he was four and his mother worked for decades as a domestic worker – a familiar tale for many South African revolutionaries. He was arrested at age 16 because of his brother's suspected sympathies with the banned Pan Africanist Congress (PAC) and was, as a result, expelled from the Lovedale College in Alice where he was studying on a bursary. Such were the injustices of being black at the time. Still, there was no denying his smarts and when he eventually matriculated he was awarded a scholarship to study medicine at the University of Natal – Non-European section, of course.

By the time he started his first year in 1966, there was a dearth of black leadership in South Africa. The ANC and PAC had been banned in 1960. The Rivonia Trial had concluded in 1964 and the likes of Nelson Mandela, Walter Sisulu, Govan Mbeki and Ahmed Kathrada were serving life sentences on Robben Island. Oliver Tambo, Thabo Mbeki, Chris Hani and others had gone into exile, and two years later Chief Albert Luthuli would be dead. Even as the 1960s saw social revolution sweeping throughout the Western world and African states gaining independence one after the other, it was a time of systematic oppression in apartheid South Africa. The Nationalists could sit back in grim satisfaction because the native was cowed.

Or so they thought.

At university Biko became quickly politicised, and in 1967 he began developing an idea that would later crystallise as the Black Consciousness Movement. His fellow black students, he found, were being condescended by well-meaning liberal white activists who nonetheless told them what to do and how to behave. There was a clear superiority/inferiority-complex delineation between white and black students that would have to change before the latter could free themselves from oppression. Blacks, Biko believed, would have to liberate their minds before they could liberate themselves.

Together with Barney Pityana he fleshed out his ideas and founded the SASO, which rejected the term "non-white" and defined all blacks, Indians and coloureds as "black". Members stressed the identity of blackness and the need for self-sufficiency, self-respect and solidarity. The idea grew as they travelled the country from campus to campus and Black Consciousness, "an attitude of mind and a way of life", came into being. It was influenced by authors, philosophers, leaders and movements all around the world, including Frantz Fanon, Jean-Paul Sartre, Malcolm X and the Black Panthers. "Black man, you are on your own" came to be the movement's rallying cry, and the likes of Mongane Wally Serote, Mandla Langa and Njabulo Ndebele found themselves attracted by the promise of a different way of thinking.

As Black Consciousness progressed into the new decade and as it spread around the country, Biko was always the face and personality behind it, but he wasn't taken in by power politics and he didn't allow himself to be dominant over others. By all accounts, he loved a drink and he loved a party, and the movement seemed to be fuelled by the social nature of its get-togethers, which often ran all night. "I would fall asleep and I would wake up and Steve would still be on his chair, talking and drinking," remembers Serote. "And the thing that struck you was his great joy at being among people. This seemed to inspire him."

Indeed, people were attracted to Biko's charismatic and genuine nature. He respected all-comers, black and white, and was interested in anyone willing to engage – sometimes rather too much, as his pretty young wife Ntsiki would discover. Having married in 1970, the Bikos

"You are either alive and proud or you are dead, and when you are dead you can't care anyway. And your method of death can itself be a politicising thing… So if you can overcome the personal fear of death, which is a highly irrational thing, you know, then you're on the way."

– Steve Biko

had two children, but the life of a gregarious travelling activist was never going to make for a stable home. Biko developed something of a reputation as a womaniser and eventually divided his affections between two great loves: Ntsiki and Mamphela Ramphele, one of the founders of the movement, whom he'd met at university and with whom there was an undeniable intellectual and passionate connection. (Today she is a hugely respected businesswoman and academic, and one-time managing director of the World Bank.) They also had two children, the first of whom died as an infant and the second of whom was born four months after Biko was killed.

And there it is: Biko's death, one of the defining moments in the history of anti-apartheid activism, and one of its most appalling.

It goes almost without saying that Biko was harassed, locked up and banned by the state for his efforts over the years, as were all the other major personalities of the movement he had inspired. In 1973 he was restricted to King William's Town indefinitely, effectively becoming his own jailer. Yet he repeatedly violated the order, taking visitors, travelling out of the area and generally furthering the movement. His defiance and demeanour seemed to aggravate the cruel men of the Special Branch no end – he never stood back when confronted by them in detention or during midnight raids on his mother's house, and in one instance he is said to have knocked out the teeth of an officer. They simply couldn't handle him any longer, and when Biko was stopped at a roadblock in Grahamstown in August 1977, his time had come. He was taken to Port

> "In South Africa, Biko and his contemporaries broke the stunned silence of their time. The refusal of a new generation of young blacks to be subservient or humiliated, even in the face of death, changed the nature of the struggle. Biko himself lived and died by this truth."
>
> *– Lindy Wilson*

Elizabeth and incarcerated naked for eighteen days before being tortured to the point of death by men who were the very epitome of what they thought the average black man was: stupid, immoral and soulless. By the time of his arrest Biko had proved that, despite every racist law in the book, he could not be beaten – except physically, with fists and chairs and weighted rubber pipes. So that is what they did. After the beatings he was chained to a grille, and left naked and dying on a blanket covered in his own urine. Four days later he was loaded into the back of a Land Rover – by this stage probably beyond saving – and driven through the night, still naked, more than a thousand kilometres to Pretoria Central Prison. He died there on a mat on the afternoon of 12 September 1977.

One of the enduring oddities of the apartheid state was the effort it took to maintain the façade that what it was doing was morally right and in everyone's best interests. So, instead of sweeping the death of Biko under the carpet – as, say, communist China or any number of Eastern bloc countries would have done – Prime Minister BJ Vorster launched an inquest just two months later (admittedly under international pressure). The evidence was presented and it was horrendously damning, as it could only be. The state's original contention that Biko had died as a result of a hunger strike was quickly changed to accidental death, but no right-thinking person could believe that a shackled prisoner had fallen against a wall and given himself extensive head and brain injuries then "shammed" severe neurological injuries for five days. In one instance, sworn statements that were supposedly read to Biko causing him to react violently were found to be dated after his death. Moreover, the apartheid state's contempt for human rights was highlighted for all to see, as in the explanation the commanding officer gave for not even granting Biko a pair of underpants to wear while shackled – so that he wouldn't try to commit suicide. But it took the presiding Chief Magistrate just one night to consider his verdict and three minutes to deliver it: Biko had injured himself in a scuffle with policemen, there was no-one to blame, case closed. It was an arrogant and thoughtless cover-up – as had occurred whenever an activist had accidentally fallen out of a prison window or slipped on the soap in the shower by mistake – but if those in power thought no-one would care once again, they were to be proved very, very wrong.*

"I am not glad and I am not sorry about Mr Biko. His death leaves me cold," the minister of police Jimmy Kruger went on record to say in the days after he died. But it certainly didn't leave the rest of the world cold, and it played an enormous role in turning and even radicalising the opinions of the international community and large sections of the local white population against the apartheid state. A young investigative journalist by the name of Helen Zille was instrumental in exposing details of the cover-up for her newspaper the *Rand Daily Mail*, which was censured by the government as a result. The long-running editor of the *Daily Despatch* in East London, Donald Woods, who was a friend of Biko and had regularly published his writing, was banned after photographing Biko's battered corpse. In 1978 he fled the country through Lesotho to London and remained an active anti-apartheid

---

* Twenty years after Biko's death, five members of the security police sought amnesty from the Truth And Reconciliation Commission for their roles in the killing and the subsequent cover-up of what happened. They were Harold Snyman, Gideon Nieuwoudt, Daniel Siebert, Ruben Marx and Jacobus Beneke. They testified that they had assaulted Biko without the intention to kill him, and they all stuck by the story that he had been injured in a once-off scuffle. No-one accepted responsibility for a decisive blow or blows. None of them received amnesty, but none of them was prosecuted. Snyman, the senior officer at the time of Biko's death, died shortly after of lung cancer.

Meanwhile, the South African Medical And Dental Council eventually investigated two of the doctors who had treated Biko at the time, Benjamin Tucker and Ivor Lang, after many years of efforts by several individuals to bring them to justice. They were found guilty in 1985 of disgraceful and improper conduct for effectively denying him treatment and thus ensuring his death. Tucker was struck from the medical roll and Lang was reprimanded.

The Biko family sued the state for his wrongful death in 1979 and settled out of court for R65,000.

> "Easily the most charismatic figure I have ever met, he was at home in any situation, all of which he would effortlessly dominate. He was one of those clever, tall, good-looking, loose-limbed charmers who could get you to do almost anything; and be genuinely concerned for your safety while you did it. All the while you were aware that this was an extraordinarily courageous man. Not just in a crowd of supporters, but alone, too, when courage matters most. The bastards who killed him were probably too stupid to appreciate what manner of leader we would end up with if they murdered our authentic leaders back then."
>
> *– Peter Bruce, Business Day editor,*
> *writing on the 35th anniversary of Biko's death, September 2012*

campaigner. His subsequent book, *Biko*, would go on to inspire the 1987 film *Cry Freedom*, starring Denzel Washington and Kevin Kline.

Biko's legacy – his legend even – has lasted well into the following millennium. Indeed, the University of Cape Town's annual Steve Biko Memorial Lecture was first delivered in 2000, and the likes of Thabo Mbeki, Trevor Manuel, Desmond Tutu and Ben Okri have spoken to mark the anniversary of his death. Prominent biographies of the man are regularly released, and his life is seldom reviewed without contention of some sort. During his lifetime many of his beliefs were heavily criticised. Some still are, and his standing on the anti-apartheid struggle hierarchy varies among different parties and organisations. And yet there remains massive admiration and respect for him in the wider population.

Within black communities his heroic appeal is obvious. Biko came to represent Black Consciousness; he was the fearless champion of the black man's identity at a time when leadership was scarce and vitally needed. And, of course, he died for his people in the process. But there was also his broader appeal, to the foreign world and to white South Africans who barely knew his name when he died. Lindy Wilson, one of his many biographers, writes, "Perhaps the thing he least set out to do was to convert white South Africans, yet the Black Conscious Movement jolted white youth into a profound self-examination that changed the political direction of a whole generation." Maybe they came to sense the personal magnetism and brilliance of the man; maybe they were won over by the fact that even in his most militant voice, and even while guiding a movement for black identity, he always preached a message of non-racism. Or maybe they were just amazed by his knowing sacrifice when they discovered that he had predicted his own death before the age of 30 and willingly faced it. He had been arrested so often and come to understand the ways of the Special Branch that he believed it was only a matter of time before they took it on themselves to kill him, as had happened to many other activists. By renouncing the movement or simply sticking to the restrictions of his banning order, he could have stopped the process and saved himself. But he was one of those rare men who disproved the notion of the great 20th-century writer John Fowles that "if a person is intelligent then of course he is a physical coward".

Steve Biko was handsome, popular, well spoken, outspoken – a born leader. He was also intelligent – an intellectual not encumbered by ivory towers. More than that, he was compassionate and all-embracing. Which is to say, he was everything the cruel men of apartheid were not, and they feared him something awful as a result. In the end, they killed him for it. But unlike so many other political deaths, the killing of Steve Biko was not in vain. He became a martyr in the most admirable sense of the word. In the lyrics of Peter Gabriel's 1980 single, *Biko*:

You can blow out a candle
But you can't blow out a fire,
Once the flame begins to catch
The wind will blow it higher.
Oh Biko, Biko, because Biko,
Oh Biko, Biko, because Biko,
Yihla moja, yihla moja [Come spirit, come spirit]
A man is dead, a man is dead.
And the eyes of the world are watching now,
Watching now.

Margaret Calvert

b. 12 May 1936

Graphic designer; co-creator of "Transport" and modern road signage; guiding hand of the modern driver (even more so than Satellite Navigation)

FONTS, LIKE FLUSH TOILETS, are generally taken for granted. Many people are happy to write an email in Outlook Express using (trusty, plodding) <u>Arial regular</u> without giving it a second thought. Or they'll create all their Word documents using the default template, even though <u>Times New Roman</u> is possibly the most boring (and yet readable) typeface in the world. Other people might try new fonts from time to time because they happen to find them more interesting or they just make a nice change. But unless you are in design or happen to be a typeface nerd, you probably don't take more than a passing notice of the way the letters on a page are formed.

For typographers and graphic designers, the vast world of type is fascinating, complex and steeped in history, and the creation of a typeface is a heady blend of art and science. Like the speakers that play your music or the screen that transmits your television pictures, fonts and typefaces* play a critical role in conveying the essence of what you're experiencing; in this case, written words – whether they're on a billboard, on a T-shirt or in a book.

---

* The definitions of "font" and "typeface" vary. For purposes here, a typeface is a complete family of letters and symbols, and a font is a subset within that family. So Minion Pro regular and *Minion Pro italics* are two fonts within the Minion Pro typeface. In practice the words are virtually interchangeable.

Take the font you are reading right now, <u>Minion Pro</u>. It is an evolution of Minion, which was designed in 1990 by Robert Slimbach, who took his inspiration from classical typefaces of the late Renaissance. Like Times New Roman and unlike Arial, it is a serif typeface. Which is to say there are little embellishments on many of the strokes of the letters; as a result, it is not as "clean" as sans-serif type, but it is considered easier to read in longer texts. In essence, Minion Pro is a flexible, widely used typeface, popular for its elegance, good looks and excellent readability. (Great for an irreverent work of non-fiction.)

If fonts are taken for granted, then there is surely no font more taken for granted than the one that appears on your average road sign. Modern road signs are so efficient at what they do that drivers just assume they've always been there, quietly guiding us on our automotive ways, whether it's down the N1 from Johannesburg to Cape Town or around some men at work on a trip to the shops. But they haven't. Modern road signs were invented, along with the font that accompanies them all, **Transport**, in the late 1950s and 1960s – by a South African woman, no less.

Admittedly Margaret Calvert was the co-inventor of **Transport** and its related family of road signs, and admittedly she moved from South Africa to the United Kingdom when she was 14, but the fact that her name is indelibly tied to what has become one of the most regularly read typefaces in the world in the last fifty years is an impressive feat nonetheless. These days she is a minor celebrity in the type-design and motoring worlds, with guest appearances in books, magazines and even on *Top Gear*.

Born in Durban in 1936, Calvert moved to the UK with her family in 1950. After school, she studied at the Chelsea School of Art in London, where she came under the tutelage of Jock Kinneir, an established designer. In 1957 Kinneir received an important, life-changing commission after – as tended to happen in those days – striking up a conversation with someone while waiting for the bus. That someone turned out to be an architect involved in the building of London's new Gatwick Airport; he was looking for a person to do the signs for the place and, hey, Kinneir looked like the right guy for the job. Kinneir took on Calvert as his assistant to help him get it done.

It was the start of a long and fruitful type-creation partnership. The success of the Gatwick signage led to a job for P&O Orient Lines, which then led to a job for the UK's Ministry of Transport – the one that would secure their legacies.

The British government had just finished work on the first stage of what would become the M1, the country's first highspeed motorway, from London to Yorkshire. Problem was there was a profusion of different and confusing road signs at the time, both in the UK and around Europe. They were "at best confusing and at worst dangerous to Britain's motorists, and threatened to be particularly so when driving at high speed on a motorway", as per the Design Museum archives.

Kinneir and Calvert's brief was to create a signage system for Britain's new motorways, and what they eventually came up with was, in design and driver-safety terms, pure genius. After much research on the topic, they worked out that there wasn't a suitable typeface for their purposes, so they devised one of their own. This was **Transport**, as it later became known, a modern sans serif with soft, friendly curves to make it more appealing than many of the modernist letters then in use. It was specifically designed for drivers to be able to read place names as quickly as possible. According to Simon Garfield, author of *Just My Type*, the key identifiers of the font are, "the curve on the end of the l, and the obliquely cut curved strokes of the letters a, c, e, f, g, j, s, t and y".

Kinneir and Calvert worked out that words would be recognised more easily when spelt out in Sentence Case rather than in UPPER CASE, as was the style at the time. They had hit on the fact that people tend to gain an understanding of a word without reading every letter within it,

TRANSPORT FONT:
The quick brown fox jumps over the lazy dog

but the exact use of the letters was particularly challenging, and their use of "careful letter-spacing on a tiling system without the loss of word-shape" was critical to their success.

It was a pioneering and time-consuming process, with many previously unconsidered aspects to investigate. For example, what colour combinations to use? They experimented with many, and finally settled on white on blue for their highway signs. (Take a cruise down your nearest highway to see how well it works.) Crucially, Kinneir and Calvert also developed a set of simple shapes, symbols and illustrations that perfectly complemented the **Transport** typeface.

"Style never came into it," Calvert later recalled. "You were driving towards the absolute essence. How could we reduce the appearance to make the maximum sense [at] minimum cost?" But even this contention belies their achievement. The system they had devised was a complete triumph precisely because all the elements came together in perfect and painstakingly designed harmony – so much so that the Ministry of Transport asked them to expand it in 1963 to incorporate signage for all roads across Britain. Here Calvert came into her own, designing many of the pictograms we still see today, such as the cow warning drivers to look out for farm animals, the schoolchildren holding hands to signal children crossing and the man digging to indicate roadworks ahead (alternatively "man opening umbrella"). The former was based on a relative's cow called Patience; the second was based on a photograph of Calvert as a girl.

The creation of brand-new road signage for all of Britain was a massive project, taking ten years to complete, by which time Calvert had become a full partner at Kinneir Calvert Associates. The end result was the Kinneir-Calvert system, which "combined a universal amalgamation

> "It is sad but true to say that most of us take our surroundings for granted. Direction signs and street names, for instance, are as vital as a drop of oil in an engine, without which the moving parts would seize up; one can picture the effect of the removal of this category of information on drivers in a busy city or on pedestrians trying to find their way in a large building complex. It is a need which has bred a sub-division of graphic design with more influence on the appearance of our surroundings than any other."
>
> *– Jock Kinneir*

of words, numbers, directions and pictograms". It was so successful that it was adapted for countries all over the world, including throughout Europe, in China, Egypt, Dubai and, fittingly, South Africa, where a modernised version also signposts our airports. Ultimately it worked – and still works in its updated format – *precisely* because it came to be taken for granted. The new road signs made instant sense and conveyed a great deal of information at speed, and they very quickly disappeared into the background of an individual's driving experience.

Kinneir and Calvert worked on many more projects down the years – for British Rail, the army, hospitals, airports and metros. Both later headed the Graphic Design Department at the Royal College of Art, and in 1980 Calvert even had a typeface, one of her own devising, named after her: **Calvert**. But her and her former boss's greatest achievement and lasting legacy is a road-signage system that still guides hundreds of millions of drivers on their way fifty years after it was designed. It's something to think about when you next pop down to the shops or navigate your way through OR Tambo International. (And hey, why not give a nod to your loo next time you pull the chain?)

Winston Churchill

30 November 1864 – 24 January 1965

Politician; orator; soldier; journalist; author; painter; drinker; smoker; hero of the 20th century – and of the South African War

IT IS, IN SEVERAL SHORT PARAGRAPHS, simply impossible to adequately distil the essence of one of the great men of history and, along with the likes of Roosevelt and Einstein, certainly one of the most influential men of the 20th century.

Oh go on, we'll give it a bash.

Because Sir Winston Leonard Spencer-Churchill, KG, OM, CH, TD, PC, DL, FRS, Hon RA* simply must be here, as one of four foreigners to qualify for this book. After all, it is what he did in South Africa that elevated him to a household name in his native England and eventually

---

* Respectively: Knight of the Garter, Order of Merit, Companion of Honour, Territorial Decoration, Privy Council for Canada, Deputy Lieutenant, Fellow of the Royal Society, Royal Academician.

paved the way for his rise to political prominence.

Winston Churchill was everywhere and everything. He saw active duty in Cuba, India and Sudan, where he participated in the last cavalry charge of the British Army, and in France in World War I. He was the man who stood up to Hitler and saw the Western world through its "darkest hour", having coined the phrase – even as everyone else, including the United States, was happy to sit by for years. Speaking of the US, he was the first honorary citizen of that fine country, one of only seven in total.

He was the voice of freedom, as epitomised in his many inspiring war speeches. "We shall fight on the beaches, we shall fight on the landing grounds," he roused. "We shall *never* surrender."

He was an influential Conservative Party politician for fifty years: Home Secretary, First Lord of the Admiralty, Secretary of State for War, Minister of Defence, Chancellor of the Exchequer, President of the Board of Trade and twice Prime Minister. And beyond politics he was an intellectual, a raconteur and great wit. He was a noted historian. He wrote dozens of books and won the Nobel Prize in Literature in 1953. He played top-level polo as a youngster and painted remarkably good Impressionist watercolours as an older man. He smoked cigars and drank whisky and famously suffered depression, his "black dog".

He was also the most quotable of quoters:

"If you're going through hell, keep going."

"He has all of the virtues I dislike and none of the vices I admire."

"You have enemies? Good. That means you've stood up for something, sometime in your life."

Churchill, all. And there were many more.

Churchill, as our non-fascist history books tell us, achieved his finest hour as Prime Minister of Britain during World War II. And given the enormity of what went on between 1939 and 1945, it is perhaps unsurprising that those cataclysmic times tend to act as a smokescreen for less globally important events that preceded them. Which is precisely why Churchill's career-forming time in South Africa is often lost from popular memory. But it is what he did here that made him famous.

It all started with something quite unusual for Churchill: failure. By this stage of his life he had spent several years charging about the world from one of Her Majesty's minor conflict areas to the next trying to make a name for himself in the somewhat novel position of soldier-cum-journalist. His mother, Lady Randolph Churchill, was a well-known beauty in her day who shared beds with the Prince of Wales and the Prince of Bismarck, among others, and who used her political pull to wangle her boy all the best posts. But she could do nothing about her son's attempt to win a seat at the Oldham by-election of 1899. Winston lost and then sat about twiddling his thumbs and wondering what an outrageously ambitious young chap might do to further his career.

Barely a couple of months later he was gifted an opportunity by the outbreak of fighting between Britain and the Boer republics in southern Africa. So, hustling as you would expect – because the young Winston was nothing if not a great hustler – Churchill scored himself a job as a reporter for the *Morning Post*, and managed to join the British general dispatched to quell the Boers, Redvers Buller, on board the RMS *Dunnotar Castle*. He arrived in Cape Town with his manservant and a drinks supply totalling 56 bottles, including 18 bottles of Scotch, on 31 October 1899.

From there things moved fast. After a stopover at the newly opened Mount Nelson – the first hotel in South Africa with both hot and cold running water – Churchill headed for Natal, which would see the majority of the early action of what was to become the Anglo-Boer War, now known as the South African War. Here the set-piece battles would be fought before the war descended into an extended bout of guerrilla engagements and the misery of the concentration camps.

Churchill was invited by Captain Aylmer Haldane to join a reconnaissance mission towards besieged Ladysmith on an armoured train leaving from Estcourt. It was to be a ride into destiny, as the train was soon attacked by a force of 500 men under Louis Botha. In response the driver sped up – as the attackers had intended, having blocked the track up ahead with large rocks. The train steamed around a bend and into the trap at a good clip, ensuring that two of the three trucks derailed and the third turned over, with a number of soldiers killed immediately.

As with many of Churchill's earlier endeavours, exactly what followed

"The Boers poured shot and shellfire into the crippled train… A shell struck and hurled [the seven-pounder] away, overturning the truck. The only newspaper correspondent present was Mr Winston Churchill, who distinguished himself by his courageous conduct, as did also Wagner, the driver, and Stuart, the stoker of the engine. The troops, who had maintained a hopeless fight with great courage, were overpowered. A few managed to escape, but the majority were either killed or wounded or taken prisoners. Mr Churchill was last seen advancing with a rifle among the Dublin Fusiliers. He is believed to have surrendered himself to cover the retreat."

– Report in The Guardian, 17 November 1899

is the subject of some debate and not a little legend. "Keep cool, men. This will be interesting for my paper," he is said to have declared before leaping into action. It seems undeniable that he played a heroic role of some sort, braving rifle shot and artillery fire, and he was instrumental in getting the locomotive detached, pushed through the wreckage and back on the line down to Estcourt with the injured. He even had the opportunity to go with, but he returned to help Haldane and his men.

"Mr Winston Churchill's conduct was that of as brave a man as could be found," Haldane would write in his report afterwards. And, indeed, had Churchill not rubbed up the wrong generals as he went about his business – Kitchener, for example, despised him for using the army to advance his political career – he may have qualified for a Victoria Cross. Depending on whose account you believed, that is.

Whatever his role on the day, Churchill was taken prisoner – by Botha himself, he would later tell people – and despatched as a prisoner of war to Pretoria where he spent his 25th birthday at the *Staatsmodelskool*, a secondary school and teacher-training institute. It was hardly Alcatraz but it was jail nevertheless and, Churchill being Churchill, he felt terribly hard done by given that there was a war going on that he should have been covering. So he announced to all and sundry that he would escape, which he did three weeks later by unceremoniously tagging on to the getaway plan of two fellow POWs – and then wholly ruining it for them. In a fit of impatience, Churchill leapt the wall of the school with just enough enthusiasm to avoid detection by the sentries while still arousing their suspicions and preventing the other two from following suit. The men who had planned the getaway were left behind and Churchill was free – without a plan, a food supply or a word of Afrikaans.

Though he may have been shot if captured, Churchill's fate didn't worry the Boers, with General Joubert referring to him as *"n klein koerant-skrywertjie"*. In fact, Churchill's release from prison had been granted days before; the orders simply hadn't arrived yet. So instead of enjoying a relaxed trip back to Natal, he now found himself trudging through the dark and dangerous Transvaal night. He managed to stow away on a coal train and alight near the mining town of Witbank, now eMalahleni, where fortune would appear to have favoured the brave. Desperately hungry, Churchill began knocking on doors in the hope of finding food, and as luck would have it the first to answer was one of the few Englishmen in the area, John Howard, manager of a coal mine.

At great personal risk, Howard fed and sheltered Churchill for a week – initially in the mine itself, until the rats ate all his candles – and eventually smuggled him on to a freight train bound for Portuguese East Africa, now Mozambique. Hilariously, his provisions for the sixteen-

"I do not concede that your Government was justified in holding me, a press correspondent and a non-combatant, a prisoner and I have consequently resolved to escape… But I wish, in leaving you this hastily and unceremoniously, to once more place on record my appreciation of the kindness which has been shown to me and the other prisoners by you, the Commandant and by Dr Gunning, and my admiration of the chivalrous and humane character of the Republican forces."

– Winston Churchill, in a letter addressed to Louis de Souza,
the Boer's Secretary of State for War, left behind after his escape

hour trip are recorded as two roast chickens, a supply of cold meat, a loaf of bread, a melon and three bottles of tea. Churchill eventually surprised the British Consul in Lourenço Marques, where he was mistaken for a fireman off a local ship due to his filthy appearance. An energising bath and a telegraph off to mama to let her know he had liberated himself, and just like that – in comic fashion and almost by mistake – the legend of Churchill had begun. Even before he made it back to Durban by ship the news of his escape ran like wildfire through the colony and back home, and he wasn't afraid to cash in and embellish where necessary. Very quickly he became a national hero in England, especially as his heroic tale was some relief after the news of heavy British defeats at Stormberg, Magersfontein and Colenso.

Churchill was keen to get back into the action, and he followed the British troops as they moved in to attempt to relieve Ladysmith. He also witnessed the disaster at Spioenkop and was among the first troops into Ladysmith itself.

Now a household name, Churchill returned to England in July of 1900 eager to capitalise on his new-found status as national hero. He rattled off two books about his South African escapades, *Ian Hamilton's March* and *London To Ladysmith Via Pretoria*, and was elected to Parliament in the general election of that year at the age of 25 years and ten months. In his maiden speech he paid generous tribute to the Boers.

Winston Churchill, MP, was on his way on the back of just eight months spent in South Africa. In the broadest possible view, it is fair to say – given how the world is not ruled by Nazis today – that those were eight months well spent. A *klein koerant-skrywertjie* indeed!

"Who on Earth is that?"
"That's Randolph Churchill's son Winston. I don't like the fellow, but he will be Prime Minister of England one day."
– *alleged exchange between an officer and Sir George White,*
commander of the garrison at Ladysmith

Johnny Clegg

b. 7 June 1953

Singer; songwriter; dancer; anthropologist; White-Zulu Great-Heart who shattered apartheid's musical borders and became a truly Universal Man

WHAT DOES IT MEAN to be a South African? Forget the "Rainbow Nation" rhetoric or those "Proudly South African" sales pitches that we've heard so often. In our evolutionary democracy – still struggling to overcome economic, ethnic, racial and linguistic divisions – what does it *really* mean to be a South African?

Johnny Clegg has the answer.

Over a musical career spanning five decades, Clegg has led the way when it comes to celebrating our collective search for a sense of being South African and embracing our universal humanity. *Ubuntu*, right? A person is only a person in relation to another person. Absolutely. But Johnny Clegg is one South African who actually walks the *ubuntu* talk. Gazing into South African pop music's turbulent history, past the flash-in-the-pan success stories and dismal dead ends for innumerable "great" musicians, Clegg is the one enduring figure who's always stood proud, forging a defiant and deeply human career.

So, how did the son of an English father and Zimbabwean mother, a man who was born in the village of Bacup, near Rochdale, England, then raised in between Zimbabwe, Zambia and South Africa, become a bona fide global music ambassador?

Kudos must go to his cabaret-and-jazz-singing mother and crime-reporting stepfather for taking the young Johnny on regular trips into the South African townships. It was there that he first encountered traditional

Zulu *inhlangwini* dancing and fell in love with the *maskandi* music of migrant Zulu mine workers who were forced to feed the Johannesburg goldfields' insatiable appetite for cheap labour. At the age of 14 Clegg coaxed Charlie Mzila, a Zulu flat-cleaner-cum-street-busker, to teach him the basics of *maskandi*. Armed only with his guitar, he followed Mzila to all the migrant labour hot spots – not something the average white kid was doing back in the late 1960s. As you'd expect, he was often bust while jamming with black musicians in township hostels and rooftop shebeens for contravening the apartheid era's Group Areas Act. But Clegg didn't let the difficulties of navigating such a complex political landscape stop him. In the meandering blues-based parables of the migrant labourers, he heard the lost chord that he'd been looking for: a way to navigate the abstract truth of just what it meant to be South African.

Now he just had to start making his own music. One migrant Zulu worker, 18-year-old guitarist Sipho Mchunu, heard about this white boy who'd earned a reputation on the streets as a pretty accomplished *maskandi* guitarist. So he called his bluff by challenging the 16-year-old Johnny to a guitar duel. This meeting at the crossroads sparked off a friendship and musical partnership that rewrote the South African musical rule book when they teamed up to form Juluka ("Sweat").

A white man fronting a multicultural rock band was, it goes without saying, a radical musical statement during the apartheid years. Seminal Juluka albums such as *Universal Men* (1979), *African Litany* (1981), *Scatterlings* (1982) and *Work For All* (1983) shattered all divisions with their singular vibrant fusion of English lyrics and Western pop melodies with Zulu rhythmic structure. Even more far-reaching were the spiritual fires of truth and reconciliation that Clegg and Mchunu's homegrown hybrid rock lit for successive generations of South African musicians. Unforgettable anthems such as *Scatterlings Of Africa*, *December African Rain* and *Kilimanjaro* have endured for decades, offering a blueprint for folk-rock activists such as Bright Blue (of *Weeping* fame) in the 1980s and the feel-good Afro-pop favourites Freshlyground today.

Since those first ground-breaking records, Clegg has sold more than five million albums. Not even Mchunu's retirement to become a

"There is a real problem. It's a cultural amnesia that is generated by the new global culture of, well, I call it the permanent present. There's a sense that you know you're permanently in the present, there's no future and no past. And you're just moving from one present moment to the next present moment. So you don't get a sense of being connected to anything. There's no continuity. And that's a spiritual desert for a lot of people. There's a need just to be part of, just, you know, to have that inner compass. It's that thing that points you in the right direction or in the direction that you feel really comfortable with. That compass is something that is very hard to get. And unfortunately the more money you have and the more you're involved in the consumer culture, the less the compass actually operates."

– Johnny Clegg

cattle farmer in 1985 could stop his flow. In 1986 he formed the band Savuka ("We have risen"), scoring a string of hit albums that included *Third World Child, Shadow Man* and *Cruel, Crazy, Beautiful World*. He followed these up with solo success stories *New World Survivor, One Life, Human* and *A South African Story*.

Across five different decades he's wowed audiences from Joburg and Cape Town to Los Angeles, Paris, Oslo and beyond with his high-energy live shows. Most notably he performed at all four of Nelson Mandela's 46664 Aids-awareness concerts, and was even joined on stage by the great man himself during his rendition of *Asimbonanga*, a song he penned about Mandela and other struggle heroes during their incarceration on Robben Island. So why is it that all his audiences spontaneously rise to their feet every time he performs this song? And how the hell did Clegg's defiant Juluka anthem *Impi* – about Zulu warriors – become a South African rugby stadium singalong? *(See Ntshingwayo Khoza.)*

Simple. Whether it's his cosmic Afro-rock ode *Scatterlings* or *Jock Of The Bushveld* theme song *Great Heart*, his music captures the experiences of ordinary South Africans trying to find out who they are. The stories he tells in his songs speak a universal truth to us, and we all recognise ourselves in them. And if you're not sure what we're on about, go listen to *Cruel, Crazy, Beautiful World*.

This deeply personal recognition has led to much deserved public recognition and numerous awards. In France, where Clegg is known as *Le Zoulou Blanc*, "the white Zulu", he was made Chevalier des Arts et Lettres (Knight of Arts and Letters) in 1991. In the United States he has been awarded honorary doctorates from City University of New York School of Law and from Dartmouth College. Back home, he has an honorary doctorate in Music from the University of the Witwatersrand (where he used to lecture in Anthropology), and in 2012 he received the Presidential Ikhamanga Award at the National Orders ceremony, the highest honour a citizen can receive in South Africa.

Despite all the awards and the praise and the general legendary status of a man who's been rocking South Africa for nearly forty years, Johnny Clegg is fundamentally just a humble South African oke trying to tell his South African story. "I'm *amadladla*, which basically means cultural driftwood," he once explained in an interview, riffing off the derogatory early 20th-century Zulu term given to those migrant farm labourers who were no longer tribal but equally not Western. "I'm just somebody who's mixed cultures and ideas. I get sustenance from broad aspects of South African history, from Zulu culture, Afrikaans, English, Jewish, from Indian backgrounds. They're all part of my consciousness. And somewhere in there I've managed to work out a place for myself. I think people get comfort from that – that it's possible and that there's this oke who's still trying to do that! You know what I mean?"

Of course we do.

Here's another way to look at it: when a gang of Saffers overseas gather together for a braai in Putney in London or St Ives in Sydney or wherever they are that's not South Africa, there's no music like Johnny Clegg's to instantly transport them home, with warmth in their hearts and perhaps a tear in the eye. And if you are home already under the African sky, well, then your braai is just *better* when Johnny's invited.

JM Coetzee

b. 9 February 1940

Author; first writer to be awarded the Booker Prize twice; winner of the Nobel Prize in Literature (2003); awkward man at a party

IF YOU'VE NEVER READ A BOOK by John Maxwell Coetzee, South Africa's most recent winner of the Nobel Prize in Literature, chances are you think he's dreary, boring and dead serious. And in the unlikely event that you ever bumped into him at a social event, you'd no doubt think the same. After all, the man is famous for writing bleak Kafkaesque allegories and being impossibly antisocial at dinner parties.

But, man, he's good.

The themes of Coetzee's writing, as with any great author, are vast, complex and the subject of numerous post-doctoral theses and literary essays. On awarding him the Nobel, the Swedish Academy described him as "a scrupulous doubter, ruthless in his criticism of the cruel rationalism and cosmetic morality of Western civilisation". He writes parables of inner isolation and human weakness and he is a pioneer of experimental narratives... And, for most readers, this all sounds scarily intellectual and way, way too heavy.

So let's just skip all the highfalutin literary analysis (there's simply not enough space, anyway) and look at one reason – *the* reason – Coetzee is so good. It's because he writes bloody well. Or, if you prefer, he is "a writer of rare acuity, with inventiveness and narrative skills that must rate among the best of our time, and an almost daunting mastery of the English language", as described by his great contemporary, André Brink.

Take this passage, for example:

For a man of his age, fifty-two, divorced, he has, to his mind, solved the problem of sex rather well. On Thursday afternoons he drives to Green Point. Punctually at two p.m. he presses the buzzer at the entrance to Windsor Mansions, speaks his name, and enters. Waiting for him at the door of No. 113 is Soraya. He goes straight through to the bedroom, which is pleasant-smelling and softly lit, and undresses. Soraya emerges from the bathroom, drops her robe, slides into bed beside. 'Have you missed me?' she asks. 'I miss you all the time,' he replies. He strokes her honey-brown body, unmarked by the sun; he stretches her out, kisses her breasts; they make love.

These are the opening lines of *Disgrace*, a depressing fictional deconstruction of post-apartheid South Africa and Coetzee's most famous book – because it won him his second Booker Prize, set him up for the Nobel and was heavily criticised by the ANC for "brutally" representing "the white people's perception of the post-apartheid black man". Its landscape is one replete with personal shame, sexual and physical violence and animal suffering, and it doesn't exactly fill the average South African with unbridled joy for the future of the country. And yet it is eminently and brilliantly readable, as much a page-turner as a Wilbur Smith novel, because of the incredible care and thought that has gone into each line.

Disgrace, like all Coetzee's novels, is a short work, a little more than 200 pages, but it is so perfectly formed that it packs in as much meaning, and quite probably took as much time and effort to write, as other novels of two or three times the length. Probably more, come to think of it. Every word has been deeply considered; none is out of place, none is missing. And yet there is no showy grandiloquence either; no trickery or word play to prove just how clever the author is. (Extremely.)

"You write because you do not know what you want to say."
– *JM Coetzee*

> "Coetzee is a man of almost monkish self-discipline and dedication. He does not drink, smoke or eat meat. He cycles vast distances to keep fit and spends at least an hour at his writing desk each morning, seven days a week. A colleague who has worked with him for more than a decade claims to have seen him laugh just once. An acquaintance has attended several dinner parties where Coetzee has uttered not a single word."
>
> *– Rian Malan, writing before Coetzee won his second Booker Prize in 1999*

Of course, it would have made quite a difference to the arc of his career and his general position in the literary world if, rather than the pained human condition, Coetzee were interested in, say, vampires and werewolves or virgins and sadomasochists. Or simply if his books weren't predicated on the "denial of pleasure principle", as Martin Amis has memorably put it. But Coetzee is who he is, and to spend some time with him or to find out about his past is to know that his writing was always going to run rather deep. Indeed, he is so unfathomable that he couldn't even write his autobiography in the first person. Rather, it is a three-part fictionalised memoir, the last of which is written as a series of interviews and notes by "a young English biographer" researching Coetzee's early career after he has supposedly died...

So there is no quick understanding of the man, but there are clues to what has shaped him and his writing. His family didn't fit the nationalist mould that a traditional Afrikaans surname might suggest; he felt isolated as a youngster; he wanted to be a poet but ended up a computer programmer in London in the 1960s. "Warmth is not in his nature," he wrote of his younger self. (Still applies.) He eventually gained a Fulbright scholarship to the University of Texas where he earned a PhD in Linguistics with a thesis that was a "computer stylistic analysis of the works of Samuel Beckett", which says rather a lot right there. Ultimately, much of his writing is effectively about him finding himself – something he still hadn't done late in life. Having moved back to Cape Town in the early 1970s, he spent thirty years teaching at UCT, then he retired and headed off to live in Adelaide, Australia, in 2002, where he would later complain that draconian new security laws reminded him of living in apartheid South Africa...

In person, he is notoriously cold. Rian Malan once called him "the stiffest man in Africa". (Mbeki was second.) He doesn't like to talk unless he *really* has to. "Speech is not a fount of truth but a pale and provisional version of writing," he explained once. In other words: why yack on when you can write?

There are numerous tales of him attending dinner parties and not speaking one word to the person seated next to him in the course of an evening. Even when tutoring at university, where he couldn't be bothered with youngsters and chose only to teach postgraduates, he would often appear almost unwilling to open his mouth. (Brink, in contrast, is affable and friendly.) But when he did, finally, it was something to behold, his mind working like one of the computers he programmed decades before. Ask him a question and he would sit calmly and quietly, sometimes for a disconcerting length of time, mentally accessing a file in the deep recesses of his brain – on his knowledge of French, say, or the works of Henry James, or pretty much any period in history – before imparting his opinion. His students, initially awestruck by his achievements, were even more impressed by the knowledge he conveyed, and if there was one thing they took from him in terms of writing skills it was the art of revision. Write, rewrite and rewrite again. Then rewrite again. The key to his brilliant, pared-down writing style.

Amis, the author of the unforgettably funny *Money*, has gone on record to say that Coetzee has "got no talent". While this is patently

"JM Coetzee's novels are characterised by their well-crafted composition, pregnant dialogue and analytical brilliance."
– *Swedish Academy press release, announcing the winner of the Nobel Prize in Literature, October 2003*

untrue (see Nobel Prize), and while Amis in turn has "got no literary awards" – as Coetzee might have retorted if he'd been bothered – it is fair to say that we do need the bursts of spontaneous, exotic, flamboyant, emotional, impossible writing that an Amis or a William Burroughs can provide. Let these rare writers roam free and inspire us with their carefree talent and wit (when they get it right). But if only the remaining 99.99 percent of the world's writers – and by that we mean *all* writers: authors, journalists, bloggers, emailers, texters, internet commenters, internet trolls, menu-makers, minute-takers – operated on Coetzee's terms, with care and precision and revision, the world would doubtless be a better place.

JM Coetzee is justly considered the greatest author South Africa has produced, a notch up on Brink and Nadine Gordimer. Whatever he writes about, whether it's the tale of a hare-lipped simpleton wandering across a war-torn landscape (*The Life And Times Of Michael K*) or a recounting of his own lonely childhood in Worcester and Cape Town (*Boyhood*), it is always compelling, if most often unlovely and disturbing. His genius is not natural and carefree; it is ruthless, disciplined, considered and measured. Read something of his, if only to see brilliance in the form that words can take on a page. Then go watch *Dumb And Dumber* or something.

Allan Cormack

23 February 1924 – 7 May 1988

Nuclear physicist; winner of the Nobel Prize in Medicine (1979); quietly brilliant inventor of Computed Axial Tomography (which, if you didn't know, is a CAT scan)

IN A WORLD OF CELEBRITY AND SELF-PROMOTION often sheer loudness wins the day, and among a motley crew of rocketeers and film stars, sportsmen and political greats, among space-exploring empire-founding record-breaking go-getters and alpha males and all-round generally superlative types, a quieter voice might easily be drowned out. But we're not going to stand for that. Because sometimes somebody with the quietest of voices does something so completely world-changing that it takes a Nobel committee to make the point.

That's what happened to our Allan Cormack.

Cormack eventually naturalised in the US and as such is one of several occupants of this book whom the Americans might try to claim, but the argument that nothing truly useful was ever invented by an American, unless you hold the "drive-thru" in inexplicably high esteem, holds true in this case. The son of Scottish immigrants – and the number of the world's great inventions that have emanated from that small nation is almost unbelievable – he was born in Johannesburg and raised in Cape Town, where he attended Rondebosch Boys' High. At a time when Sailor Malan was gaining fame as a fighter-pilot hero of World War II *(see Sailor Malan)*, Cormack was quietly going about his studies at the University of Cape Town, where he was awarded his Bachelor's in Physics in 1944 and his Master's in something appallingly complicated called Crystallography the following year. In his spare time he liked walking on the mountain and listening to music. How lovely.

After a stint at Cambridge as a research student, where he married an American girl, Barbara Seavey (they met in Quantum Physics classes – really), Cormack returned to Cape Town to lecture on Particle Physics at Groote Schuur Hospital. At the time he was the only nuclear physicist in town, so the job was a rather lonely one. To keep himself busy he took up a "hobby", playing with some mathematical theories he had on Computed Tomography (CT). As you can see, Allan Cormack was rather the opposite of the medical rock star who would pace Groote Schuur's august corridors a decade later. *(See Chris Barnard.)*

Cormack's hobby turned out to involve extremely complex mathematical algorithms that used X-ray "slices" of a human body to piece together a three-dimensional image. With not much more than a desktop calculator and an X-ray machine, he had invented the Computed Axial Tomography scan, now known as the CAT scan.

There was a problem though: no-one was interested in these findings, partly because computing power was so slow in the 1950s that the necessary calculations took an age to complete. After a brief sabbatical to the US, Cormack's theories were published to a deafening silence in the early 1960s. And that might have been that, but for the work of a fiendishly clever electrical engineer working at the EMI music company in England who had independently had a similar idea without any knowledge of Cormack's work. Godfrey Hounsfield was also a shy and retiring type who liked mountain rambles and listening to music – it took a certain type of genius, clearly – and he moved fast, developing a machine and scanning a preserved human brain, then a cow brain that he bought from a local butcher. His first workable scans took several days to complete and required the use of a mainframe computer. In 1975 Hounsfield scanned himself; that same year a spinal cyst was diagnosed using a full-body scanner he had built.

Despite the vast costs involved due to the computing power required, the machine was very well received. Suddenly doctors could "see" inside a patient's body and discover diseases and damaged tissue without resorting to the scalpel. It took only another four years before Cormack and Hounsfield were jointly awarded the Nobel Prize in Physiology or Medicine, despite neither of them being medical doctors. "Few medical achievements have received such immediate acceptance and met with such unreserved enthusiasm as computerised tomography," was the verdict at the ceremony (where Cormack and Hounsfield met for the first time). "It literally swept the world."

The invention of the CAT scan led to numerous developments in diagnostic medicine, and the machine has now been saving lives for nearly forty years. It is also used for nondestructive testing of various objects in industrial, biological and astronomical fields – for example, the US military uses them to detect defects in ageing nuclear weapons – and has been a virtual supporting actor in a variety of medical dramas down the years, most notably *House*.

Having succumbed to cancer in 1998, Allan Cormack was posthumously awarded the Order of Mapungubwe, South Africa's highest honour at the time, in 2002. (Another recipient that year was a certain N. Mandela.) Quite right too, because Cormack, who died of cancer in 1998, wasn't going to shout about it.

"It had a profound effect on radiology, liberating with the first step, the brain of both patient and doctor from the constraints of traditional imagery. It introduced the concepts of digital data acquisition, sophisticated interactive display systems and powerful image processing to *in vivo* biological studies, at the same time providing a stimulus and scientific environment for other major developments to follow, including Magnetic Resonance Imaging. CT provided, for the first time, quantitative information about tissue density differences in uniformly thin slices of tissue by employing collimated X-rays directed only at the layer under investigation."

– *Extract from Radiology journal's entry on Computed Tomography*

Basil D'Oliveira

4 October 1928/1931 – 19 November 2011

Ageless cricketer who might have been one of the greats; spark that ignited the sports boycott; picture of human dignity amid political upheaval

BJ VORSTER, PRIME MINISTER OF THIS BENIGHTED LAND at the height of what became known as the D'Oliveira Affair, opined thus: "The matter has passed from the realm of sport to the realm of politics. Leftist and liberal politicians have entered the field of sport."

It was 1968, and Vorster was arguing that Basil D'Oliveira, a coloured cricketer from Cape Town who was now playing cricket for England, did not deserve to be picked on merit for the upcoming English tour of South Africa, and that his late inclusion in the squad had come about due to political pressure from the anti-apartheid lobby. In reality the exact opposite was true – he *did* deserve to be picked and his original exclusion from the side had been due to political pressure from the South African government. The best thing about Vorster's little rant is that we can prove he was wrong, empirically and scientifically, because D'Oliveira went on to average a shade over 40 in Tests, that crucial statistical watershed that (until fairly recently) elevated an international cricket player from useful to world class.

Had all been right on the planet, Basil D'Oliveira would have had a long and illustrious career playing for the nation of his birth, South Africa, and in all likelihood would have averaged far better than 40 seeing as he started his international career far later than he should have. Of course, in apartheid South Africa he had no chance. A black Bradman would never have played for South Africa in the 1960s; hell, in those days a black Superman wouldn't have played. So "Dolly" had to fight his way to the highest level as an international cricketer in the face of not one, but two cricketing systems entrenched in racial thinking.

D'Oliveira was superb, and he became a legendary figure in "non-white" cricket circles in Cape Town in the 1950s. Strong and brave, he had a powerful bottom hand and a great eye, the required attributes when you learn your cricket playing in the streets and then graduate to uneven pitches and substandard fields – which was the lot of coloured cricketers back then. He once scored 225 in 70 minutes. On another occasion he hit 46 runs off an 8-ball over. He also bowled tight away-swingers that would eventually earn him 551 First Class wickets.

No matter his obvious talent, D'Oliveira would have been destined for no more than the black and coloured leagues were it not for the intervention of the BBC broadcasting legend John Arlott. Arlott, as the voice of cricket, had been feted on his arrival in South Africa for the first time in 1948, and treated as a true celebrity. While he would no doubt have preferred to remain polite throughout, the fact that it was 1948 – the year the Nats came to power and began to implement DF Malan's disastrous dream for this country – meant he returned to Britain utterly appalled. Never one to hold back, it was on-air comments such as this that got BBC newscasts banned in South Africa: "The existing government in South Africa is predominantly a Nazi one… Anything can happen to a native in South Africa – any form of violence, carrying through as far as murder – and you can rest assured that the person who kills him or ill-treats him won't suffer in any way at all."

And so it was Arlott to whom Basil D'Oliveira wrote in the late 1950s, and it was Arlott who became hugely motivated in getting this unheralded South African nobody a side to play for in England. Despite his many efforts the counties weren't interested, but a club side, Middleton, found themselves short a player when their overseas professional left them stranded. They were desperate enough to call on the skills of a complete unknown, and all of a sudden D'Oliveira was on his way to England in 1960 with the promise of £450 for a season's cricket.

D'Oliveira was 29, nearer the end than the beginning of a modern

> "No Test player has had to overcome such tremendous disadvantages along the road to success as the Cape coloured D'Oliveira. Admirable though his achievements were against the West Indies in 1966, undoubtedly his triumph in ever attaining Test status was more commendable."
>
> *– Wisden entry on D'Oliveira's selection as Cricketer of the Year in 1967*

cricketer's career – or so he told people at the time. In later years he admitted to his biographer, Pat Murphy, that he'd lied about his age because he was worried the English wouldn't fancy his long-term chances if they knew the truth. Murphy now claims that D'Oliveira was born in 1928, not 1931 as most of his biographies attest. Either way he was, in his own words, "over the hill", and he was still schooled in the land of his birth. He marvelled at the sight of white waiters and white labourers and was amazed he could share a dressing room with his white teammates.

He had a tough start. It was cold, he spoke more Afrikaans than English and he missed home, but in time he settled and he was good enough to come out on top of the league's batsmen, pipping one Gary Sobers for the spot. Arlott's job was done and henceforth D'Oliveira's talent spoke for itself. Middleton soon became Worcestershire, where his 1,691 runs helped the county retain the 1965 Championship. The following year at the age of 35 – or possibly 38 – Basil D'Oliveira was selected for England.

This alone was an astonishing achievement. British prejudice certainly had nothing on South Africa at the time, but the English side of 1966 was not quite as all-embracing as the demographics of recent years might suggest. There were no Nasser Hussains and Devon Malcolms back then, and *Cricinfo* notes that Roland Butcher was "the first black player to represent England" – in 1981. By being selected for England, D'Oliveira had climbed a huge mountain and he'd thrown sand in the eye of local prejudice and apartheid ideology in the process.

He performed well against the touring West Indians, scored his debut century against India in his fifth Test,* and in 1967 he was made *Wisden's* Cricketer of the Year. There was a series against Pakistan and a return tour to the West Indies, and before too long the inevitable cropped up – an impending tour of South Africa, in 1968.

Rumours had it that on Vorster's initiative D'Oliveira was offered £40,000 and security for life if he made himself unavailable for the tour. Either way, massive pressure was put upon the selectors – from London and from Pretoria – and they initially caved in by picking several injured and out-of-form players. D'Oliveira himself had endured a dip in form, but he'd been a last-minute inclusion for the final two Tests against Australia and produced consecutive innings of 87 not out and 158, his highest Test score. The English cricket selectors in the form of the Marylebone Cricket Club (the MCC) became a focus for the increasing revulsion the world felt about apartheid. Nineteen MCC members quit in disgust. So when one player dropped out of the tour due to injury, D'Oliveira's selection was virtually inevitable.

Our apartheid overlords were nothing if not men of principle, and of course competing against a coloured player in an international contest was anathema to them, so the next step was equally inevitable: the tour was cancelled. D'Oliveira would have relished the opportunity to play Test cricket in the country of his birth but the opportunity was gone, and he would in fact never play a First Class match in South Africa. While it looked at the time like Vorster had won the battle, the war would eventually go to D'Oliveira and the thousands of coloured and black cricketers who he effectively represented during the affair. As *Wisden* so adroitly put it, "both Vorster and apartheid would be dead before South Africa played cricket against England again".

It was an international bust-up of huge proportions, and it forced the vacillating hand of the International Olympic Committee to ban South Africa from the 1968 Olympics in Mexico. The general sports boycott

---

* D'Oliveira scored 109 and an unbeaten 24, steering the English to victory in the second innings. This was the same Test in which Geoff Boycott was criticised for selfish batting. He scored 246 not out off 555 balls and was dropped for the next match.

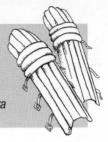

> "This is a fairy tale come true. Six years ago I was playing on mudheaps. Now I have played for England and met the Queen. What more could I possibly ask?"
>
> *– Basil D'Oliveira*

followed, hitting hard in sports-loving South Africa. This was real tangible progress in the battle against apartheid, all because a talented and gentle man had exposed the backward doctrine for what it was.

And amid all the brouhaha, D'Oliveira played on with great dignity. He became a much-loved figured in his adopted country and he didn't miss an England game in four years, once again giving the lie to Vorster's assertion that his selection had been political. He picked up three more hundreds in that time – against Pakistan, Australia and New Zealand, all highly rated – and he eventually ended with 2,484 runs and 47 wickets from 44 Tests.

In the end Ali Bacher had it best: "He showed conclusively that blacks in South Africa, given the same opportunity as whites, had that ability, talent and potential to become international stars." Indeed.

It is fitting that South Africa and England now compete for the Basil D'Oliveira Trophy because, while the man himself was always generous to a fault in his thanks to Britain generally and in his acceptance of first an OBE and then a CBE, he really should have had a long and successful career with South Africa. And because of what he endured, players such as Herschelle Gibbs, Ashwell Prince and Makhaya Ntini have done just that. Quite the legacy.

Ernie Els

b. 17 October 1969

The Big Easy; golfer with the Rolls-Royce swing; multiple Major winner; vanguard for the globalisation of golf; wine-maker; autism campaigner; generally lovely guy

ERNIE ELS IS, WITHOUT DOUBT, *not* the best golfer to ever represent South Africa. He may not even be the second best given the incredible talents of one Bobby Locke, a man who was kicked off the US tour in 1949 for, they say, being too good, and who then went on to win four Open Championships.

Superior to both Els and Locke was a South African golfer who could, on playing record alone, stroll into these pages wearing silly multicoloured trousers if he felt like it – as is the wont of the golfing man. Except that in his case his trousers would be black and he wouldn't stroll; he would march with righteous purpose and determination. But Ernie Els gets to appear here because he is a superb golfer in his own right with one of the most aesthetically pleasing swings in the game, because he's probably the nicest professional sportsman around, and because the head of state he's photographed with is Nelson Mandela, not BJ Vorster. Besides, we think Ian Player is far more interesting than his brother. *(See Ian Player.)*

The Big Easy is just that – big and easy, which is how they breed 'em out in Kempton Park. In fact, he's such an easy-going and generally lekker fellow that it's only appropriate to refer to him using his first name.

Ernie was one of those multitalented outdoorsy South African kids who excelled at all sports growing up in the 1970s, but especially at golf and tennis. He started playing golf at the age of eight and caddied for his dad Neels at the Kempton Park Country Club; he'd won the Eastern Transvaal Junior Tennis Championship by the age of 13. You'll still spot him on TV in the crowd at Wimbledon occasionally, perhaps wondering about a tennis career never pursued, but it was the fact that he was playing off scratch by the age of 14 that pushed Ernie into golf full time. At that age he travelled to San Diego where he won the Junior World Golf Championship, beating Phil Mickelson into second place.

From the start it was Ernie's fluid, easy-looking swing that caught the eye, disguising as it did the tremendous power with which he struck the ball – to the point that the more relaxed he is the further he hits it. (He has spoken of how he always drives much further off the tee when operating at 80 percent.) When he was on song he hit the ball miles, his approach irons were beautiful, he was one of the best out of the sand and he was notably calm under pressure with a putter. Those who saw him in his early days predicted big things, and they weren't to be disappointed.

After going pro in 1989 and winning locally and internationally over the next few years, the Big Easy hit the big time good and proper in 1994, the year he won his first World Match Play Championship and his first Major, the US Open at Oakmont. There would be more of both. In fact Ernie's casual calm under pressure meant he was made for match-play golf – where golfers play head-to-head rather than against the field – and he would go on to win three consecutive Match Play Championships up to 1996, then three more from 2002 to 2004, and another one for good measure in 2007. He is Big Easily the most successful Match Play golfer of all time. Which is not to forget his four Major victories, won in three separate decades, including a further US Open and two Open Championships. Or the fact that he holds the record for time spent ranked in the world top ten – at around fifteen years – or that he's won more than sixty tournaments across the planet. As a measure of Ernie's durability, the prize money for his first US Open in 1994 was $320,000; for his second Open Championship in 2012 it was more than $1,450,000. (Which is nice work if you can get it.)

With stats like this, it goes without saying that Ernie has had many amazing years in golf. 1997 was a scorcher. He picked up the Johnnie Walker Classic, defended his Buick Classic title and added that second US Open to his collection after a thrilling final-round showdown with Tom Lehman, Jeff Maggert and Colin Montgomerie at the Congressional in Maryland. Those who saw it won't easily forget the four battling it out in the final two pairings down the back nine, with Ernie chipping in at the 10th before executing an approach at the 17th that is still regarded

"Els is one of those guys who like to make sure they are caught up on their foot-dangling, the sort who likes nothing more than to sit silently with a friend for 10 minutes with his hat tipped over his face, then say, "Isn't this great?" He likes his lager and is likely to be found drinking it with a bunch of caddies. In fact, he is more often going to bed at five in the morning than getting up at that hour. 'Ernie is so laid-back it's frightening,' [Colin] Montgomerie says."
– Rick Reilly, from his review of the 1997 US Open, writing in US Sports Illustrated

> "'The Big Easy' has long been Els's sobriquet, capturing his rolling gait and apparently nonexistent pulse in the crucible of major championship combat. It crystallises, too, the liquid elegance of his swing."
> — *Oliver Brown, writing in The Telegraph*

by those in the know as one of the best golf shots ever played under pressure. As described by Rick Reilly of *Sports Illustrated* magazine, he "put his slowest and sweetest swing of the day on an unforgettable 5-iron that flagged the pin and stopped eight feet behind it". It was the shot that would set up the tensest of victories, by a solitary stroke, with the win taking him to the top of the world rankings for the first time.

2002 was also epic, with Ernie winning the Heineken Classic, the Genuity Championship and then, the pinnacle of golf, the famous Claret Jug at The Open at Muirfield. But there has been golfing heartbreak too, as is inevitable in an extended career in a game of such psychological torment, where fate and fortune play such a role. Most notably disappointing was his inability to really capitalise on five years of consistent Major performances from 2000 to 2004. Yes, he won at Muirfield in that time, but he also recorded five second places in twenty Majors and thirteen top-ten finishes – more than Tiger Woods who was then at the peak of his powers. Probably his greatest regret will be not winning the Masters, having come second, sixth, fifth, sixth and second in that time. But golf is a funny game, one in which players of proven class like Colin Montgomerie never crack a Major, while outsiders and journeymen like Rich Beem and Todd Hamilton can pick up one (or, in the case of Padraig Harrington, three) from nowhere…

Fast forward to 2011 and it looked like the great man's golf ambitions were shot. Ernie was inducted into the golfing hall of fame, usually a sign that a career is coming to an end, and he endured a poor year generally, falling out of the top 50. As a result he suffered the embarrassment of failing to qualify for the 2012 Masters, having missed only one major, through injury, in twenty years.

> "For some reason I've got some belief this week. I feel something special can happen. I feel I've put in a lot of work the last couple of – let's call it the last couple of years, especially the last couple of months. So something good is bound to happen, so hopefully it's tomorrow."
>
> *– Ernie Els, before playing the final round of The Open in 2012*

"Obviously in March I looked like an absolute fool," he said later that year. "People were laughing at me and making jokes about me and really hitting me low, saying I'm done and I should hang it up." He had been particularly upset by comments made by David Feherty at an exhibition match and admitted later that he had fallen "into a pit of despair".

How did the Big Easy respond? He won the 2012 Open Championship at Royal Lytham, that's how.

Having started the day six shots off the pace, he let Australian Adam Scott suffer a meltdown as he quietly went about his business, eventually winning by a stroke. "Sport has been seldom been more cathartic or so gloriously improbable," declared *The Telegraph*. "With a second Open triumph that left the patrons of Royal Lytham open-jawed in incredulity, Ernie Els cemented his restoration from the dead men of golf."

He had been a 45-1 outsider at the start of the tournament and, as Ernie explained in his own inimitable way, winning the Claret Jug again after enduring such a terrible time was "quite satisfying… so everything is groovy at the moment again".

What he didn't say was, "David Fehe-who?" – because he is the most gracious of winners. In his acceptance speech he sympathised with his "buddy" Scott, cracked a few jokes, gave a shout out to Nelson Mandela and generally wowed the crowd. No surprises there – although his caddie Ricci Roberts's later revelation that Ernie didn't celebrate the win with a large night out on the town was perhaps unexpected, given his previous reputation for enjoying the occasional drink or seven.

Unlike most of his contemporaries, Ernie has embraced the global nature of the game of golf, and has played all over the world in European Tour-sanctioned events. This, however, has irritated the US PGA organisers who despatched a snotty letter to him in 2004 in which they demanded he play more events on their tour. He characteristically publicised the letter and told the PGA to get stuffed. "Don't start putting a padlock around me because that's not going to work," he said. "I think they need to understand the golfing world has changed through the years. There is a world outside of America and I am part of it."

Damn right. And it's this fantastic attitude that means we've got to see him playing so much here in South Africa. No wonder the guy is one of the most popular players in the world. And Ernie's proud of his global appeal: "I have been doing this all my life. You can't start telling me, hey, come over here and leave the rest of the world. It's not going to happen that way."

When not telling the PGA and David Feherty to take a hike – rare outbursts, admittedly – and playing golf in Guatemala and Japan and South Africa and wherever the hell else he feels like it, he's designing golf courses and golf clubs, which have been received very well. He also runs a foundation aimed at getting talented but poor South African kids into professional golf. And you can add to Ernie's all-round nice-guy appeal the fact that he has raised millions of dollars for autistic children through another foundation, Els For Autism. Having married his long-term girlfriend Liezl in 1998, Ernie has two children, the second of whom, Ben, was born autistic in 2002. Unsurprisingly, it's been a rough road for the family, but Ernie has used his personal wealth and great international influence to create much awareness for the affliction. And finally there's the wine, a pastime he's has been pursuing since 1999 with great success.

So Ernie Els will be remembered, one suspects, as far more than just a great golfer with a languid and beautiful swing, a big heart and an easy smile. All of this is true, of course, but it's more likely that, in time, as the golfing heroics fade, Ernie will be remembered for simply being a great South African.

Brenda Fassie

3 November 1964 – 9 May 2004

Drug-addled   tantrum-throwing   controversy-courting Afro-pop sensation; the Madonna of the Township; the Queen of Kwaito; Ma-Brr

IT WAS, ACCORDING TO *TIME* MAGAZINE, "pure Brenda".

During an explosive performance on her US debut in Washington in 2001, having sung for three hours straight, her breasts fell out of her dress during a particularly excitable dance move. Unperturbed, Brenda Fassie thrust them at the stunned audience, shouting, "This is Africa!" Coming, as it did, years before Janet Jackson's famous wardrobe malfunction during the Super Bowl, this was Fassie at her pioneering best. But, as *Time* explained, America was not ready for such revelations.

"The promoters asked me not to do that again," she said afterwards.

Ah yes. That was Brenda Fassie alright. Hyper-energetic, frenetic, and not a little mad. With her, you never knew what you might get because she was, it is categorically impossible to deny, a bit of a handful at times.

It all started in Langa, Cape Town, where she sung as a preschooler, making money from tourists. By age 15, her reputation had grown to the point that Soweto-based producer Koloi Lebona came to see what all the fuss was about. She auditioned for him, with her mother playing piano, and he was immediately struck by her voice. "I knew it was the voice of the future," he later explained. Fassie's mother agreed to let Lebona mentor her, and the young singer joined him and his wife in their home.

After a fitful start, her break came in 1983 at the age of 19, by which time she was fronting the wonderfully named Brenda & The Big Dudes. The song in question was written by a teenager called Melvyn Matthews, it was called *Weekend Special* and it would propel Fassie into stardom.

Matthews would later reminisce fondly about the time: "She had difficulty pronouncing English and cut corners quite a lot. She sang in her Xhosa-ised English, tinged with clicks. But her passion made up for everything. Even at that age she was an emotional artist who would turn any song into a Brenda song. She had feeling, timing, melody, heart and rhythm. She lifted my lyrics to a chaotic beauty I had never imagined."

The lyrics were, of course, about being someone's casual shag – his "weekend special" – and the song was a groovy number that had almost instant appeal. Listening to it today, three decades on, the '80s factor is undeniable but it is streets ahead of so much other cringeworthy pop of the time – both local and international – and it's hard to deny that Fassie's energised singing is what makes it. *Weekend Special* went on to become one of the fastest-selling records of its time in South Africa, generating more than 200,000 sales and rousing dance floors across Africa, and in the US, Europe, Australia and Brazil. Fassie followed up with the platinum-selling *Too Late For Mama*, more catchy bubblegum Afro-pop.

Fassie's singing had fast become a modern, youthful antidote to the struggle songs and toyi-toying of the townships but, as *ThisDay* noted, her "music was pure township, and township during the Eighties was political by definition". Whatever her original intentions, she had forged a powerful connection to young black South Africans, and as the turbulent '80s rumbled on she wasn't afraid to add her voice to the fire. In 1990 she recorded *Black President*, a song with an unambiguous message about Nelson Mandela – even at that late stage in the apartheid game it had the honour of being banned.

With her success came the mayhem. By this stage she had teamed up with the producer Chicco Twala – "the South African Quincy Jones", as he was later known – a man who would battle for most of their on-again-off-again twenty-year relationship to keep her from harm. "My daily struggle was to rescue her from those around her," he recalled when she died. On one occasion he "literally dragged her screaming and kicking from a dingy R29-per-night Hillbrow hotel".

There were repeated visits to drug rehab, there was a brief marriage to an ex-convict and there were numerous affairs with both men and women. She started missing concerts and ran into debt, largely because of her irrepressible, sometimes naive, generosity. Not to mention her habits… She was struggling with a cocaine addiction when the world of fast cars and seedy hotels caught up with her: in 1995 she woke up next to the drug-saturated corpse of her lesbian lover.

These were tough times and her reputation suffered, but Fassie's popularity and talent remained undiminished. She kept recording, and in 1998 she proved even her harshest critics wrong with the release of *Memeza*, perhaps her most polished record, which went on to sell 500,000 copies that year. With Twala once again guiding her, she had reinvented herself as a kwaito star and she was on a roll: for four consecutive years she produced the best-selling album of the year – *Memeza, Amadlozi, Nomakanjani* and *Mina Nawe* – and she won an array of South African Music Awards (Samas) and two Kora Awards for Best Female Artist along the way. It was an incredible comeback, and the royalties came flooding in – though they would be squandered in due course.

Fassie's behaviour was always volatile. Anyone in the music industry who encountered her would have a story to tell, and she had a schizoid relationship with the press. Accepting an award for best-selling album at the Samas, she pulled back her dress and showed the assembled guests her legs. "Nice, hey?" she said, to much amusement. Then, in tears after receiving the award, she returned to her table only to launch a vicious attack on Lesley Mofokeng, then of the *Sowetan*, who had written about some of her sexual exploits. The *Sunday Times* loved it. "Hurling a box at Mofokeng," it reported, "she threatened to 'kill him and his family'. There was a stunned silence as Fassie screeched that Mofokeng was a 'homosexual who sleeps with men to get stories'. She said she would find out where Mofokeng lived and wreak vengeance on him."

Yvonne Chaka Chaka, once Fassie's bridesmaid, recalls having beer thrown over her: "Brenda arrived, a bit high. I don't know what had angered her, but she just *gooi*'d me a glass of beer." And Therese Owen was on the receiving end of her affections too: "If you don't let me come home with you, I shall destroy your interview and then you'll have nothing to write about," Fassie told the stunned journalist.

There was also an affair with Sindi Khambule, characterised by public displays of affection and much-reported domestic violence. At one point Twala and Fassie spent a night in jail together after the producer had been called in to break up a particularly nasty fight between them. Twala spoke frequently of his concerns for his star, believing that it was only a matter of time before she self-destructed. And so it happened.

In April 2004 Fassie was rushed to hospital with breathing problems that led to an asthma attack and then a heart attack. There were vigils and prayer meetings. Fans drove through the night from as far away as Lesotho and the Cape to be at the Sunninghill hospital. Her brother, Thembi, played *Black President* and *Weekend Special* from a radio next to her bed. The Mandelas – both Nelson and Winnie – visited. So did President Mbeki. But Ma-Brrr was gone.

EMI, with which she had recorded 15 albums and more than 150 songs, issued a statement: "A hero has fallen". The world had been robbed of that brilliant voice and that outrageous, authentic personality. Somewhere along the line Fassie had picked up the nickname the "Madonna of the Townships". It was utter balls. Brenda Fassie was a South African original, and she died too soon.

Mahatma Gandhi

2 October 1869 – 30 January 1948

Lawyer; political activist; railer against British imperialism on two continents; developer of nonviolent protest; influencer of freedom fighters in South Africa and across the world

WHICH WAS SOUTH AFRICA'S FIRST black political-resistance movement? The ANC? The PAC? Nope, it was the Natal Indian Congress, established by Mohandas Karamchand Gandhi in 1894.*

---

*The ANC was founded in 1912, the PAC in 1959.

Gandhi was a man who would go on to become an icon of liberation, the man who refused to raise his fists in anger and in so doing guilted Britain into setting India free after a century of the Raj. But what often flies under the radar about this pint-sized giant of the 20th century is not that he spent some time in South Africa, but rather that he spent two decades here, almost entirely in the cause of helping South African Indians avoid oppression. And it was, in fact, his time here that launched him to greatness.

Before we get there, though, let's deal with something up front. Like everyone else on our list – and yes, that includes Nelson Mandela – Gandhi was hardly the purest of the angels sent from heaven. Despite being lionised almost beyond recognition after the liberation of India, a perfectly understandable phenomenon in a new country needing heroes, he was, like all of us, a complex human being with his own array of blemishes. Less rose-tinted readings of history make it pretty clear that, especially early on, Gandhi wasn't particularly interested in the fate of black African people, writing of them in disparaging and racist terms often enough for us to have to accept that he was man of his time. While Churchill famously referred to Gandhi as "a half-naked fakir", Gandhi himself wasn't averse to speaking of "uncivilised kaffirs". He was also sexually peculiar. His parents arranged his marriage at age 13, he fathered four children before choosing to become celibate for religious reasons, and he almost certainly took a male lover while living in Johannesburg. In older age he chose to test his celibacy by sleeping naked with the adolescent daughter of his nephew – which is disturbingly Michael Jackson-ish. And, evidently, he was mighty vain too.

So, worthy of damnation? Probably not. But one tends to require some pretty awesome moral credentials to get away with some of these behaviours with not much more than a raised brow. Luckily, Gandhi had these in spades and it was in South Africa that they first came to the fore.

Gandhi is known for his advocacy of nonviolent mass protest, and it was this methodology that started with the Natal Indian Congress and would continue under the auspices of the ANC for many decades.

Though a strategic shift towards more violent rebellion in South Africa took place in the 1960s, what Gandhi began in 1894 was effectively finished by Nelson Mandela and the ANC collective in 1994. Exactly 100 years after the formation of a movement to advance the cause of Indian people in this country, the moment came when another movement succeeded in freeing the entire nation.

But first Gandhi had to head from Bombay to London, in 1888, to enter training as a barrister, which he completed after three years. After an unsuccessful sojourn back home he was offered £105 for a year's work at Dada Abdulla and Company in Durban to assist on a complex civil case requiring his translation skills, which was to be heard in Pretoria. He accepted, and arrived at Port Natal-Durban in May 1893.

Indians had been brought to the Colony of Natal en masse to work as indentured labourers on its sugar-cane plantations from 1860 onwards; 150,000 of them would be imported over the next five decades, with many staying on permanently. By the time Gandhi arrived there was a thriving Indian population in Durban, with smaller communities having sprung up elsewhere. It didn't take long for him to realise that his poorly esteemed brethren were caught between twin perils: imminent legislation that would leave them disenfranchised under British rule in Natal, and overt and violent racism in the Boer republics.

As a barrister Gandhi took on the affectations of an English gentleman in how he spoke and how he dressed, but this could not disguise the colour of his skin. Only two weeks after his arrival he was, very famously, booted off a train in Pietermaritzburg for refusing to move from first

"It seemed beyond his capacity to also take on the cause of the Africans amidst whom he and the Indians of South Africa lived. Yet Gandhi's platforms in the opening decades of the 20th century, including his nationalism, were stepping stones to a common humanity, and also to a future politics of an African-Indian alliance in South Africa."

– *Rajmohan Gandhi, grandson and biographer*

to third class. It was to be a revelation, the date – 7 June 1893 – that his activist career began. A statue of Gandhi now stands where the incident took place. Not long after, he was beaten up by a Pretoria coach driver for refusing to sit on the floor to allow space for a white man.

These incidents fired up the little man's sense of injustice. Once finished in Pretoria, where he saw that the conditions of Indian traders was even worse than in Natal, he was due to return to India, but for news received at a farewell dinner that the government in Natal intended to disenfranchise the Indians there. He felt morally impelled to stay, and so stay he did – for another twenty years. His work to get a petition together wasn't enough to get the bill stopped, but it was enough to make people both in Britain and India aware of this man called Gandhi.

With the help of others, Gandhi formed the Natal Indian Congress later that year, giving Natalian Indians a cohesive political voice for the first time. After a brief trip back to India in 1896 to fetch his family, he returned to Durban where he was met by a furious mob that had been misinformed of his intentions – they had been told he was coming with hundreds of Indian families to settle in Natal, and he was attacked and beaten once he'd made it on to dry land. Typically, he refused to pursue police investigations.

By 1899 the Boers and Brits were at war, much of it taking place in the Natal interior. While it might have made more sense for Gandhi to fall in with the Boers, he urged Indians to side with the British, the thinking being that if Indians wished to be full citizens then they had better behave that way. He formed the Indian Ambulance Corps, which numbered up to a thousand volunteers and helped injured soldiers on the battlefield – including at Spioenkop near Ladysmith in January 1900, a battle that was disastrous for both Boer and Brit.

(As an aside, it is often suggested that the fact that Indians helped the British in the South African War was the real motivation for their complete banishment from the Free State during apartheid.)

In 1906 Gandhi again sided with the British in the Bambatha Rebellion, a bloody and brief Zulu rebellion against British taxes, and he again carried stretchers. But it was in the Transvaal, during the last six years of his time in South Africa, where Gandhi refined his *satyagraha* ("firmness in truth") policy of passive resistance that would become such a powerful force in his struggle for Indian independence. The Transvaal government infuriated South African Indians by first demanding that they register and have their fingerprints taken, and later ruling that only Christian marriages were legal, so it seemed natural for Gandhi to continue the battle there. He settled on a small-holding outside Johannesburg called Tolstoy Farm, where he shunned materialism, found "spiritual purification and penance" and organised peaceful marches and demonstrations, the mass burning of registration cards and similar nonviolent gestures of resistance. (His family was left neglected in Natal.) In 1913 Gandhi led a march of several thousand Indians across the Transvaal-Natal border in protest of an Act restricting Indian migration between provinces; his followers were ordered not to resist arrest, beatings and whatever else may be thrown at them, and Gandhi found himself in jail afterwards, by now a familiar occurrence. When he was later sentenced to a year's imprisonment, Indians around the country reacted in sympathy by striking and closing their businesses on a massive scale.

In the face of this well-organised and morally irreproachable defiance, Jan Smuts had no choice but to back down on most of the Indian demands. Though South Africa would remain a country of much racial inequality for a long time yet, Gandhi had made an enormous difference

"When he died, people mourned because some goodness, some power for love and peace and justice, had been taken from the earth. Like most of us, he did not recognise some of his faults. But once he recognised a fault, it was doomed. His power of will, his power to decide to do this or not to do that, his power to abstain if he thought that abstinence was needed to make him a better instrument of God, was one of the things that brought him the admiration of millions."

– *Alan Paton, writing in the foreword to Fatima Meer's biography of Gandhi* in regard to the "Asiatic question". He had also made a name for himself around the world. It was, he felt, time for him to take his passive fight to the country of his birth.

By the time of his departure from South Africa in 1914, Gandhi had earned the sobriquet Mahatma, meaning "great soul", which would come to be his recognised name. Before setting sail he sent a pair of sandals he had made in jail to Smuts as a gift. At the time Smuts was glad to see Gandhi gone, writing, "The saint has left our shores, I sincerely hope for ever." But part of Smuts's own greatness was his willingness to learn and evolve, and in an essay to commemorate Gandhi's 70th birthday in 1939 he wrote, "I have worn these sandals for many a summer since then, even though I may feel that I am not worthy to stand in the shoes of so great a man."

Gandhi's time in South Africa made him what he was, and gave him the opportunity to take the *satyagraha* to India where, too, a government would have no choice but to eventually capitulate. Unfortunately the principles of *satyagraha*, so admired by the leaders of the ANC in the 1940s and '50s, ultimately failed here. After Sharpeville, and with much regret, Mandela and co formed Umkhonto we Sizwe to meet force with force. But that's hardly Gandhi's fault, and speaks more of the brutality of the apartheid regime. Given what he overcame, Gandhi's dedication to nonviolence here in our especially violent little corner of the world stands as a beacon of hope and selflessness.

Ironically – or perhaps predictably – Gandhi was assassinated in 1948 in New Delhi, shot at close range by a Hindu extremist. A week later two million people attended his funeral procession. In 2010, on the 62nd anniversary of his death, a small portion of his ashes was scattered in the waters off Durban.

*(See **Nelson Mandela** and **Jan Smuts**.)*

Herschelle Gibbs

b. 23 February 1974

Cricket star; 438 champion; sporting prodigy; entertainer; party man; wastrel; loveable rogue

BASIL D'OLIVEIRA MADE HIS APPEARANCE earlier in the book as a cricketer and man who transcended the game he played and the time he lived in; a fine human being who required courage and integrity, as well as skill, to get to the top of his profession. He was an exceptional player, certainly, but the reasons for including him here go well beyond cricket. So we've cleared another cricketing spot – and we've gone and given it to Herschelle Gibbs. Surprised?

Though there are so many world-class South African cricketers to choose from, we've opted for the guy whose career statistics are, if we're brutally honest, nothing more than very good – and who always hit the news for the wrong reasons. Indeed, Herschelle Gibbs must be the only sportsman in South Africa who it seems appropriate to caricature, not actually playing sport, but with a joint in his mouth…

What about the *best* cricketer we've ever produced? Pollock, Richards or Kallis? Graeme Pollock is widely acknowledged as one of the finest batsmen to have graced the field, a player whose average of 60.97 stands him behind only Donald Bradman in the rankings of Test greats. Barry Richards was considered even more dangerous than Pollock by many of the bowlers of the day, a man whose legend was stunted only by the pariahdom of his country at the time. And then there's Jacques Kallis, still playing, the greatest all-rounder of them all – and if you're going to argue for Sobers then it's a tie and nothing less.

We've also been blessed with many tremendous fast bowlers. Since readmission in 1992, Allan Donald, Dale Steyn and another great Pollock, Shaun, all have career figures more impressive than Gibbs's. You could also argue for Jonty Rhodes, the player who revolutionised fielding (and general energy) as a weapon in a team's armoury – or for his prototype, Colin Bland, the guy who did it originally way back in the 1960s. Bland was so good that he once hit three stumps one after the other in a fielding exhibition before a tour match in England in 1965. The keeper, Dennis Gamsy, who was behind the stumps at the time, wasn't paid his attendance fee as a result – because he hadn't been required to do anything…

Or we could try the historical option, the ground-breaker, a fellow by the name of Jimmy Sinclair, who scored the first hundred for South Africa in 1899. He in fact hit our first three centuries, one of which is still by measure of time the fastest in South African Test history: 80 minutes. Sinclair's story is a fascinating one. He is credited with putting South African cricket on the map as a swaggering all-rounder, and he has the remarkable distinction of having escaped a Boer prisoner-of-war camp during the South African War because he wanted to make the tour of England in 1901. He also played a rugby Test for the Springboks against the British Isles.

The truth of it is that any man who's walked onto the cricket field in South African colours and made a little magic has a measure of brilliance in him. So why Gibbs?

Well, it sure isn't for his wholesome values and gentlemanly demeanour. In fact, in that department he makes for a cataclysmic comparison with D'Oliveira, a quiet man whose ascent to the heights of the game was always accompanied with grace and humility. Gibbs, on the other hand, is the perfect example of why sportsmen should *not* be seen as role models, someone "as poorly equipped for the trials of daily life as any human being can safely be", as Telford Vice once described him. He has been involved in match-fixing, dope-smoking and racial-abuse controversies, and was banned for the former for six months, collateral damage from the Hansie Cronje affair. ("Looking back now, it was probably one of the most stupidest decisions I have made," he would later say.) He has hit the headlines for fathering a love child, driving under the influence and being one half of a particularly tacky divorce. Never one to restrain himself in an interview, he famously admits to only having read one book in his entire life, his *second* biography. It was called *To The Point*, and it was published in 2010 to widespread critical disdain and immediate sales success, with readers lapping up scurrilous details of drinking bouts and sexual conquests. Reviewers, including his first biographer Colin Bryden (perhaps peeved that Gibbs hadn't read *Herschelle: A Biography*), denounced it as "sordid", "depressing" and "cringeworthy". Amazingly, despite criticising several

> "Gibbs is about as close as cricket has come to producing a punk rocker, a figure who veers too close to self-destruction too often for the likes of those who prefer their cricketers unblemished by the real world."
>
> — *Telford Vice*

senior Proteas players in the book, Gibbs professed the hope that he would be selected to play for his country again, both in the book and in interviews afterwards. A sporting genius he may be, but a genius genius he isn't. This is the man, after all, who went to a disciplinary hearing – for calling Pakistani supporters a "bunch of fucking animals" during a 2007 Test match at Centurion – and emerged with two beers in hand.

But Gibbs's embarrassing decision-making and his hurricane of a private life belie two things. First, he is a nice guy. No, he's never going to be first pick in your Trivial Pursuit team, but he is a lot more genuine and approachable than many other sportsmen out there, and if there's one thing that Herschelle wants it's for everyone to be having a good time. And second, in those moments when he defied his lack of worldly nous and the personal demons stampeding about his head, he was simply sensational to watch on a sports field.

This was never as pronounced as when he was at school, before the distractions and pitfalls of living in the limelight presented themselves. As a cricketer, his youthful talent was obvious. He scored somewhere in the region of 3,500 runs for his school First XI, an almost impossible figure that would have been more but for his selection to Western Province senior teams from the age of 16. In his first match for the A side, against Northern Transvaal, he made a good-looking 14 before being caught in a legside trap off the wily left-arm spin of Willie Morris. (It would prove to be something of a metaphor for Gibbs's life.) His fielding was astonishing from the start. While still in matric, he was awarded "catch of the year on TV" for a blinding running take at mid-on, and he made it on to the field as 12th man during South Africa's first Test match since readmission, against the West Indies in Bridgetown in 1992.

Amazingly, many knowledgeable observers considered him a better rugby player than cricketer. In 1990, his under-16 rugby coach wrote, "Herschelle Gibbs is a genius. He has magic in his hands, magic in his feet. If he wants it, he could become one of the legends of rugby football." The doyen of schoolboy rugby, Basil Bay, praised his "extraordinarily high rugby IQ" and his all-round game at fly-half. He could kick, run, step, distribute and tackle; his game had no flaws, except perhaps that he wasn't always motivated against weaker opposition. In 1992 he single-handedly won the Craven Week final for Western Province against the Free State, scoring two superb individual tries. That same year, he broke his school 100-metre sprint record – for the second year in a row – running 10.9 on grass with no training and no starter blocks.

And, even more amazingly, the sport he favoured the most was soccer. Having finished his First XV rugby duties, he would race off to play for his club, Rygersdal, the game often delayed for his arrival. In one instance he arrived with only five minutes left to play; he was sent on immediately, scored the equaliser and then pocketed the winner in extra time. He was invited to Arsenal trials but couldn't make the trip due to a lack of funds. Wise heads believe he could have made a stellar name for himself playing soccer.

Unsurprisingly, Gibbs was selected for SA Schools for all three major sports. He was eventually steered towards a career in cricket because of his early provincial success and the safety and longevity that it offered. (He probably could have made careers for himself in table tennis, squash or golf, if he'd put his mind to it; anything with a ball.)

Two decades later and it's fair to say that those who watched him on the sports field as a 16- and 17-year-old will be somewhat disappointed with his overall efforts. "Only" 14 Test centuries. "Only" averaging 42 in Tests and 36 in One Day Internationals… "Could have done better," his report card might say.

But in his more inspired moments, when he wasn't distracted by off-the-field shenanigans or taking the wrong advice, he could briefly deliver his fans to cricketing nirvana. As when he would dance up the pitch and drive an opening bowler (Brett Lee, say) on the up over extra cover, or when he would hook the same bowler, possibly in the same over, off a good length and on the front foot, cleanly and without any doubt of the ball's destination. When he wanted, he had every shot in the book and could hit any ball to the boundary.

There were, of course, many exceptional knocks and moments down the years. In 2002 in Durban Gibbs scored a match-winning fourth-innings century against an Australian team that featured one of the

> "Herschelle's innings was amazing on several levels, not the least of which was that we almost dropped him before the game. Graeme and I seriously debated whether we should play him because, yet again, he'd been out the night before and was not in great shape. We were close to our wits' end with him. Herschelle knew that I knew, Vinnie Barnes knew and Graeme knew – we were the only ones. And he knew he was very close to the edge. Maybe he knew he needed to produce something special... and he did! It was a typically majestic Herschelle innings. No, better than typical – one of his absolute best."
>
> – *Mickey Arthur, South African coach*

greatest bowling attacks of all time;* in 2003 at Newlands he rattled off 228 runs in a day against Pakistan; at the 2007 World Cup in the West Indies he hit six sixes in an over against the Dutch. But his natural brilliance was eventually encapsulated in one astonishing innings of wonderful, instinctive batting that only he could ever have delivered for the Proteas.** And, almost by fateful necessity, it came on the back of a tremendous hangover that had him coming perilously close to being dropped on the morning of the game.

The game, of course, was the 438 win over Australia at the Wanderers in 2006, one of the finest days in South African sport. Close your eyes for a moment and recall that beautiful, beautiful day. No lesser authority than *Wisden* officially deemed it "The Greatest ODI", and it easily ranks as the Proteas' best limited-overs win, not least because the team had to break a raft of records to get there, they scraped in by a solitary wicket in the last over of the match and, in doing so, they won a series against

---

* Glenn McGrath, Brett Lee, Jason Gillespie and Shane Warne. Ironically Gibbs was eventually out to the part-time offspin of Mark Waugh.

**AB de Villiers may contest this at some point.

the best team in the world. But, of course, the day belonged to Gibbs and the 175 runs he scored off 111 balls.

Neil Manthorp outlined the innings in *The Proteas: 20 Years, 20 Landmark Matches*: "He started relatively slowly for his first 50 runs (46 balls), but he upped the pace sufficiently to reach the then-fastest ODI hundred for South Africa (another 33 balls) and then simply exploded as he stepped down the pitch and smashed ball after ball through the covers and down the ground, collecting his last 75 runs in just 32 balls, by which time he had hit 21 fours to go with his seven sixes."

Gibbs eventually fell in the 32nd over with the score on 299, caught at long-off trying to hit his third six in a row. There was still much drama to come, but the fates ensured that it would be enough to secure both a South African victory and a spot for Gibbs as the ultimate hero on a day replete with heroics. No-one who saw his performance, whether South African, Australian or neutral, will ever forget it.

The sad, and possibly predictable, end to the cricket career of Herschelle Gibbs sees him, according to his Twitter account, as a "T20 specialist travelling the world!" He now plies his trade in India, Australia, New Zealand and wherever else he can make a buck or two from 20-over cricket. Financial incentives aside, it probably seems natural that he would gravitate towards the most abbreviated version of the game, with its limited attention span and "entertainment" sideshows, and many would argue that he came on the scene ten years too early. But perhaps the opposite is true. Because the modern world of professional sports – so scrutinised, so overthought, so rehearsed – was never really Gibbs's playground. If only we could have seen him playing soccer, rugby and cricket in amateur times. Ah, what could have been…

John Herschel

7 March 1792 – 11 May 1871

Astronomer, biologist, chemist, mathematician, inventor, philosopher, photographer and all-round wonder-brain; plotter of the southern skies; temporary resident of Cape Town

THE ENTRY BEFORE THIS belongs to Herschelle Gibbs. Right here you've got John Herschel. From Herschelle to Herschel on a double-page spread and you have two of the most diametrically opposed individuals in this whole book living side by side. One is quite possibly the most intellectually gifted individual of the lot, and the other is… well, not. And even if you've never heard of John Herschel before, you don't win any prizes for guessing which is which. They do have something in common, though: their brilliant all-round ability in their respective fields of expertise. In Herschelle's case, he shone when participating in any ball sport whatsoever, and in an amateur age he might have made a name for himself playing three or four of them. With Herschel, it was science. And whereas modern science has, like modern sport, specialised to such a degree that it's virtually impossible to excel beyond one discipline, Herschel lived in an age when science was in its infancy. He got to play with the lot of it, and even helped to invent a few offshoots.

If you have a passing interest in astronomy then you probably do, in fact, know the Herschel name. Father and son, William and John Herschel, were giants of the field and perfected the construction of the first large reflecting telescopes in England in the late 18th and early 19th centuries. Of course, neither of them were South African. But if you live in the southern suburbs of Cape Town you'll be familiar with the name, too. Herschel Girls School is one of the best schools in the country. Naturally, there is a link, which is why John Herschel finds himself in these pages: back in the 1830s he spent some of the most productive years of his life plotting the southern skies from what is now the leafy suburb of Claremont in Cape Town.

An Eton old boy and graduate of Cambridge, John Herschel seemed destined to follow in his father's multitalented footsteps. Among other things, William Herschel discovered Uranus and infrared radiation, coined the word "asteroid" and wrote 24 symphonies. So it's clear where John got his all-rounder abilities. He was 42 when he came to the Cape in 1834, by which time he was a revered man of science: an astronomer, mathematician, chemist, inventor and thinker of considerable renown. Among his many achievements, he had helped found the Royal Astronomical Society and he won various rather important-sounding awards for his re-examination of double stars catalogued by his father. In coming here, he hoped to further enhance William's work by completing a grand survey of the heavens that the two of them had begun in England, a task that could only be fulfilled in the southern hemisphere, where the area of the sky not visible in the north could be studied.

Herschel would not be the first international astronomer to use Cape Town as a base for his observations. In the early 1750s a Frenchman, Louis de la Caille, working from a house in Strand Street, spent time studying the skies. He named fourteen constellations not visible from Europe (from where the ancient Greeks had named the rest), and in so doing completed the Celestial Sphere. In a nod to his surroundings, he called one of them *Mons Mensae*, Latin for Table Mountain, which thus became the only geographical feature on the surface of the Earth represented by a constellation. Though it is small and rather insignificant, De la Caille intentionally positioned it just below the Large Magellanic Cloud, a heavenly representation of the Tablecloth. (Like, shuwow, man.)

On arrival in Cape Town, Herschel settled with his family on a large estate below the eastern slopes of the self-same Table Mountain. He called it Feldhausen, and set about erecting his state-of-the-art 20-foot reflecting telescope in a clearing on the estate known as The Grove.

Over the course of the following four years, Herschel completed his visual telescopic survey of the entire sky – "probably still the only man to have done so", according to late UCT professor of astronomy Tony Fairall. In the process he discovered approximately 2,100 double stars and 1,700 nebulae, and made countless other observations. He befriended and frequently collaborated with Thomas Maclear, Her Majesty's Astronomer at the Cape at the time, for whom the highest point on Table Mountain is named. Together they took accurate measurements of Halley's Comet when it appeared in the night sky in 1835.

But Herschel's vast intellect and thirst for knowledge extended far beyond his astronomical interests, even in Cape Town. Though he spent up to sixteen hours a day making and recording his observations,

An 1860s etching of the night sky over Cape Town, from *The Midnight Sky* by Edwin Dunkin. The Milky Way dominates, with the Southern Cross and Pointers prominent (**1**). *Mons Mensae* or Table Mountain (**2**) appears to the right just below the Large Magellanic Cloud, acting as its Tablecloth (**3**).

> "Here stood from MDCCCXXXIV to MDCCCXXXVIII the reflecting telescope of Sir John FW Herschel, Baronet, who during a residence of fours years in this Colony contributed as largely by his benevolent exertions to the cause of education and humanity as by his eminent talents to the discovery of Scientific truth. Erected MDCCCXLI."
>
> *— Inscription on the obelisk monument situated in what is now The Grove Primary School, which was erected in 1842 at a cost of £300*

he became an important public figure in the young town, population 15,000 at the time, and contributed significantly to the schooling system with ideas that were considerably ahead of their time. With his wife Margaret's help, he produced 131 high-quality botanical drawings of Cape flora, which were eventually published in 1996 (as *Flora Herschelia* by Brian Warner and John Rourke; it's superb). In 1836 Herschel met the young Charles Darwin when the HMS *Beagle* arrived at the Cape; Darwin took great inspiration from the older man's writings, eventually referring to him as "one of our greatest philosophers" in the very first paragraph of the *The Origin Of Species*. Even from afar, his thoughts still influenced the great thinkers of the day back in England, including Charles Babbage, the first guy to imagine (and design) a computer. Herschel was a force of scientific and philosophical intellect; Cape Town was far poorer for his eventual departure in 1838.

After his return to England, Herschel spent years collating the work he had done, eventually publishing *Results Of Astronomical Observations Made During The Years 1834-1838 At The Cape Of Good Hope* in 1847.

Herschel and his family retained ties with the Cape for many years after, and astronomy in South Africa benefited hugely due to their influence. In time, the Cape Observatory, which later became the South African Astronomical Observatory, developed into a world-renowned institution. Today its primary telescopes are based in Sutherland, while the headquarters remain in the eponymous suburb of Observatory. The best astronomers on the continent are to be found in the vicinity.

With a little imagination it is possible to suppose that Herschel's genius extended, in some way, to the awarding of the multibillion-dollar Square Kilometre Array (SKA), one of the biggest and most expensive scientific projects in the world, to South Africa in 2012.

Today, Feldhausen estate has become a middle-class residential area behind the Cavendish Square shopping centre in Claremont. The land from which Herschel observed the heavens is home to The Grove Primary School, which was founded in his honour and is still run along the educational lines he promulgated at the time, and there is a large obelisk on the very spot where his telescope stood. The obelisk, completed in 1842, is a national monument, one of the oldest in the country; it is regularly visited by astronomers and historians, as well as classes from Herschel Girls School, down the road. The roads themselves serve as markers of Herschel's time spent in the Cape: School, Grove, Feldhausen, Obelisk, and of course Herschel Close, Road and Walk.

In the years after John Herschel's Cape excursion, he added untold value to the fields of astronomy, biology, chemistry and photography, a word he came up with, along with the photographic terms "negative" and "positive". He named the major moons of Saturn and Uranus and implemented the Julian Day system in astronomy. He performed pioneering studies on colour blindness and ultraviolet radiation, and translated Homer's *Iliad*. He was made a baronet by Queen Victoria and, on his death, was buried in Westminster Abbey next to Isaac Newton. In the words of Tony Fairall, Sir John Herschel was "one of the world's great scholars". That he performed some of his finest work in Cape Town, South Africa is a badge of honour for the city and country. Herschel and Herschelle: two brilliant all-rounders.

Waddy Jones

b. 26 September 1974

Rap-rave frontman of Die Antwoord; musical chameleon; journeyman-turned-superstar; hard-working long-persevering post-ironic zef star living an exaggerated existence

TRUTH SURELY IS STRANGER THAN FICTION when you think that a 30-something suburban Saffer white rapper armed with little more than a pickpocket's dexterity went culture-slumming, hijacked the best bits for himself, discarded the chaff, and created the zeitgeist with zef. And if that doesn't make any sense whatsoever that's because we're talking about Ninja from Die Antwoord, a modern music phenomenon that, in the grander scheme of things, makes about as much sense as a white guy with a faux-ironic hairstyle rhyming the phrase "poes cool" with "poes you" and getting away with it.

But Ninja, also known as Waddy Jones, more properly known as Watkin Tudor Jones, didn't just stumble into the big time by accident. Jones's story is one of perseverance, of metamorphosis, of sheer will and determination. After years of falling, getting back up, then falling again, he finally got a break in early 2010 when his new "rap-rave" band Die Antwoord "went all up on the interweb worldwide". They'd released a couple of singles as YouTube videos months earlier and all of a sudden they went viral, generating huge online interest and resulting in so many visits that it crashed the server that hosted the band's website.

"The response to Die Antwoord was a total mind-fuck," Jones says. "It was like being on an acid trip. I'd been rapping for twenty years and all of a sudden there was overload. It made no sense. You can make your confusion work for you. You have to drive into it. When you see that people are paying attention, then you have to push that motherfucker into the red."

All of a sudden the world had another nugget of trivia from that place famous for apartheid, Mandela and the Soccer World Cup. What was refreshing was how, instead of the usual cuddly rainbow-nation portrait, the band presented an entirely new view of South Africa to the world. An almost incomprehensible one, in fact. And with it came Ninja, an entirely new South African. "Blacks, whites, coloureds, English, Afrikaans, Xhosa, Zulu, *watookal.* I'm like all these different things, all these different people, fucked into one person," he declares in the lead-in to *Enter The Ninja*, the band's first big hit.

Ninja, it seems, had found The Answer: next-level beats with punch-line-heavy raps, a healthy dose of swearing and a visual identity as strong as the music was. Throw in some crude posturing, a pint-sized sexy singer chick with a fringe – Ninja's baby-mama Yo-Landi Vi$$er – and it all made for a thoroughly entertaining experience. Zef.

Essentially it was cheesy techno music with a liberal lashing of irony which, in a post-ironic world, was perhaps not always received as a rather extravagant piss-take. While South Africans thought it was pretty funny – a really slick joke, maybe a step or two up on Vernon Koekemoer – the world couldn't get enough. In a flash there was an international record deal with Interscope records. David Fincher wanted Yo-Landi for *The Girl With The Dragon Tattoo*. There was an offer to direct their next video from *District 9*'s Neill Blomkamp. A short movie with Harmony Korine. Collaboration with Roger Ballen. Front-row seats at New York Fashion Week. An Alexander Wang campaign…

An overnight success? Not quite.

Watkin Tudor Jones, a Parktown Boys' High old boy, tasted success fairly early. Two years out of school, in 1995, his band The Original Evergreen managed to get signed to Sony but Jones quit because they weren't taking rap as seriously as he thought they should. What followed was "a whole lot of contractual eff-ups", like not being allowed to record for three years, so Jones dressed up in his dad's three-piece suit and rapped the Johannesburg club scene as Max Normal – dress code strictly formal. During this time there was also a memorably regrettable stint as a Channel O presenter. ("I was the token white guy. It was the worst experience of my life. Getting exposed to the whole of Africa on this whack show.")

After the recording moratorium lifted, and building on the success of Max Normal, Jones put together a group by the same name. "The band started doing big, big shows where you couldn't see the back of the crowd and chicks were flashing their tits and nobody was listening. But I didn't trust the manager. He wasn't my cup of tea." Thus Max got axed and Jones stopped rapping for two years, spending all of his time drawing and writing and experimenting instead. *Constructus* was an experimental limited-edition hard-cover book. But now he felt he had veered too far into his dark side and, wanting to be as accessible as possible, he put out a new album, *The Fantastic Kill*, rapping under the moniker MC Totally Rad and doing a soft-toy range. Then he decided to resurrect Max Normal as a corporate hip-hop outfit that had Visser – not yet Vi$$er; actual name Anri du Toit – doing PowerPoint presentations and Jones trying to sell an animated series called *Spoek Mathambo* to the SABC. All of which sounds batshit crazy, certainly, but then Jones has never been known for marching to someone else's beat.

> "It doesn't matter why people like you. It just matters that you do something with it."
>
> – *Ninja, a.k.a Waddy Jones*

Jones realised he was overcomplicating things and that he needed to simplify his approach; after a decade and a half in the business it was time for another personality shift. So, being very smart about being stupid, and in order to appeal to the widest audience possible, he then turned himself, one crude prison tattoo at a time, into his current incarnation. Enter the Ninja. And what a change it was.

"It's cool playing the bad guy," he reckons. "It's like playing in a film where you get to play a character and go a bit crazy. It's nice poking fun at people who are horrible. It's cool to throw opposites together. Draws a lot of attention. Interesting things happen when you combine them. I think about that a lot."

And now, along with Yo-Landi, Ninja lives an "exaggerated existence" of Business Class flights, collaborating with Diplo, playing festivals with Aphex Twin, international fame and rolling cash registers – and you would think that all this would've changed the guy who used to be known as Watkin Tudor Jones.

Not so. After a year of honeymooning with Interscope Records, the label that represents 50 Cent, Lady Gaga, Eminem and Madonna, Die Antwoord threw a million dollars in the company's face and released their second album *Ten$ion* on their own.

"If you try to make songs that other people like, your band will always be shit," explains Jones-as-Ninja. "You always gotta do what you like. If it connects, it's a miracle, but it happened with Die Antwoord."

Ntshingwayo Khoza

c. 1810 – 21 July 1883

Quick-witted Zulu general who inflicted upon
Britain its most embarrassing colonial defeat

THERE IS A VERY LONG AND SCHOLARLY book about Zululand of old called *The Washing Of The Spears*. Oddly, it was written by an American, Donald Morris, who had yet to visit South Africa when it was published in 1965. Nonetheless it is considered the definitive text on the Zulu people from the time of Shaka to the destruction of the kingdom in 1879. And yet in that book there is but a sentence on the man who orchestrated Britain's greatest-ever colonial defeat. His name was Ntshingwayo kaMahole Khoza, and he deserves wider recognition as a great South African leader of men.

Britain would get its comeuppance at a place the Zulus called *iSandlwana*, today known as Isandlwana, a mountain shaped like the Egyptian Sphinx that adorned the cap badge of the 24th Regiment of Foot destined to be slaughtered there. And the road to Isandlwana was beset with classic colonial shenanigans. The High Commissioner for Southern Africa, Bartle Frere, had decided that the solution to the Zulu "problem" was a quick and decisive war. In and out. This despite direct orders from Whitehall specifically instructing him to avoid a "native war". But Frere figured that if he presented it as a *fait accompli* to his overseers in England then all would be well. After all, these Zulus were, in his words, just "a bunch of savages armed with sticks". *(See Bartle Frere, 50 People Who Stuffed Up South Africa.)*

So it was that Frere issued an impossible ultimatum to King Cetshwayo without the sanction, or even knowledge, of the British government.

Prime Minister Benjamin Disraeli and Queen Victoria had no idea what a Zulu was, nor where Zululand might be.

But they were going to find out.

Under the leadership of Lord Chelmsford, the British invaded Zululand on New Year's Day 1879, crossing the Buffalo River at Rorke's Drift and eventually setting up camp at the foot of Isandlwana. And it was Chelmsford who, against convention, then split his force to take a large party to investigate rumours of an impi in the mountainous country to the south, with approximately 1,400 men remaining in camp. It was a move typical for the lack of respect it showed for the Zulus' martial abilities, with Chelmsford assuming that his enemy would prefer to harass the unwieldy British column from mountainous countryside. The last thing anyone expected was for the Zulus to actually stand and fight.

The main Zulu army was, in fact, not far away. News of the British invasion had reached Ulundi quickly, and King Cetshwayo despatched his army, under Khoza, to repel the invaders. And he was very clear: the Zulu army was not to cross the border into Natal, but to drive the British back across the Buffalo River – known to them as the Umzinyathi – and to leave it at that. His intention was to keep the moral high ground, and in Khoza he had a man who would make it happen.

Khoza was tall and striking. He wore the traditional married man's headring, along with a most thunderous scowl. In January 1879 he was 70 years old and yet, along with his 22,000-strong impi, he ran barefoot to meet his enemy, some eighty kilometres away from Ulundi. Local lore has it that the swathes in the grass cut by the impi were still visible six months later.

As the British should have known, Khoza had under his command a fearsome army. Folk, even today, seem to fall into the trap of disrespecting the Zulu war machine, but they were fit, they were unquestionably brave and they were well trained. Armed with just "sticks", theirs was to be a mighty achievement.

Khoza ensconced his force in a gulley a few kilometres from the great plain at Isandlwana, where he had his men sit in silence on their shields. He had not planned to fight on the 22ⁿᵈ of the month because it was new moon, an inauspicious time in the Zulu calendar. But by luck an expeditionary force of British scouts stumbled across the ravine, and stared in utter disbelief at what they had found: the main Zulu army. The scouts turned and fled, carrying their crucial news back to the man left to guard the British camp, an unbloodied half colonel by the name of Henry Pulleine. And the news was this: the Zulus are not hiding in broken country to the south, they are right here, and they are going to stand and fight.

Khoza and his troops had been rumbled; the element of surprise was lost. We can only speculate what he and his generals had initially planned for Isandlwana, but Khoza's genius now was to immediately react to the change in circumstances and call for the attack. He went on to execute King Shaka's famous "horns of the buffalo" pincer movement. *(See Shaka.)* The British were aware of these battle tactics, but they likely never contemplated that Khoza would use them to such staggering effect, and on such an enormous scale.

Soon Khoza's army was visible on the escarpment to the north, and the Brits had set out a line to meet them.

Before we continue, though, let's take a moment to discuss the enemy Khoza's troops would meet, because it is not only the Zulu army that warrants a posthumous restoration of dignity. British soldiers, too, suffered under history as written by the apartheid state, which revelled in the idea of the rooinek wilting hopelessly under the African sun, and put the Boer commando firmly at the top of the South African fighting-man's tree.

"Ntshingwayo lived and died in the defence of the life and rights of his people. He was a patriot and a hero. The sacrifice he and so many others made during the colonial wars against the indigenous people of this country must not be forgotten."
– *Ronnie Kasrils, then Minister of Water Affairs and Forestry, at the renaming of Chelmsford Dam to Ntshingwayo Dam, which supplies Newcastle, August 2000*

This particular British contingent was mainly from the industrially depressed valleys of Wales, often forced by poverty to take the Queen's shilling. They were from places with names as exotic to us as Isandlwana would have been to them: Llanelli, Pontypridd, Aberstwyth and Caernarfon. They knew little of geopolitics, and their letters home make for some emotive reading.

These men from Wales had marched the 250 kilometres from Port Elizabeth to King William's Town, where they had fought in the last skirmishes of the Border Wars. Afterwards they had marched another 700 kilometres to Durban, and then several hundred more on to Isandlwana, where they would die. They would have looked a bit ramshackle. Their helmets would have been dyed with tea to make them stand out less. Their boots and uniforms would have been torn and worn. These were hardened, tough, leathery-tanned veterans, due for return to Britain; to dismiss them as lily-livered Poms blundering ineptly about the place does both them, and Khoza's men, a scandalous disservice.

But back to the battle, where Khoza didn't tarry. He sent his men in. It was 8am and it was already more than 30°C. The right horn ran out of sight to the north and west to cut off the road back to Rorke's Drift and Natal. The left horn swung far and wide, overwhelming a British rocket battery in the process, and the main head and the chest advanced at a sprint across the plain towards the mountain. This was the cream of Khoza's force, the young buck regiments, the Zulu paratroopers, and they ran into a withering hail of bullets.

Before long the gloriously named Zulu regiments were pinned down in a vlei. The *uVe*, the *umCijo*, *isaNqu* and the *inGobamakhosi*, the Benders of the Kings, who are name-checked in Johnny Clegg's iconic *Impi*, about this very battle. But it was the *uMbonambi*, on the left horn, who advanced, running though entire British companies as though they weren't there. Eventually the head and the chest of the Zulu assault advanced to within striking distance of the main British army, which began an orderly retreat, all the time laying down a deadly enfilade fire that was cutting the Zulu army to shreds.

Unbelievably, in the midst of all of this, an eclipse of the sun occurred.

All along the river Chelmsford's army lay asleep,
Come to crush the children of Mageba
Come to exact the realm's price for peace…
Hopeless battalion destined to die
Broken by the Benders of Kings…
They came to the side of the mountain,
Scouts rode out to spy the land,
Even as the realm's soldiers lay resting
Mageba's forces were at hand.
And by the evening the vultures were wheeling
Above the ruins where the fallen lay,
An ancient song as old as the ashes
Echoed as Mageba's warriors marched away

– Selected lyrics from Impi by Johnny Clegg and Juluka.
(Mageba was an early Zulu king, from the mid-18th century)

For those on the battlefield, one can only imagine the terror.

It was in the campsite that the British had made a mistake, because Pulleine, perhaps in panic but probably because he just never thought it necessary, had failed to order that camp be struck. And it is impossible to retreat in an orderly fashion through a pitched camp.

It quickly turned into a rout. Fleeing soldiers, bottle-washers, drummer boys, cooks and all the hangers-on you'd expect with a British column ran over the saddle of the mountain to find, to their horror, the road to Rorke's Drift blocked by none other than the *inDluyengwe* regiment, the Leopard's Lair, among others. Pulleine's men were cut down and disembowelled, an honour bestowed upon a brave enemy soldier so that his spirit may escape. It was respect at its most gruesome. Stragglers veered off the road and blundered through thick bush towards the Buffalo River several kilometres away. To this day, the white cairns under which their bodies are buried line the route to Fugitive's Drift, named in their honour, where to their horror they found the river in full spate.

In less than two hours it was over. Khoza had watched from the escarpment, directing his generals where necessary. When all was said and done, just 55 white men had escaped with their lives.

The stories of this battle are many and amazing. Not too far from Dundee in northern KwaZulu-Natal, Isandlwana is well worth a visit. It remains unspoilt, and its cairns and memorials tell their grizzly tale with a quiet serenity that belies the violence of the day. It is on the battlefield itself that visitors get a real sense of the scale over which Khoza directed his army.

It's really important, this. The stunning Zulu defeat of the British came against a hardened and technically superior force armed with modern Martini-Henry rifles, a couple of artillery pieces and a rocket battery. The victors fought with assegais and some old rifles and muskets. Using the topography, which he knew intimately, and reacting to events quickly and decisively, Khoza's tactical brilliance cannot be underestimated. For this battle alone, he deserves to be hailed as one of the greatest generals to grace the planet.

Tragically, Khoza's success at Isandlwana, and the scale of the massacre, would assure the destruction of the Zulu nation. Victorian Britons did not like to read of disembowelment over their breakfasts. Exactly 1,329 of the Queen's soldiers lay dead, and anywhere between 1,000 and 6,000 thousand Zulu warriors lay with them. Chelmsford's force, returning in the dark, would describe their horror at the way the grass was slick with gore, gutted corpses strewn everywhere, and vultures having spent the afternoon feasting. It is a scene that is terrible to contemplate, and retribution was inevitable.

For the record, King Cetshwayo's impi was destroyed at Ulundi less than six months later, on 4 July 1879. The British came with Gatling guns. Up on a koppie, directing events, Khoza would have been with the king. Watching the Zulu nation die, he would have recalled a time in his boyhood before it had even come into being as a proud and mighty force, a time before Shaka.

Khoza died when Cetshwayo was returned to Zululand from England after his exile, in 1883. Zululand had been sliced into thirteen separate chiefdoms by the British. It was the classic divide-and-rule strategy, and it worked as Zululand descended into civil war and internecine blood feuds. The Mandlakhazi attacked Cetshwayo and his clan in 1883. The king was injured and Ntshingwayo Khoza was killed – an ignominious end to a great general.

There's an engraving at a memorial at Isandlwana for a colonial company, the Natal Carbineers. The great Zululand historian David Rattray always used to say that, with a word or two changed here and there, it would also make a fitting memorial to Khoza and his men.

> *Not theirs to save the day,*
> *But where they stood,*
> *Falling to dye the Earth*
> *With brave men's blood,*
> *For England's sake and duty*
> *Be their names sacred among us.*
> *Neither praise nor blame*
> *Add to their epitaph,*
> *But let it be simple as that which*
> *Marked Thermopylae.*
> *Tell it in England those*
> *That pass us by,*
> *Here, faithful to their charge,*
> *Her soldiers lie.*

*(See **Simeon Khambula**.)*

Simeon Khambula

c.1800s

*Soldier; loyal and brave leader of men; provider
of evidence, annoying to some, that it wasn't only
the Brits who wanted to smash the Zulus*

THE EAGLE-EYED READER might note that this chapter is alphabetically
out of place. By rights, Khambula ought to precede Khoza. But we're
breaking the rules on this one. Hopefully the reason will make itself
quickly apparent.

The previous entry is about a great Zulu patriot and general, a man
whose skilful conduct on the battlefield meant his army stuck it to the
Brits in no uncertain way. But before we wrap up Khoza's astonishing
story, we need to make and illustrate the point that the Anglo-Zulu War
of 1879 was far more complicated than innocent little Zululand being
duffed up by big ol' Britain.

One fact that won't sit comfortably with many people is this: more
than half of Lord Chelmsford's force that invaded Zululand in January
1879 was made up of Zulu-speaking black people. And they weren't
forced to fight the Zulus. They wanted to.

This is because Zululand was hardly some benign Switzerland of
southern Africa. It was, in fact, the Britain of the area, the big military
outfit ruled by an indomitable monarch with a fondness for empire and
war. And it was inevitable that when the people of the area, so similar
in so many ways, were to encounter each other at battle it would be
somewhat cataclysmic.

The region had only recently settled down after the depredations of
the Mfecane, the dreadfully violent ripple effect caused by the sudden

militarised expansion of the Zulu empire under Shaka. *(See Moshoeshoe I and Shaka.)* The Battle of Blood River had marked the high tide of the Zulu-Boer conflict, and after Mpande came to the Zulu throne in 1840 and the British began to colonise Natal not long after, the incredible upheaval of the preceding decades began to fade. The people of Zululand and Natal lived in relative peace alongside each other for many years, but after the death of Mpande in 1872 the new King Cetshwayo reprised an old tradition known as the "washing of the spears", which proclaimed that a Zulu man could not marry until he had bathed his assegai in the blood of an enemy (and after which Donald Morris had named his book – *see Ntshingwayo Khoza*). This was hardly progressive. And a canny commentator might consider the southeastern territories of South Africa circa 1878 and note that Cetshwayo and his impis had limited enemies in whose blood they might bathe their spears.

That thousands of black people were likely fed up with this frightening sabre-rattling and general intimidation, and were quite excited about getting some revenge on the region's big bully on the back of a British invasion, is evident in the fact that they signed up to fight alongside the colonial and imperial forces of Queen Victoria, the "Great White Queen". People had been fighting each other in the hills of Zululand long before the Brits arrived – their arrival merely complicated a situation that already existed. Sadly, the fighting would continue long after they left, and this all probably goes some way to explain the ever so torrid and occasionally murderous nature of ANC-IFP politics in KwaZulu-Natal in the modern age.

As for the British, some of the empire's officers didn't much care for being assigned to so-called native regiments, but one chap, Colonel Anthony Durnford, loved his Edendale Horse contingent very much indeed. (Durnford was considered an odd fish at the garrison town of Pietermaritzburg. An Irishman often seen riding his beloved white charger, Chieftain, he struck up a firm friendship with John Colenso, the first Anglican bishop of Natal, and a far firmer friendship with the bishop's daughter, Frances. It was a dalliance that scandalised Victorian Pietermaritzburg.)

In 1873 Durnford was dispatched to deal with a Hlubi gunrunner called Chief Langalibalele. He was sent with a ragtag troop of Tlokwa men and the rather ridiculous order not to fire first. The translator assigned to the expedition was Elijah Khambula, a missionary-educated man who would unfortunately not return. In short, there was a firefight. Durnford was injured – his arm would hang uselessly by his side for the rest of his life – and Khambula was killed, which upset Durnford greatly.

But Khambula had a son, Simeon, who would sign up to fight at the side of the charismatic Irishman when word came that there was to be a British invasion of Zululand in 1879. Indeed, tribal elders exhorted their men to join in the fight once Durnford had requested a mounted force from the Edendale area, and Sergeant Simeon Khambula was one of a large group of local forces to do so.

> "We all know the cruelty and the power of the Zulu king… and if he should subdue the queen's soldiers and overrun this land he will wipe out all the native people who have dwelt so long in safety under the shadow of the Great White Queen. Shall we not gladly obey her, when she calls for the services of her dark children?"
>
> – Daniel Msimang, local elder,
> encouraging his people to join the British invasion of Zululand

On the fateful day of 22 January 1879, Durnford found himself on the receiving end of the left horn of the Zulu impi's attack at Isandlwana, with Khambula at his side. As the sheer number of Zulu soldiers threatened to overwhelm Durnford's contingent, they would, as they had practised in the lead-up to the invasion, mount their horses, beat a hasty but organised retreat, stop, halter their horses, and lay down a withering fire until the impi was nearly upon them. Then, seeing as the battlefield at Isandlwana is pretty huge, they would repeat the process over and over. And they might have carried on doing this all day, but for the fact that as they carefully retreated into the saddle of the Sphinx-like mountain, two things began to happen: Khoza's impi started overrunning the main British line and Durnford's troops began running out of ammunition.

Not far from the spot where the memorial for the Natal Native Contingent stands at Isandlwana today, Durnford ordered his men to fix bayonets and make a final stand – except, that is, for Khambula and his mounted Edendale Horse, numbering a few dozen riders. They were, he ordered, to "secure the koppie", a position with no tactical or militarily use. Khambula would later recount how he begged Durnford to come with him, and how he knew he and his men were being sent away so that they might be saved. But Durnford was adamant. He gave Khambula the reigns to his beloved Chieftain, and ordered him off the battlefield.

Khambula was hugely moved and upset, for Durnford and his soldiers were soon dead and disembowelled. The sergeant ordered his own men to stick together, and they attempted to harry the Zulu warriors as they chased down British stragglers on the way to Fugitive's Drift. His troops made several telling stands before retreating and managed to save a number of otherwise doomed and terrified British on the way.

Upon reaching the Buffalo River, the border between Zululand and Natal, Khambula had his men lay down covering fire so that the fugitives could cross without being attacked. On seeing the approaching Edendale Horse, the Zulus briefly retreated, allowing Khambula and his men to cross the flooded river, shouting at the remaining British to cling to his men's stirrups as they went. From the Natal bank, his men turned and fired into the Zulus until their ammunition ran low.

Already a hero of the battle by any standards, Khambula now did something astoundingly brave, given the scale of the slaughter he had just witnessed. Instead of running directly for the safety of the British garrison at Helpmekaar, about fifteen kilometres into Natal, he and his now diminished force of men made for the little mission station at Rorke's Drift, a couple of kilometres upstream – the same point at which the invasion of Zululand had commenced. The company of men stationed there, just 110 strong, had heard the guns of battle and had by now received the news that their regiment had been devastated by the Zulu army and that one wing of that same Zulu army, estimated at

4,000 warriors, was (against Cetshwayo's and Khoza's orders) hotfooting it towards the little mission station to indulge in a little spear-washing. Turns out that right horn of the impi had never really got stuck in, and those young men wanted to return home and marry their girls.

Khambula and his men assisted with preparing the defences, creating a redoubt and using supplies to shore up defensive walls, but his courageous offer to help defend the station was, somewhat curiously, declined. There was no room to keep his men's horses in the small station, and sacrificing the horses was clearly not the done thing. Instead, he was tasked with harassing the Zulu force as it approached, which he and his troops did before they were eventually forced to retreat to Helpmekaar.

(In the end the small British company was able to repel the Zulu onslaught in one of the most celebrated defences in military history. In a night of fighting that saw nearly every defender wounded or injured in some way, but only seventeen killed, they held off their attackers, killing hundreds of Zulus and winning eleven Victoria Crosses in the process.)

Simeon Khambula had stood up for what he believed was right as much as had Ntshingwayo Khoza. He, like so many other people living in Natal at the time, was fed up with Zulu bullying and violence, and had chosen to side with the colonisers. It was, no doubt, a devil's alternative, but Troop Sergeant-Major Simeon Khambula of the Edendale Horse served Her Majesty with great bravery and for this he received a Distinguished Conduct Medal – "from the hands of an English general," noted the Reverend Owen Watkins. "Had he been a white man, he would have received the Victoria Cross." Indeed he would have, but Victorian prejudice would not allow such a thing. No doubt it will strike many as odd that so many men would go into battle to risk their lives for, and would show such extraordinary loyalty to, a colonial system that would forever regard them as children, as second-class citizens.

But it makes sense to turn this around. Perhaps, given the choice, this really was the lesser of two evils. If it was life under Victoria or life under Cetshwayo, history would appear to suggest that thousands were ready to fight for a life under a fundamentally racist system and to be ruled over by the Great White Queen. Funny how it all worked out in the end.

Chad le Clos

b. 12 April 1992

Swimmer; Olympic champion; Phelps conqueror;
potential future Phelps; son of YouTube sensation

AT THE 2008 OLYMPIC GAMES Team South Africa won one medal. One single solitary sad and lonely medal. A silver. Well done to longjumper Godfrey Khotso Mokoena for sparing us complete *and utter* embarrassment in Beijing, but the mild depression that followed was haunting, that's for sure. (Made even worse by our team appearing at the opening ceremony in Crocs, for the love of sweet mercy.)

By contrast, at the 2012 Olympics in London we won six medals: three golds, two silvers and a bronze. The comparative relief was so overwhelming that even now we feel obliged to name all the winners here, if only out of sheer gratitude. They were, in chronological order:

GOLD Cameron van der Burgh – swimming – men's 100m breaststroke

GOLD Chad le Clos – swimming – men's 200m butterfly

GOLD Sizwe Ndlovu, Matthew Brittain, John Smith, James Thompson –
rowing – men's lightweight four

SILVER Chad le Clos – swimming – men's 100m butterfly

BRONZE Bridgitte Hartley – canoe sprint – women's K1 500m

SILVER Caster Semenya – athletics – women's 800m

Van der Burgh, it must be mentioned, broke the world record to win his race and he could easily feature in this book. Caster Semenya does, for slightly more complex reasons *(see Caster Semenya)*. And the rowing boys could be here just for participating in the tensest, most exciting race of the entire Games.

While we're at it, it's only fair to consider other recent outstanding Olympians. Penny Heyns, one of the world's great breaststroke swimmers, is the obvious one, with her record-breaking double golds at the Atlanta Olympics in 1996, followed by a bronze in Sydney; Josiah Thugwane won one of the hardest-earned and least predictable of all athletics golds, the marathon, also in 1996; and, if you witnessed it, you'll never forget our equally unexpected world record in the 4x100m freestyle relay in Athens in 2004.

But only one South African has beaten Michael Phelps, the most decorated Olympian of all time: Chad le Clos.

It may seem unfair to spend too long discussing the guy who our guy beat, an American, in an entry dedicated to our guy, but the greatness of Phelps needs to be made manifest to appreciate Le Clos's achievement. Besides, it's unlikely Le Clos would object; Phelps has been his hero for many years and he actually told him as much in London. So as quickly as possible, then, the rundown on Phelps goes like this. He has 22 Olympic medals. Twenty-two! The entire country of South Africa has to go back to Thugwane's gold in Atlanta to beat that haul. He has eighteen gold medals from three Olympics. South Africa has 23 from seventeen. Of the 48 men's swimming events raced since the Athens Olympics in 2004, Phelps competed in half of them, medalled in 46 percent of them and won 38 percent of them. If Michael Phelps were a country, he would be coming 12th on the gold medal table since 2004. He is the best ever swimmer there has ever been. Ever.

Which is all a rather long-winded way of saying that Le Clos's achievement was something truly special.

The race itself, the 200-metre butterfly final, was a cracker. There was no way the world-record holder was going to be beaten in one of his strongest disciplines except by the narrowest of margins, and Le Clos had to come from third on the final turn, and several metres behind the champ, to pip him by a fingernail. But pip him, he did. Phelps seemed to make a basic timing error in his final lunge for the wall, allowing the late-surging Le Clos to take victory by just 0.05 seconds. In the crowd Princess Charlene of Monaco, who used to give Le Clos lifts as a kid to the Pinetown swimming pool where they both trained, was ecstatic, while around South Africa stunned fans fell off their chairs.

Three days later, Le Clos won silver to Phelps's gold in the 100-metre version of the event, a result that was far less surprising to those watching, but one that elevated the young Durbanite into the rarefied atmosphere of multiple Olympic medal winners, an honour that only fourteen other South Africans share.

And the lovely thing about his success is that he's such a likeable guy too. He blubbed during the national anthem, he has an amazing relationship with his dad (and, presumably, his mom), he's well spoken and respectful and, hey, he's friends with a princess. But if you're a South African sports fan, what's particularly palm-rubbingly endearing about him is that he's just starting out. Le Clos originally intended to use London 2012 as preparation for Rio de Janeiro 2016; he wasn't thinking about gold medals. So if he's beating the world's greatest Olympian as a stepping stone to future Games, we can only imagine what he has in store for us in Rio. He is already a virtual shoo-in to win at least one more gold and thus join Penny Heyns and Charles Winslow – tennis singles and doubles, Stockholm, 1912 – as our only double gold Olympians, but perhaps he has grander ambitions. Perhaps Chad le Clos is South Africa's Michael Phelps in the making. But even if he isn't, he *beat* Michael Phelps. Did we mention that?

BBC: And here is Chad's father, Bert. My word, what a performance?

Bert Le Clos: Unbelievable, unbelievable, unbelievable! I've never been so happy in my life, it's something undescribable! Tonight, it's like I died and went to heaven, whatever happens in my life now is plain sailing, it's plain sailing.

BBC: And there is your boy down there, I think he could hardly believe it, not just that he's won the gold medal but that he's beaten Michael Phelps.

BLC: This is unbelievable! Look at him! He's beautiful! Look at that! What a beautiful boy! [Bert apologises for getting carried away]

BBC: Tell us a bit about Chad, when he decided to swim and how he's got this good.

BLC: He is unbelievable. He is committed like you cannot believe. He is the most down-to-earth beautiful boy you'll ever meet in your life. Look at him, he's smiling like me! I love you. [to Chad, who is doing a victory lap]

BBC: [laughing]

BLC: Is this live?

BBC: Yes, you're fine! And his mum is here as well, how many more friends and family members have you got here?

BLC: My other son is here, the small one, and he's somewhere up there, I can't find him. We had to get tickets all over the place, you know. It's not easy to get tickets.

BBC: I know, we're aware, but you were here for the most perfect moment in your son's life and it sounds like the most perfect moment in yours.

BLC: Ah, unbelievable, unbelievable. Thanks, Great Britain! [he raises his fist]

BBC: Thank you and congratulations.

BLC: Thank you very much!

– BBC interview with Bert le Clos after his son won gold in the 200m butterfly

Albert Luthuli

c. 1898 – 21 July 1967

Teacher; tribal chief; ANC legend; Nobel Peace Prize winner; committed nonviolent nonracial reconciler; the best president we never had

To READ LET MY PEOPLE GO, Albert Luthuli's autobiography, is to understand something about this country that is, unfortunately, rather depressing. We miss our opportunities. We do it all the time. Case in point: Luthuli. Because as Harold Macmillan's winds of change swept the continent of Africa in the 1960s, and nation after nation attained their freedom, fate offered us the perfect man for the job in South Africa – a man who believed with absolute sincerity that South Africa belonged to all those who lived in it, black and white. But we had Verwoerd and his jackbooted mob of fascist troglodytes stuffing up the place.

Despite his very real commitment to nonviolence and nonracialism, despite his insistence that peaceful disobedience was as far as the ANC would go, all Luthuli ever got back from the government was bans, banishment and bullets. So an opportunity for great leadership would be missed – just as it would be with Tambo and Sisulu and Biko. And the result, effectively, is the government we have today. Say no more.

Imagine the odds, if you will, of a black boy born near Bulawayo in 1898 going on to win a Nobel Peace Prize. Long, you might say, and you'd be right. But it happened.

In 1908 Luthuli moved back to his ancestral home in Groutville, Natal with his mother after his father, John, had died. After school, he turned down a scholarship to Fort Hare – the standard and eventually well-worn route into the ANC – and instead took up teaching at a school near Newcastle, where he would spend the next fifteen years.

In 1936 he was elected chief of the Mvoti Mission Reserve and was forced to leave the school, but it was his work here that would give him the experience he would later need in the ANC during some very dark days indeed. In that same year, the government started removing from blacks what little rights they had in regard to land ownership and the vote. It was a process that radicalised people not historically involved with politics or protest – Albert Luthuli being among them – and it culminated in the establishment of the Non-European Unity Movement in Bloemfontein in 1943. Luthuli joined the ANC and quickly became quite the star in the Natal branch. But things were about to get worse.

The election of DF Malan, and the official implementation of apartheid in 1948, changed the landscape completely. It's easy to forget just how fast and how incredibly technically proficient the apartheid government was in its move to socially engineer this country; so much so that Verwoerd's "skills" in this respect would have to be considered brilliant in their way. Fortunately, as a result of Hertzog's previous laws, the ANC was at least organised by this time.

By 1950 the ANC was being squeezed by its more militant youth wing and the increasingly oppressive advance of apartheid. As a result, large-scale peaceful protest became the favoured mode of rebellion, resulting in, inevitably, the infamous Riotous Assemblies Act and the Suppression of Communism Act, which made such protest illegal. It also got Luthuli into trouble; in 1952 the government booted him out of his role as chief in the Mvoti region.

And that's when Luthuli got the *moer* in.

"Who will deny that thirty years of my life have been spent knocking in vain, patiently, moderately and modestly at a closed and barred door?" he railed. "Has there been any reciprocal tolerance or moderation from the Government, be it Nationalist or United Party? No! On the contrary, the past thirty years have seen the greatest number of laws restricting our rights and progress until today we have reached a stage where we have almost no rights at all. It is with this background and with a full sense of responsibility that, under the auspices of the African National Congress, I have joined my people in the new spirit that revolts openly and boldly against injustice and expresses itself in a determined and nonviolent manner."

Within a month, Luthuli was elected head of the ANC and received

"Despite the regime's efforts to silence him, the Luthuli name became a colossal symbol of peace and unity, far beyond the horizons of Groutville and even the borders of South Africa. We stand today on the shoulders of such giants. The Chief chose a life of hardship and persecution when he demanded 'Let my people go!' In doing so he taught us a very important lesson – that real leaders must be prepared to sacrifice all for the freedom of their people."

– *Nelson Mandela, speaking in 2007*

his first banning order. It was the first of many to come, and there would be jail time, too. But wherever he spoke, he had one abiding theme: "South Africa does not belong to any one race or tribe; it belongs to all who live in it, black and white, and no government can justly claim authority unless it is based on the will of all the people."

As the fifties wore on, Luthuli became increasingly frustrated. He was appalled by the evictions in Sophiatown and District Six, but he refused to countenance violence, even in the face of criticism from the likes of Robert Sobukwe. Heavily influenced by the success Gandhi had enjoyed, he remained committed to nonviolence. *(See Mahatma Gandhi.)*

In 1955, at the Congress of the People, the Freedom Charter was written and adopted. It marked a high point for nonviolent protest against apartheid. JG Strijdom, South Africa's new Prime Minister, wasn't impressed, and 156 people were rounded up to face what become known as the Treason Trial, Luthuli among them. *(See Winnie Madikizela-Mandela.)* The trial dragged on for years, with Luthuli often banished to his home in Groutville.

But then everything changed. In 1960 police opened fire on an anti-pass demonstration in Sharpeville; a minute later 69 people were dead or dying. Within a week the ANC and the PAC were banned. South Africa was booted out of the Commonwealth, a State of Emergency was declared and as many as 18,000 people were rounded up. Luthuli himself was assaulted by police while in detention. Speaking on the fortieth anniversary of his death, Nelson Mandela described his reaction: "[I]t was hard for us to take. A man of immense dignity and achievement, a lifelong Christian and a man with a dangerous heart condition, was treated like a barnyard animal by men who were not fit to tie his shoes."

Without Luthuli's knowledge, Mandela and company went on to establish Umkhonto we Sizwe (MK), but even Luthuli was beginning to see that nonviolence just wasn't working. And so he wrote: "The ANC never abandoned its method of a militant, nonviolent struggle, and of creating in the process a spirit of militancy in the people. However, in the face of uncompromising white refusal to abandon a policy which denies the African and other oppressed South Africans their rightful heritage – freedom – no-one can blame brave just men for seeking justice by the use of violent methods; nor could they be blamed if they tried to create an organised force in order to ultimately establish peace and racial harmony."

So it was not without unhappy irony that, as this abandonment of nonviolence became necessary, Luthuli was awarded the Nobel Peace Prize "for a religious-political creed his organisation now found irrelevant", to quote the activist and writer Es'kia Mphahlele. Luthuli was awarded the prize in 1960 but was initially prevented by the government from leaving the country. He accepted it in Oslo the following year, delivering a memorable and eloquent speech.

> "It is welcome recognition of the role played by the African people during the last fifty years to establish, peacefully, a society in which merit and not race would fix the position of the individual in the life of the nation. This award could not be for me alone, nor for just South Africa, but for Africa as a whole."
>
> – Albert Luthuli, in his Nobel Prize acceptance speech, Oslo, December 1961

After the raid on the MK headquarters in Rivonia, and the trial and imprisonment of Mandela, Sisulu and the rest, and with Tambo in exile, the movement had been dealt a very serious blow. Even though he was pinned down in Groutville, Luthuli did his best to carry on leading the banned ANC until his death in 1967. Nearly 70 and mostly deaf, he was "hit by a train". But most of his supporters reckon he was murdered, and 45 years later the circumstances remain highly suspicious.

His death pretty much marked the end of nonviolence in the battle to end apartheid and, while he has been criticised by some for his unending efforts to negotiate an end to apartheid, the fact that the Nationalists were so blind cannot, in the final analysis, be laid at Luthuli's feet. He was a good man, one of the best, and a golden opportunity missed – as happens way down here at the bottom tip of Africa.

Winnie Madikizela-Mandela

b. 26 September 1936

Liberation heroine; source of hope and strength in the darkest days of apartheid; ex-wife of Nelson Mandela; maker of grave ethical mistakes; lightning rod for apartheid-era hatred and post-apartheid reactionary white hostility

A TYPICAL DAY IN THE LIFE OF WINNIE MADIKIZELA-MANDELA

"STOMPIE." It's pretty much all they can say.

There is a breed of South African for whom the word "Stompie" is the story of Winnie Madikizela-Mandela. A life lived. Everything in that one word. And the reason is because it is how they wish it would be. They wish her life could be distilled to this one word, which speaks of an unforgivable deed committed at the height of PW Botha's State of Emergency; this word that means, without question, that the name of Winnie Madikizela-Mandela will be stained forever and ever, amen.

But, to the spittle-lipped fury of those who loathe what she stood for, those who fear her strength and her repeatedly proven desire to speak truth to power – be that power black or white – it isn't the end of the story, is it? The word "Stompie" doesn't tell the tale of Winnie Madikizela-Mandela. It doesn't even begin to.

Unlike her erstwhile husband, Madikizela-Mandela took a far less conciliatory tone with the formerly advantaged. She still does. She has been unable to forgive or forget, it would seem, and when we put away the racial sunglasses through which it's all too easy to see life, and we consider what the apartheid state did to her family, it's hardly a surprise at all. The question at stake is whether Madikizela-Mandela's crimes outshine her contribution to our country's transition to democracy. Many South Africans would argue that they don't. But more still – given that South Africa is now fully democratic – think exactly that.

Born into relative prosperity in 1936, Winnie Madikizela was another protagonist of the struggle to emerge from the Transkei. Her father Columbus was a minister in Kaizer Matanzima's cabinet; her mother, Nomathamsanqa, was a science teacher who died in 1944 when Winnie was eight. Four years later the National Party was elected to power on a wave of Afrikaner nationalist fervour, and with it came a sea change in the country's race relations. Black South Africans had long been treated as second-class citizens, but the Nats had specfically campaigned on the idea of apartness, an official doctrine that would come to underscore every tenet of South African society. The speed with which the new government moved to separate and classify was shocking. One of the first major laws, passed in 1950, was the Population Registration Act, one of the pillars of apartheid, which required that citizens be classified as white, Indian, coloured or black. Madikizela was clearly the latter – the wording of the legislation was intentionally vague, and a person's racial classification was, in fact, not always clear – and, as such, was allowed into the Jan H Hofmeyr School of Social Work in Johannesburg in 1953, the first institution in the country to train black social workers. (It was forced to close in 1960 due to government neglect.)

Shocked by conditions in an Alexandra township hospital, Madikizela become interested in politics, and eventually, in 1957, met and caught the eye of a married father of three called Nelson Mandela. It was an understandable attraction. He was tall and handsome and active in the ANC – she described it years after as "a dual romance" – and she was a very, very beautiful woman who would grow into something of a goddess as she moved through her twenties.

Nelson and Evelyn Mandela were divorced in 1958, quickly replaced by Nelson and Winnie Mandela, an apparently far more suitable pairing.* Personal relationships aside, these were monumental times, with Mandela enduring the protracted Treason Trial that had seen the state arrest 156 ANC members in 1956, including him, Albert Luthuli, Walter Sisulu and Oliver Tambo. Tambo was released after preliminary hearings and went into exile in 1960 to lead the liberation struggle from abroad, but Mandela and 29 others had to wait until the following year before being acquitted. Winnie had tumbled willingly into the deep end of struggle politics, and it wasn't long before she was forced to stay afloat on her own.

Nelson was rearrested in 1962 after seventeen months on the run, and this time, at the Rivonia Trial, the verdict would not go in his favour. In 1964 Winnie Mandela found herself a single mother of two young children and the wife of a man sentenced to life imprisonment on Robben Island. And it is then that this young woman's remarkable resolve shone though – because it is easy to be brave and courageous

---

* Nelson and Evelyn had grown apart since the death of their first daughter while still in infancy, and the subsequent birth of their fourth child, in 1954, when Evelyn converted to the Jehovah's Witnesses. Her new-found religion forced her to prioritise worship and remain politically neutral at the same time that her husband was forging a path to becoming the most famous politician of his age. It was an untenable situation and they fought bitterly; Nelson, so they say, had found solace with other women by the time Winnie came on the scene.

"She offers a symbol of contradiction, of subversion, of disrespect, of impatience, an anarchic symbol that appeals to those who have nothing at stake in the available status quo."

– Desiree Lewis, journalist

when you have your comrades around you or your husband by your side, but real character shows through when you are alone. And Winnie didn't simply endure; she rebelled against all the brutal machinations of the apartheid police state, becoming a rare public voice against the regime in the face of ceaseless abuse and harassment.

From the early 1960s through to the moment the ANC was unbanned, Winnie Mandela was subject to a barrage of legal restrictions. She represented a difficult challenge to the apartheid authorities. Given the high profile of her husband, the usual slip-on-a-bar-of-soap-in-the-showers trick – that is, murder – was out of the question. But they were desperate to shut her up. She was initially restricted by law to the Mandela house in Orlando, Soweto, but she was not one given to listening to apartheid judges. In 1969 she was arrested under the Terrorism Act and was slammed into solitary confinement for eighteen months – on death row. A more chilling and drawn-out horror is hard to imagine. On her release, she was put under house arrest in Soweto again, which she naturally ignored. She was repeatedly arrested, banned and imprisoned over the years for a variety of violations.

As the 1970s ground on Winnie began to adhere to Black Consciousness principles, establishing the Black Women's Federation. This earned her banishment, along with her 16-year-old daughter Zindzi, to Brandfort, a dusty Afrikaans-dominated town in the Free State about fifty kilometres outside Bloemfontein, where they were dumped in a house with no floors, ceilings, running water or electricity. "It was the hardest thing for me to take as a mother," she later wrote in her biography. "That shattering experience inflicted a wound that will never heal."

In the course of her time in Brandfort – eight years by the end of it – Winnie enjoyed the privilege of constant death threats and, of course, continual harassment from the Security Branch. Nevertheless, she adapted to life in the Free State, politicising the local township and taking in local and international visitors. Eventually, when the Brandfort house was firebombed in 1985, she simply upped and returned to Soweto – illegally but without consequences.

Now, it is true that this is a book about brilliant South Africans. Not saintly ones. Not even terribly nice ones. If that were the case, then Winnie Madikizela-Mandela – and several other names besides – would have no place here. Because Winnie's life was one of two halves; the first admirable and, yes, brilliant in its way; and the second filled with undeniably repellent behaviour. And it is the late 1980s, at the height of the madness of the Botha regime and the apartheid endgame, that seem to mark the almost schizoid break in her legacy, for this was when Winnie Mandela did much to tarnish her reputation. There was the Mandela Football Club, a gang of her bodyguards implicated in a range of criminal activities in her neck of the Sowetan woods. There was Stompie Seipei, kidnapped on

her orders, assaulted by her and others, and later found dead in a field. And there was her notorious fondness for necklacing which, if clarity is needed, was the act of pinioning someone's arms with a tyre soaked in petrol and setting it alight; the victim, usually a suspected collaborator or informer, would take fifteen or twenty minutes to die. "With our boxes of matches and our necklaces, we shall liberate this country," Winnie once famously said. And the Truth and Reconciliation Commission eventually agreed with many of the accusations held against her, declaring that she was "morally accountable" for what the Mandela Football Club did. After pointed requests from Desmond Tutu, she admitted that "things went terribly wrong".

Unsurprisingly, in retrospect, Winnie's transgressions became a cause célèbre for the dying apartheid regime, and they remain one for her detractors today. She was, as she described it herself, "bitter" at her and her family's treatment, and though she often chose to portray herself as the personification of the cause – "I have ceased a long time ago to exist as an individual," she said in 1985 – it is undeniable that she has taken to the VIP life in post-1994 South Africa, seemingly relying on "donations" to fund it. The actions of the Mandela Football Club and a subsequent conviction for fraud – not for her own benefit, as it turned out – are, of course reprehensible. But some mitigating truths remain.

Winnie was allowed to visit Nelson on Robben Island, but they were not allowed physical contact, and though she was at his side as he left the Victor Verster prison on 11 February 1990, an event that was broadcast all over the world, the time past and the sheer awfulness  of what had been done to the Mandelas meant there was no hope for the marriage. It had been 27 years and Winnie had been unfaithful. (One of the most high-profile cases being an affair with a young Dali Mpofu, then about half her age.) Albertina Sisulu she was not. And Albertina's enduring love for her husband is, in this instance, perhaps more praiseworthy than Winnie's moral weakness is damnable. *(See Walter and Albertina Sisulu.)* Twenty-seven years is rather a long

> "I am a living symbol of whatever is happening in the country. I am a living symbol of the white man's fear."
>
> – *Winnie Madikizela-Mandela*

time, and of the many things it cost the Mandelas, one of them was their marriage. So when Winnie Madikizela-Mandela – as she came to be known after the divorce, in 1996 – is pulled over by a white cop these days, as happens from time to time, and she behaves appallingly, seen in the context of what white policemen have done to the Mandelas over the years, it is perhaps to some extent understandable.

You don't have to like Winnie Madikizela-Mandela, but you do have to ask yourself why she remains so incredibly popular to so many people all these years later. It is because she and her husband came to represent the hope of black South Africa during the 1960s, '70s and '80s, and, while no-one had even seen a new image of Nelson's face in that time, Winnie was always on the frontline. She was, effectively, the face of the revolution. Unlike a populist of the calibre of a Julius Malema, though, she had the intellect to back up the role that history had bequeathed her – hence her longevity after so much controversy.

Winnie Madikizela-Mandela may ultimately have failed as an individual, on several levels, but she fought long and hard for her people in a war that many of her current critics were not even aware of at the time – or, worse, simply chose to ignore. And so it becomes clear why she remains enduringly popular – first on the ANC's National Executive Committee list at Polokwane – and is still seen by many as the rightful Mother of the Nation, and why she continues to speak truth to power, be it to Jacob Zuma or whomever else.

Only in a country like South Africa, with our fractious and tumultuous past, could a person like Winnie Madikizela-Mandela feature among its most brilliant individuals.

Miriam Makeba

4 March 1932 – 10 November 2008

Grammy Award-winning singer; political exile; fashion trendsetter; world music ambassador; Africa's most iconic diva

MAMA AFRICA

IN A CAREER SPANNING FIVE DECADES she was a singer, actress and political activist. She serenaded American president John F Kennedy at his birthday in Madison Square Gardens alongside Marilyn Monroe. She performed for statesmen including Cuba's Fidel Castro, Ethiopian Emperor Haile Selassie, France's François Mitterrand and our own Nelson Mandela. She toured with Hugh Masekela, Dizzy Gillespie,

Nina Simone and Paul Simon. She brought the fire to the "Rumble in the Jungle" between Muhammad Ali and George Foreman in Zaïre. She had five husbands and lived in Johannesburg, the United States, France, Guinea and Belgium. Hell, she even had three private audiences with the Pope. She was Miriam Makeba, the first African woman to win a Grammy Award, the Empress of African Song, Mama Africa.

Zenzile Miriam Makeba, the sixth child of an illegal beer brewer and a Swazi sangoma, showed remarkable talent growing up in Orlando East, singing at church fundraisers and in amateur competitions. But what a stretch of the imagination it must have been to envision this young girl from the townships going on to become the godmother of African folk-blues and the most influential African diva of the 20th century.

One of the many musicians and artists to emerge in the 1950s from Sophiatown, the vibrant cultural hub of black Johannesburg at the time, Makeba honed her chops with South African doo-wop pioneers the Manhattan Brothers and her own girl group the Skylarks. As a mark of the times, her bands weren't permitted to record songs in English, and Sophiatown would be rezoned entirely before the end of the decade and renamed Triomf, its black, coloured, Indian and Chinese residents all dispatched to separate suburbs under the Group Areas Act. But for Makeba, and some of her more talented black co-performers, there would be a way out of South Africa altogether.

In 1959 she landed a starring role in the seminal black jazz opera *King Kong*, which saw incredible success in South Africa before it was later taken abroad. That same year she appeared in the anti-apartheid documentary *Come Back, Africa*; she was flown to Venice for a screening and so her international career began. She wouldn't return for another thirty years, the apartheid government having deemed her an

"Miriam Makeba's voice is as majestic and contoured as the Magaliesberg."

— *Christopher John Farley, journalist*

undesirable revolutionary and revoked her passport; she was not even allowed to return for her mother's funeral in 1960. Various countries came to her aid at the time and she would ultimately hold at least nine passports; she became a citizen of the world and, in time, the physical embodiment of Africa.

Building on the rapturous reception she received during her residency at New York's legendary Village Vanguard nightclub, she released her eponymous debut album that same year. She was 28 years old and she stepped confidently onto the world stage with a swinging mix of traditional Xhosa wedding songs, airy African jazz moods, mellifluous Indonesian lullabies and infectious Calypso romps. It was a compelling portrait of a young artist in exile.

Much of the album's magic lies in the "exotic" timbres of her Xhosa singing – as on *Qongqothwane*, known as *The Click Song*. On this interpretation of the traditional wedding song – with two lines of lyrics that loosely translate to "Diviner of the roadways, the knock-knock beetle / It just passed by here, the knock-knock beetle" – she enchanted American audiences with the onomatopoeic range of vocalised Xhosa vernacular clicks. *Time* compared this distinctive sound to "the popping of champagne corks" and hailed Makeba as "the most exciting new singing talent to appear in many years". American journalists were so seduced that from the first rhapsodic reviews in *Billboard* magazine in 1960 Makeba was tagged as the Click-Click Girl.

While *Qongqothwane* would become her signature tune in live performances over the next five decades, Makeba herself had a love/hate relationship with it. As a vocal proponent of Black Consciousness she was all too aware of its novelty value as an exotic signifier of African-ness.

She may have once worn leopard-print bikinis on the cover of *Drum* back in the late 1950s, but by the '60s the times they were a-changing. "Black is beautiful," was the Pan Africanist rallying cry. And Miriam turned her consciousness quest into a Proudly Pan Africanist aesthetic of beauty that would inspire fashion rages for decades. She braided beautiful long corn rows on the cover of 1974's *A Promise* and 1978's *Country Girl*, and she rocked a fierce afro for *All About Miriam* in 1996.

"I see other black women imitate my style, which is no style at all, but just letting our hair be itself," she explained simply. For Miriam, being herself meant embracing her globetrotting reality. She freely mixed Xhosa gear with Parisian accessories, displaying a modish melting pot of ancient techniques, Afro-erotic flair and high-fashion ideas.

Her music became progressively more Afro-conscious too. In 1966 she became the first African artist to win a Grammy Award for her album with Harry Belafonte, *An Evening With Belafonte/Makeba*. It was a landmark global pop recording, boasting roots-driven African ballads such as *Mailaika* alongside succinct political commentaries like *Ndodemnyama Verwoerd!* ("Watch out, Verwoerd!")

But it wasn't just her music that earned Makeba the status of Mama Africa. It was also her politics. Her marriage to Black Panther activist Stokely Carmichael in 1968 pretty much put the kibosh on her American career. US labels cancelled her record contracts; promoters blacklisted her tours. But that didn't stop Makeba, who spent the next two decades promoting the cause of African liberation as Guinea's United Nations delegate and a member of Paul Simon's worldwide *Graceland* tour of 1987/8. Then came her triumphant South African homecoming in 1990.

Although always regarding herself as a singer and not as a politician, Makeba's fearless humanitarianism earned her numerous international awards, including the 1986 Dag Hammarskjöld Peace Prize and the Unesco Grand Prix du Conseil International de la Musique. But she remained gracious and down to earth, a homegrown sister until the end. "Everybody now admits that apartheid was wrong, and all I did was tell the people who wanted to know where I come from how we lived in South Africa," she said. "I just told the world the truth. And if my truth then becomes political, I can't do anything about that."

"My life has been like a yo-yo. One minute I'm dining with presidents and emperors; the next I'm hitchhiking."

– *Miriam Makeba*

> "Her haunting melodies gave voice to the pain of exile and dislocation which she felt for 31 long years. At the same time, her music inspired a powerful sense of hope in all of us. She was South Africa's first lady of song and so richly deserved the title of Mama Africa. She was a mother to our struggle and to the young nation of ours."
>
> *— Nelson Mandela, on the death of Makeba in 2008*

On her return from exile she continued to spread her message of freedom and humanitarianism on stages in South Africa and around the world.

Appropriately Makeba died singing. After a life of song, she finally collapsed on stage in Italy in 2008, having just performed of one of her most famous hits, *Pata Pata*.

Today her voice lives on. It is present in the rhythm of the Conakry evening wind and in the shadows of dimly lit jazz joints in Soweto. It haunts Harlem's hipster hot spots and echoes through the hills of the Eastern Cape. It's audible in the music of a generation of jazz divas. Miriam Makeba lives on, visible in the current craze for Afro-centric designs on ramps from Paris to Dakar, Joburg to Milan. Most importantly she lives on inside so many South Africans. She's the soul sister we can look to for fashion advice and a best friend to party with. She's the girl of our dreams, a babe with the beguiling elegance of Grace Kelly and the fire of Bette Davis. Finally, she's Mama Africa, a mother to our nation of misfits and orphans, paupers and King Kongs.

Sailor Malan

24 March 1910 – 17 September 1963

*Group Captain in the Royal Air Force; World War
II hero; Battle of Britain ace; natural-born fighter
pilot; tremendous shot; leader of men; legend*

"PRESSURE IS A MESSERSCHMITT UP YOUR ARSE."

So said the fine Australian all-rounder and World War II pilot Keith
Miller when asked in later years by Michael Parkinson how he managed
to stay so cool and collected on a cricket field. It is surely one of the
better examples of a great sportsman putting life in perspective. After
all, playing a ball game, even on the international stage, is nothing
compared to so many stress-filled occupations out there – and not much
trumps the responsibility of piloting fighter planes during a war.

Miller flew Mosquito fighter-bombers in 1944 and 1945 and was, in
pretty much everything he did, a total legend. If the Aussies ever publish
their take on this book he'll be one of the first on their list. But the
pressures of his wartime activities, though considerable, were a league
below those faced by the pilots of the Royal Air Force (RAF) who fought
the Battle of Britain over the summer and autumn of 1940, defending
the United Kingdom against the bombers of the German Luftwaffe.

These were desperate times, the most critical few months of the war
in terms of Allied survival, with Britain enduring wave after wave of
airborne assault. Hundreds of aircraft from both sides were involved on
a daily basis. Spitfires and Hurricanes of the RAF scrambled, often three
or four times a day, to meet squadrons of German bombers and their
Messerschmitt fighter escorts as they crossed the Channel, leading to

great wheeling dogfights in the skies over southern England. It was an immense, unprecedented clash, the first major campaign to be waged entirely in the air, and the attrition rate was astonishing. About 3,200 aircraft were shot down in total. In August 1940 the Luftwaffe lost close on 800 bombers and fighters, the RAF more than 400 fighters. Nearly 140 planes were destroyed on the 18th alone, in what came to be known as The Hardest Day. The future of Britain – and thus Europe and the free world – hung in the balance for three-and-a-half months.

But even as their cities were bombed, their planes shot to pieces and their friends killed in action, the fighter pilots of the RAF kept returning to the air to fight. And ultimately, though there were fewer than 3,000 of them – of whom one-sixth would be killed and many more wounded or taken prisoner of war – they prevailed. The arrival of winter eventually signalled the Luftwaffe's defeat and Hitler's first setback; the fighter pilots of the RAF had repelled the Nazi menace and delivered Britain its finest hour.

Unsurprisingly these brave young men, mostly in their early twenties, were looked upon with awe and reverence. Even as the fighting raged they were deemed heroes. Eventually they would come to be known as "the Few", as immortalised by Churchill, and one of the greatest of them all – if not *the* greatest – was a boy from Wellington, South Africa: Adolph Gysbert Malan, otherwise known as "Sailor". By Keith Miller's definition, here was a man who could handle the pressure – and dish it out in spades.

Though he possessed within himself the indefinable ability to pilot an aeroplane, shoot down other aeroplanes and not get shot down himself, Adolph Malan had no inkling of this until he was in his mid-twenties. A stubborn, independent kid, by all accounts, he decided as a 13-year-old that he wanted to be a sailor, and he entered cadet school in Simonstown soon after. At 17 he joined the Union Castle Steamship Line before spending eight years travelling the world, serving on nine different ships – hence his nicknames when he finally joined the RAF in 1936 at the age of 25: first "the Admiral", then plain old "Sailor". (Malan evidently didn't enjoy sharing a first name with Hitler; he became known generally as Sailor and was called John by his wife and close friends.)

Malan signed up to the RAF just in time; a year later and he would have been too old to qualify. But the sailing had endowed him with confidence and discipline and he quickly excelled in training school. In retrospect, it was perhaps not that surprising because, like Miller, Sailor Malan was a natural. Good-looking, not averse to brushes with authority and supremely confident, Malan was born to be a fighter pilot. In old black-and-white photos from the time he looks like a cross between François Pienaar and Connery-as-Bond. With his hair slicked back and a pair of Aviator sunglasses, he was an original Top Gun. Appropriately for such a hero, he was seen as sociable and always up for a drink, but slightly reserved – something of a brooding hero, then.

In November 1936 Malan was posted to Number 74 (Fighter) Squadron, known as the Tigers. His reputation quickly grew. He was considered by fellow pilots as "formidable" and "completely professional, so on the ball". His piloting skills were good, but it was his air gunnery that set him apart, including his ability to deflection shoot; that is, judge during a turn the passage of your bullets so that the plane you're attacking flies into them. By the start of the war Malan had been promoted to Flight Lieutenant.

In the action that followed from May 1940 onwards, it was soon apparent that Malan would translate his potential as a Spitfire pilot into combat victories. Five days before the evacuation of Dunkirk commenced, he claimed his first victims, two German bombers. He brought them down within minutes of each other, and was elated. "I'd tasted blood at last," he wrote later. "The release from tension was terrific, the thrill enormous. I'd been wondering for so long – too long – how I'd react in my first show. Now I knew. Everything I had learnt had come right. There was hardly time to feel even scared."

Malan's fighting prowess was brought to the fore as the war intensified, and he secured his first Distinguished Flying Cross (DFC) by early June for displaying "great skill, courage and relentless determination in his attacks upon the enemy". With excellent eyesight, good physical strength and a high "G" threshold, he was built for the job. But he was more than just a gifted dogfighter; his command from the air and tactical awareness was similarly impressive, and after the first combat

SAILOR MALAN'S TEN RULES FOR AIR FIGHTING

1. Wait until you see the whites of his eyes. Fire short bursts of one to two seconds only when your sights are definitely "ON".
2. Whilst shooting think of nothing else, brace the whole of your body: have both hands on the stick: concentrate on your ring sight.
3. Always keep a sharp lookout. "Keep your finger out."
4. Height gives you the initiative.
5. Always turn and face the attack.
6. Make your decisions promptly. It is better to act quickly even though your tactics are not the best.
7. Never fly straight and level for more than 30 seconds in the combat area.
8. When diving to attack always leave a proportion of your formation above to act as a top guard.
9. INITIATIVE, AGGRESSION, AIR DISCIPLINE, and TEAMWORK are words that MEAN something in Air Fighting.
10. Go in quickly – Punch hard – Get out!

(Abbreviated version, copied and kept by many World War II RAF pilots)

contacts with the Luftwaffe he played a key role in revising the RAF's dated formations, as well as various other flying and combat strategies. In time he would develop his Ten Rules For Air Fighting, which pilots across Fighter Command would learn as gospel.

On the night of 18/19 June, Malan's legend – if it needed securing – was secured. Observing that bombs were falling near Westcliff-on-Sea where his wife had recently given birth to their first child, his paternal instincts kicked in and he was granted permission to take off and defend their wellbeing. Night flying in Spitfires was notoriously difficult, due primarily to the glare off the exhausts, but Malan took to the air without support shortly after midnight and shot down two Heinkel 111s within half an hour.

This type of behaviour – flying in to combat at night on a whim and unsupported – is rather frowned upon in modern air forces, but World War II was a different era in so many ways. The RAF had only been in existence for a little more than two decades and, well, it clearly seemed like the sensible thing to do at the time. In fact, Malan was later awarded a bar to his DFC (essentially a second DFC) for his efforts. Given the pressures on pilots at the time, including the incredible number of combat sorties flown and the inevitable fatigue that followed, these behavioural curiosities were, on reflection, perhaps not that surprising. With a widespread reputation for partying and skirt-chasing, fighter pilots were partial to a drink or three and it was not uncommon for them to go in to battle – that is, against the German Luftwaffe, not the Abyssinian Aero Services – on the back of a hangover. They generally thought themselves invincible and would frequently fly ill or injured.*
Malan himself flew for a while with his back encased in plaster after suffering a forced landing when his engine failed.

They were cheeky too. In April 1943, a French pilot, Lieutenant Baoul Duval, was shot down over France near his hometown in April 1943; he escaped back to England shortly afterwards, with a bride in tow…**

But not all their stories of mischief and skylarking ended well. In April 1941 Pilot Officer Peter Chesters of 74 Squadron brought down an ME109 over Kent and, to celebrate, chose to perform a victory roll over his aerodrome – but he misjudged the manoeuvre and promptly crashed into the parade ground. "A daft way to die," as his friend and fellow pilot John Freeborn recalled with some understatement many years later.

---

* The other legendary South African fighter pilot of World War II was Marmaduke Pattle from Butterworth in the Eastern Cape, who Roald Dahl described as "the Second World War's greatest flying ace". Having fought in North Africa and Greece (with Dahl), he was shot down over Athens in April 1941 while flying against recommendations under the influence of flu and combat fatigue.

** Equally cheeky here is another story about Keith Miller, which appeared in his obituary in the *Sydney Morning Herald*: "After duelling with Messerschmitts in his Mosquito one night, he made an unauthorised detour over Bonn because it was Beethoven's birthplace and he was a lover of the classics."

Sailor Malan, however, was blessed with the intelligence, skill and luck a pilot needs to survive a war. Though he was shot up on occasion and suffered his fair share of mechanical failure – often calmly resolved in the heat of battle – he flew with great success until the middle of 1941, claiming dozens of kills in the process. Victory counts are generally contentious and differ from source to source, but Malan probably downed 32 to 42 planes in total, with many more damaged. He claimed three or more victories in a day on four separate occasions. (As perspective, it is estimated that less than 40 percent of the Few scored a single victory, and only 8 percent qualified as "aces", having shot down five or more enemy.)

Malan's golden run came after the Battle of Britain, in June and July of 1941, when he shot down or damaged 20 Messerschmitt 109s in 20 days. In one case, his reflector sight malfunctioned but he managed to adjust for the error once he'd worked out what the problem was. He was the RAF's leading ace at this stage, having battled the toughest opposition the Germans would muster during the war.

By now he had been promoted from Squadron Leader to Wing Leader, and in 1943 he would become Station Commander of Biggin Hill, the top fighter aerodrome in Britain. Like all RAF pilots (as opposed to their German counterparts), he was placed on mandatory rest, and when he returned to combat his increased responsibilities left him with far less time to fly; when he did it was seldom as lead pilot. But by this stage he had already won the Distinguished Service Order (DSO), also with bar – the first fighter pilot to win two DFCs and two DSOs. Already a hero, he trained new pilots and toured the USA on a public relations trip to secure support for the Allied effort. Malan's standing was such that Churchill agreed to be godparent to his child in 1941 (following the deaths in action of the two friends he had originally asked). After the war, Battle of Britain pilot and later RAF Air Commodore Al Deere described him thus: "Malan was the best. A great shot and splendid Wing Leader. He had the maturity of years and experience behind him. Others were good but he was the greatest."

In 1946, Malan left the RAF and returned to South Africa with his wife and children. Feted wherever he went, he found himself becoming a figurehead for the anti-fascist Torch Commando movement that emerged in the 1950s in opposition to the National Party's increasingly authoritarian governance. Not only a legend in the air, he was a man of morals, too. Having spent time working with the Oppenheimer family in Johannesburg, he eventually took up sheep farming outside Kimberley, becoming something of "the country gentleman".

Sailor Malan died in 1963 at the age of 52, the victim of Parkinson's Disease. It was a tragically early end to a great life. A memorial service was held at Biggin Hill, and it included these words from Air Chief Marshal Sir Charles Elworthy: "We mourn the passing of a fine officer and gallant comrade who was in the forefront of the Battle of Britain, a man who fought bravely and led fearlessly at a time when courage and leadership in the air was our only safeguard. His name will live on in the history of the Royal Air Force and in the minds and hearts of men of courage everywhere." It will also live on in the annals of great South Africans.

Captain Sailor Malan; you'd be his wingman any time.

"Never in the field of human conflict was so much owed by so many to so few."

– *Winston Churchill, on Battle of Britain fighter pilots, August 1940*

Nelson Mandela

b. 18 July 1918

Saint, hero, icon, saviour and unquestionable moral titan to some; perpetually misunderstood political hero, reconciler and complex human being if you think about him for a while

THERE'S NOT MUCH NEW that we can tell you about Nelson Rolihlahla Mandela. Everybody knows the basics. How he was born into a Thembu dynasty, how he tended cattle as a boy in 1920s Transkei. How he went to Fort Hare, where he met Oliver Tambo, and then Johannesburg, where he met Joe Slovo and Ruth First, and was mentored by Walter Sisulu. You know about the ANC, MK, Rivonia and Robben Island. And if you don't, well, you're not going to find too much of it here.

The picture you have in your head of Mandela is a mirror into your own soul. But if you stop and think about it for a bit, it's possible you might not like the reflection.

The gravest misrepresentation is that Mandela – or Madiba, as he is often called, sometimes by those wanting to sound a bit too familiar – is just a nice old gentleman, a benign and happy grandfatherly figure who only ever wanted black and white people to get along. Something like the personal embodiment of the McCartney song *Ebony And Ivory*, and about as complex. In this incarnation all Mandela desired was to end apartheid, draw a line under the past and put his feet up while fondly tousling the hair of the bouncy giggling Rainbow Nation. Then the crying would stop, and the beloved country would frolic off into an idyllic future.

Add to that a fuzzy sense of saintliness, as though this is a man who has never done *any* wrong, and the end picture can become a wilful misunderstanding of the past – and, dare one suggest it, somewhat racist. Many people seem to like the idea of an affable, harmless darkie content with the status quo. Historically, though, the moment Mandela has said something vaguely revolutionary, condemnation has been rapid.

So when he told the British government to engage in talks with the IRA in the 1990s, people were outraged, even though John Major did just that after he came to power two years later. When he denigrated Dick Cheney as a "dinosaur" in 2002, the White House briefed against him. He strongly condemned NATO's action in Kosovo in the late 1990s. He caused fury when he said that Tony Blair was the "foreign minister of the United States". He was apocalyptically angry about the US invasion of Iraq in 2003.

When still in the public eye, Mandela was in fact the perpetual activist, forever calling out injustice where he saw it. And he saw it in places those who dared to dismiss him as a congenial old simpleton didn't like.

It may seem like madness to some, but there are people who really don't understand that Mandela, quite naturally, viewed political liberation as only the first step to uplifting black South Africans from a subservient existence bequeathed to them by more than 350 years

"The time comes in the life of any nation when there remain only two choices – submit or fight. That time has now come to South Africa. We shall not submit and we have no choice but to hit back by all means in our power in defence of our people, our future, and our freedom... We of Umkhonto we Sizwe have always sought to achieve liberation without bloodshed and civil clash. We hope, even at this late hour, that our first actions will awaken everyone to a realisation of the disastrous situation to which the Nationalist policy is leading. We hope that we will bring the Government and its supporters to their senses before it is too late, so that both the Government and its policies can be changed before matters reach the desperate state of civil war."

– Extracts from the original manifesto of Umkhonto we Sizwe, first released in December 1961 to coincide with its first attacks against government installations

of oppression of one sort or another. The first democratic elections of 1994 were, of course, just the start to fixing things. Mandela may have been keen to forgive – famously keen, in fact – but he sure as hell wasn't interested in forgetting.

So, for example, the image of Mandela portrayed in *Invictus* is, for want of a better word, unabashedly white. Mandela did not, in fact, spend his entire presidency making friends with Afrikaner rugby players. Yes, he worked famously for reconciliation, and for many white South Africans the memory of the great man appearing on the Ellis Park pitch at the 1995 World Cup final wearing a Springbok jersey is the defining image of the post-liberation era. *(See François Pienaar.)* There is no doubt he had a gift for making iconic gestures. But for many, many more South Africans, Mandela's time in charge was marked by something most middle-class South Africans can't even imagine. Like getting a house to live in. Or a constant electricity supply. Never mind a vote.

The fact is that Nelson Mandela's presidency marked a fundamental revolution in the way this country approached the governance of the land and the people living in it. How could it not? With able assistance from his deputy Thabo Mbeki, Mandela pursued a radical agenda to change, as fast as he could, the lives of poor black people. He launched the Reconstruction and Development Programme (RDP), introduced the Land Restitution Act, the Basic Conditions of Employment Act and the Labour Relations Act, and heralded the creation of a progressive and world-acclaimed new constitution. This was radical stuff, especially considering just how cowed and conservative South Africa was in the early 1990s.

But he didn't just realign the architecture of the country. He worked on the ground too, and got things done. The Mandela presidency – which was one term only, remember – saw the building or upgrading of 500 clinics. Nearly three million people were housed; two million were connected to the grid; three million got running water. Another 1.5 milllon children were brought into the education system.

Amazingly, some people still wonder why the majority of South Africans vote for the ANC!

Indeed, the sentimental picture of a doddery, gentle, kind Mandela does a great disservice to the ANC, especially at a time when its reputation is in crisis. Under the corrupt and seemingly disinterested leadership of Jacob Zuma, following the paranoid and ultimately divisive Mbeki

> "Mandela is a myth, a man who could have been dreamt up by the magical fictions of a Gabriel Garcia Marquez."
>
> *– Mandla Langa*

era, the party has rapidly haemorrhaged its reputation as a progressive nation-building entity. It is – to call it bluntly – in the process of looting the country and reducing to tatters our status as a gateway to Africa. But still. The ANC of old liberated South Africa. Though Nelson Mandela was strategically promoted as the personification of the struggle, he did not ride in on a white stallion and, God-like, gift us all a chance at a future all on his own. Many brave men and women liberated this country. Mandela was certainly the greatest of the lot, but he is the quickest of them all to acknowledge the collective role of everyone involved.

Mandela was a tough, brave and ruthless leader in a liberation movement. Having initially adhered to the ANC's nonviolent approach, as per the teachings of Mahatma Gandhi, he changed tack after the Sharpeville massacre of 1960. The following year he co-founded Umkhonto we Sizwe, the Spear of the Nation, and was sent abroad to drum up support. He received military training and studied tactics of warfare, and went on to oversee bombings on government buildings and institutions that were symbolic of apartheid. The Umkhonto leadership had identified four forms of possible violence: open revolution, terrorism, guerrilla warfare and sabotage. They aimed to use the latter approach only, avoiding human casualties at all costs, but Mandela later admitted that the ANC violated human rights during the struggle, and the Truth and Reconciliation Commission found that the organisation routinely used torture. This is not something we lay at Mandela's feet. But it is because he was willing to face up to the ugly truth about the way in which some of his comrades acted, and to do so publicly, that we mention it. Mandela has no delusions of saintly grandeur. He leaves that to us – to the likes of the embarrassingly twee and middle-class suburban muppets who like to sing him songs on his birthday, as if he's a child.

"I do not... deny that I planned sabotage. I did not plan it in a spirit of recklessness, nor because I have any love of violence. I planned it as a result of a calm and sober assessment of the political situation that had arisen after many years of tyranny, exploitation, and oppression of my people by the Whites... During my lifetime I have dedicated myself to this struggle of the African people. I have fought against white domination, and I have fought against black domination. I have cherished the ideal of a democratic and free society in which all persons live together in harmony and with equal opportunities. It is an ideal which I hope to live for and to achieve. But if needs be, it is an ideal for which I am prepared to die."

– Extracts from Nelson Mandela's opening statement at the Rivonia Trial, 20 April 1964

No, Mandela features here not because he is a kind and gentle old man. We love him greatly and admire with awe his legacy of reconciliation and his genuine desire for a nonracial South Africa. Of course. We bow to his huge contribution towards averting violence and killing and general mayhem, especially after the murder of Chris Hani in 1993, a time in our history when civil war seemed almost inevitable. We are forever grateful for his insistence that South Africa belongs to all who live in it, white or black, and we can never thank him enough for his speech at the Rivonia Trial, which ought to be writ large in the halls of Parliament. We marvel at his capacity for the symbolic gesture, for having tea with Betsie Verwoerd (in Orania!), for insisting that his assistant be a young Afrikaner girl. We'll love him forever for making PW Botha look so doltish and stupid, and for out-living him too.

But that's only one element of the story. Mandela is a complex, fascinating, flawed human being. As his third wife, Graça Machel, has said, "He is a symbol, but not a saint." He finds himself in these pages because, generally, he could never be excluded from a list of fifty brilliant South Africans. But specifically he is here because he was a militant and radical revolutionary ready to die, and to bomb, for the cause – after half a century of nonviolent protest by the ANC at the treatment of black South Africans, it was unfortunately what this country needed to wake it from its moral slumber. It was a lengthy process, but eventually it succeeded, and so it is Mandela, the warrior, we salute.

Thabo Mbeki

b. 18 June 1942

President of South Africa (1999-2008); creator of the black middle class; ironic source of whatever hope we might have for the future

SUN. TIMES 6·2·00 © ZAPIRO

IT IS TRUE THAT OUR FORMER PRESIDENT had a long and starring role in *50 People Who Stuffed Up South Africa*, and with good reason. His rampaging paranoia about, variously, the West, white people, Western medicine and the media gave us, in no particular order, as many as 300,000 early deaths from HIV and Aids, a crime pandemic we still haven't managed to bring under control, the crisis called Eskom, xenophobic attacks and (not unrelated) the continued reign of a tyrant in the nation to our north. His win-at-all-costs, forged-in-exile tunnel vision gave us the abuse of state institutions such as the National Prosecuting Authority and our spy agencies, and led us, ultimately, to the ANC's moral collapse at Polokwane, the utterly disastrous presidency of Jacob Zuma, and another bunfight at Mangaung.

But – and inevitably there is a but – Thabo Mbeki also, ironically, gave us the one shot we have of fixing all of these things. And we're not talking about his apartheid-era negotiations here. (Sure, he performed well in that arena, but that was a collective effort – from both sides – and if we really had to narrow it down and apportion all the credit to one person, we're inclined to give it to a certain Mr Mandela.) No, in this case we're talking money – and specifically its distribution in South Africa. That there is capital left in this nation, that investors are still here and that despite our great challenges multinational companies still see us as the gateway to the next growth frontier, Africa, is the result of Thabo Mbeki's sane fiscal policies.

It is, we must (almost) apologetically report, capital and capitalism that has made rich countries rich. It is capitalism and the City of London – you know, bankers – that prop up free healthcare in Britain, for example. And without wealth, contrary to what the commies believe, we cannot uplift the poor.

Thabo Mbeki may not have enjoyed the company of capital and capitalists, but he understood that growing the largest economy in Africa at 5 percent a year could potentially create the jobs the country so desperately needs, while expanding our tax base at the same time. He understood that he could, via legislation, ensure that when the middle class grew, it would also grow blacker and blacker.

Mbeki also understood perception. He knew that, while Washington and London might not enjoy his policies on HIV or Zimbabwe or whatever else, British and American capital only cares for returns. And so the fiscal and policy frameworks that his government presented to the world were solid and stable. Capital likes solid and stable, which is why foreign investors arrived with bags of money during Mbeki's time in charge. Equally, capital dislikes flaky and shaky, which is why this endless wittering about nationalising the mines since Mbeki's departure, and an unshakeable sense that the ANC is so riven with strife that it can't even say anything assuring about security of tenure in this country, has moved the ratings agencies to mark us as "negative". In other words, Mbeki fired up the economy – don't forget, an economy that the Nats had squeezed dry as the apartheid endgame reached fever pitch – and his successor has set us up for a ratings downgrade and hiked borrowing costs and the weakening of the rand… All of which comes with the very real threat of impoverishing ever more those who just cannot afford it.

Mbeki might not have liked it – he spoke often and clearly about the inequities of the globalised world, the failure of the Washington Consensus and about how liberalised African economies were not attracting the investments they'd hoped for – but he did understand it, and he did, where he could, use it to the benefit of South Africa.

Adam Habib, professor of Political Science at the University of Johannesburg, explains it thus: "When the ANC came into power in 1994, it confronted a number of pressures. It inherited a nearly bankrupt state, was confronted with an ambitious set of expectations from the previously disenfranchised, and an investment strike by the business community. To get investment and growth going, the ANC leadership felt that they had to make a series of economic concessions most of which was captured in the Growth, Employment and Redistribution strategy (Gear)."

First under the Mandela presidency and then into his own first term, Mbeki was the driver of Gear, which focused on things like privatisation, budget-deficit reduction and the removal of exchange control. He faced great reluctance from Cosatu and the SACP and was accused of selling out the revolution – an alienation of the tripartite alliance that would come to haunt him further down the road – and the programme was far from faultless. But it was in the words of RW Johnson, one of Mbeki's harshest critics, "his finest hour".

"While [Mbeki] may have cruelly thrown the textbook on Aids away, he has followed it to the letter on economics. As a result, SA has less debt, lower inflation, higher tax revenues and access to cheaper financing than at any time in the past 20 years."
– *Business Day editor Peter Bruce, writing in 2002*

And it is the pragmatic legacy of empowerment and economic stability, embodied in the rise of the black diamond, for which the former president gets a few lines in this book. It may be true that he had his hands on the helm in easier economic times, but this is hardly his fault. It may be true that the current bunch of gangsters leading this nation, economically illiterate as they seem to be, are squandering this legacy, and that they can't even extricate themselves from the Junior Common Room of the mind. But that, too, would not be his fault.

Left-wing types like to prattle on about how the rich got richer under Mbeki's conservative fiscal regime. That may be so. The point is, however, that so too did a great many of the poor. In a country such as ours that is an undeniably brilliant achievement and, though Thabo Mbeki subsequently demolished his reputation as a leader in various other fields, he deserves at least a modicum of credit for his economic efforts.

*(See **Thabo Mbeki, 50 People Who Stuffed Up South Africa.**)*

Eric Merrifield
& Aubrey Krüger

Eric Merrifield: 1914 – 1 December 1982
Aubrey Krüger: b. c. 1935

Harbour engineers; inventors; ocean tamers

SOMETIMES IN LIFE THE SIMPLE ROUTE IS BEST. Take the mousetrap, for example. In 1894 William C Hooker, of Abingdon, Illinois, patented the first-ever spring-loaded snap-trap. It is a "spring-actuated jaw" attached to a wooden board, with a hinged trigger on one side and a locking bar on the other. Bait is placed on the trigger, the jaw is primed, and when your resident mouse comes tiptoeing along for a nibble the locking bar disengages and the jaw slams shut. Bye-bye, mousy. This simple device is so effective at what it does that in more than a century since its invention no-one has come up with a better, more efficient, more cost-effective way of catching mice. Not for nothing the phrase, "Build a better mousetrap and the world will beat a path to your door."

In the 1960s, South Africa came up with an invention that is not only simpler than the mousetrap, but one that has a far mightier role to play around the world. It is the dolos, a giant, oddly shaped concrete construction with no moving parts whatsoever, and its job is to tame oceans. Plonk several hundred, or even several thousand, of them in a row along a harbour breakwater or a shoreline and they offer immense protection against the relentless erosive power of the sea.

The dolos takes its name from the Afrikaans term for an ox's knucklebone because of their similarity in shape, often described as "an H with one leg turned through 90 degrees". It is *slightly* more refined than that – there's a bit of a taper in the design and there are usually eight angled surfaces, not four – but that's pretty much it. The key to success is the way they interact with each other when packed together. Unlike rectangular breakwater blocks that aquaplane and move about in heavy running seas, dolosse scatter the energy of the waves and actually lock closer together over time. Even though they can weigh up to thirty tons, they are also easier to handle than rectangular blocks.

About the only thing complicated about the dolos is working out who invented it. For a long time the East London harbour engineer Eric Merrifield was given all the credit. Dolosse were originally known as Merrifield Blocks and he received the international Shell Design Award, among other prizes, for his efforts. But after Merrifield's death, the unheralded Aubrey Krüger, a junior draughtsman, claimed to have come up with the prototype of the dolos, using several sections of broomstick and some string. Merrifield, so this version of the story goes, was simply the man in charge who had dished out the instructions for a new concrete structure to be designed, and then managed the invention into being. Either way, they both worked for the South African Railway & Harbour Services at the time and, since it was invented on company time, the dolos was considered its property. And it was never patented. Given that there are – from Tristan da Cunha to Hong Kong harbour and throughout more than a hundred countries in between – millions and millions of the things holding back the ocean all around the world, that was probably not the soundest financial decision ever made.

So, to Merrifield and Krüger and whoever else was involved in the creation of the dolos go great kudos and acknowledgment – but no financial fortune. Between them, they built a better ocean-restraining structure, but the world did not beat a path to their doors.

"If I had patented my design, I would be a millionaire."

– *Eric Merrifield*

Moshoeshoe I

c. 1786 – 11 March 1870

King of the Sotho (1822-1870); warrior; diplomat; humanitarian; the reason why there is a small landlocked country in the middle of South Africa

IN THE WORLD OF BUSINESS, if your company can hold its ground during recession, the chief exec is likely to feel as if he or she has done well. If the economy contracts and your company doesn't, it's considered a good effort. And, of course, if your industry faces a storm of bad luck, sectoral collapse and as desperate a recession as the world has experienced since 2008, it's really rather good going if your company merely survives without being merged or closed down. Just ask anyone in the aviation or motor industries.

So can you imagine being the ruler of a small mountain kingdom where on one side you have the barbarous rise of a bloodthirsty tyrant, Shaka Zulu, and on the other you have heavily armed Trekboers with a hunger for land, lots of it, and a complete disdain for the indigenous folk of the continent? Throw in the British, who saw themselves as natural overlords in the region, and you'd think you were Saab in 2011. This, throughout much of the 19th century, was the impossible situation that faced the nascent nation of the Basotho, who inhabited that often harsh but always beautiful place we now call Lesotho.

Back in the early 1810s the South African map looked nothing like it does today. South Africa didn't even exist. Neither did the Natal Colony, the Orange Free State or the Transvaal. The British had only taken over the Cape Colony from the Dutch at the turn of the century and were doing their level best to acclimatise to life at the bottom of the continent by regularly engaging in running battles with the Xhosa on their eastern border. Further afield Shaka was on the rise, building his Zulu nation and preparing to lay waste to those who stood in his way. Not far in the future 4,500 British settlers would land at Algoa Bay in the 1820s, and a trading post would be established at Port Natal in 1824. The Great Trek would follow in the 1830s and '40s, as the Boers migrated north and west. It was to be a century of upheaval, expansion and much violence, and no-one could have rated the chances of the small Basotho nation surviving any of it, let alone all of it. But it did, and it's no accident that Maseru's airport is today called Moshoeshoe I International, named for the kingdom's founding monarch. It was Moshoeshoe whom fate dealt the circumstances described above, and it is Moshoeshoe who is a bona fide historical hero to the folk of Lesotho.

There is a popular image of Moshoeshoe as a gentle soul but it isn't entirely fair. Probably the most famous illustration of him today shows him as a serene-looking older man, rather like Morgan Freeman in a top hat – but he started out as an ambitious and brazen chance-taker. In his youth he was a noted cattle raider, a pastime he would continue to pursue into his kingship. It is said that Moshoeshoe gave himself his name in a praise poem he composed for himself – as we do when we're king, should the mood take us – in which he described himself as "like a razor that trimmed all of Ramoheng's beards", a reference to repeated cattle raids on a rival chieftain as he was coming to power. And he found himself in power in interesting times.

The Mfecane came to the people of southern Africa as nothing had before. With Zululand as its epicentre, it rippled violently across the land for around 25 years from 1815 onwards as fleeing tribes fell upon one another in their desperation to escape the savage brutality of Shaka's impis. *(See Shaka.)* It is worth pointing out that the Mfecane went on to have an impact deep into sub-Saharan Africa, through large portions of South Africa and into what we now call Swaziland, Botswana, Zimbabwe, Mozambique, Malawi and Zambia. There is a place on the Caprivi strip, which borders Angola, that carries a Zulu name, Katima Mulilo, which translates loosely as "the place where the fire was eventually put out".

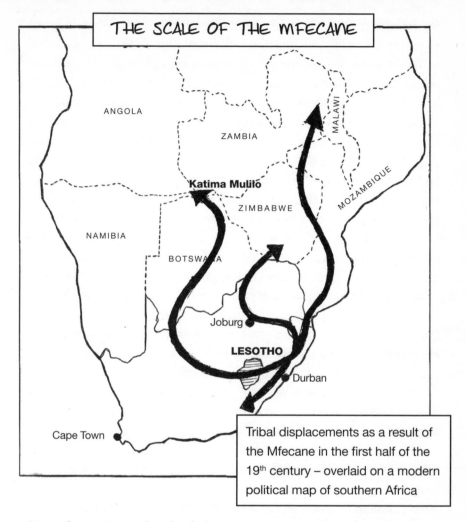

THE SCALE OF THE MFECANE

ANGOLA

ZAMBIA

NAMIBIA

BOTSWANA

Katima Mulilo

ZIMBABWE

MALAWI

MOZAMBIQUE

Joburg

LESOTHO

Durban

Cape Town

Tribal displacements as a result of
the Mfecane in the first half of the
19th century – overlaid on a modern
political map of southern Africa

Given the continental scale of what was going on in the early 1820s, those folk living in Butha-Buthe – now northern Lesotho – were gravely close to its heart. The town was Moshoeshoe's Paris to Shaka's Berlin, circa 1939, and the young king was destined to be attacked by many of the participating peoples of the Mfecane. He would require a canny mixture of military means, diplomacy, pragmatism and open-mindedness to the modern rapidly changing world to keep his realm intact, which meant he wasn't above paying tribute to Shaka or cutting deals with the British.

But he also fought off the advancing Nguni tribes as and when it was necessary. So trying were the times that he was forced to move his capital to Thaba Bosiu, a small elevated plateau near modern-day Maseru that the Sotho could use as a natural fortress. He managed to hold off the invaders when there was fighting and buy them off when he could.

People displaced by the Mfecane were forced to flee in search of security. The Tlokwa, led by the famous regent queen Mma Nthatisi, settled near modern-day Ficksburg after raging battles with Hlubi and Sotho forces. Her son, Sekonyela, who was said to be vain and cruel, eventually ruled the Tlokwa once they were established as a formidable tribe themselves, and even married a daughter of Moshoeshoe, but his love of war and his lack of tactical nous saw him and his 35,000 people lose their mountain citadel to Moshoeshoe in 1853, effectively ending one of the most extraordinary conflicts of the era. *(See Mma Nthatisi.)*

But the Mfecane and its ripples were only half of Moshoeshoe's woes. In the 1830s Trekboers started appearing in the west and pulling off their favoured trick of simply demanding land. Jan de Winaar settled his people on land near Matlakeng in 1838, a fateful year for trekkers generally. *(See Dingane, 50 People Who Stuffed Up South Africa.)*

Moshoeshoe knew little of white people. So instead of doing a Dingane Special and murdering the wizards, he sent for the French missionary Eugene Casalis, whom he installed as a kind of foreign-policy advisor and translator for dealing with Boers and Brits. Eventually Moshoeshoe told De Winaar's people that they could run their livestock on his land so long as they accepted his authority – but, of course, once the Boers "felt strong enough to throw off the mask," to quote Casalis, they reverted to their land-stealing ways.

Throughout the 1850s and '60s Moshoeshoe's leadership was sorely tested. He was never beaten in battle, though, and seemed to have an uncanny knack of picking his fights perfectly. Over the years he overcame both British and Boer forces. After defeating British forces in 1851 and in 1852, Moshoeshoe acted fast to exact a diplomatic solution, well aware that if the Imperial army really came for him in force he'd be crushed.

After defeating the Tlokwa in 1853, peace reigned, but in 1854 the

British briefly decided that they had no further interest in southern Africa beyond the Cape, and withdrew from the region. (They would, as history attests, rapidly change their minds about that, especially when the world's richest gold supply was discovered on the Witwatersrand.) This left the Sotho vulnerable to attack from the newly founded Boer republic of the Orange Free State. And indeed, it wasn't long in coming: in 1858 the Free State declared war over land claims in the formerly British Orange River Sovereignty.

It's extraordinary to contemplate, really. Trekkers had only first arrived in the region two decades before. Even their best efforts at justifying their actions – it was "abandoned" land, being about the extent of it – were just laughable. One can only suppose that these folk, for whom a major reason for trekking was their distaste at the British ban on slavery, didn't feel it necessary to even consider the niceties of what is right and what is wrong when dealing with blacks generally and the Sotho specifically. So war it would be.

Moshoeshoe suffered his most damaging losses to the Boers. In the first of three wars, Senekal's War, the Boers were repelled and Moshoeshoe responded by sending raiding parties into the Free State. In 1865 the Boers attacked again. Moshoeshoe looked to the British for help, but his appeals fell on deaf ears. Eventually he sued for peace and ceded a great deal of land to the Orange Free State. Unsatisfied, the Boers attacked one more time. In 1867 they still couldn't reach Thaba Bosiu, but the situation was dire. After consulting Casalis, Moshoeshoe appealed again to the British and submitted to becoming a protectorate of the British Empire the following year, thus using the British desire to contain the Boers to protect his own country. It was, he realised, the only way it would not be destroyed.

In three wars Moshoeshoe had lost half his kingdom, mainly productive arable land to the west that became known as the "Lost Territory" – land now owned by white farmers in what we call the Free State. Basutoland became a Crown Colony in 1884, and would only gain its freedom, as the Kingdom of Lesotho, in 1966.

But it did gain its freedom as an independent state, and it was because of Moshoeshoe's wit and diplomacy that this was possible. Other, more famous southern African tribal leaders ultimately failed, most notably Shaka, whose nation was first beaten into submission then swallowed by the new behemoth created in 1910 – the Union of South Africa.

So it is true that the times of conflict in which he ruled were seldom easy, and that large tracts of land were lost by means foul and fouler, but Moshoeshoe did what no other achieved. He rode out the Mfecane, that perfect storm, and he managed to keep his nation and his cultures distinct and intact in an extraordinarily violent and volatile time.

King Moshoeshoe I died in 1870 after nearly fifty years as leader of the Sotho people. Possessed of a great foresight, he had ruled as though he was aware that Shaka would burn out, that his savagery would not go unpunished, and that even the worst of the violence of the Mfecane would eventually dissipate. He had seemed also to know that the only way to safeguard his people a century into the future was to negotiate with Britain as best he could. The colonists would come and then they

"Moshoeshoe was a humane man. Unlike Shaka, he respected the dignity of every person, he ruled by consultation and consent, and he rarely imposed the death penalty. His was a self-disciplined and integrated personality. He abstained from drinking alcohol and smoking cannabis, for he declared that they would prevent him form making wise decisions. He was a selective innovator, quick to appreciate the advantages of guns, horses, new crops and literary education. Above all, he was a realist and a patriot... To preserve the cohesion of his people he kept one foot in the conservative and traditionalist camp, even while placing the other in the modern and Christian. He acquired a deep understanding of the changing power relationships in the southern African state system of his day and, matching his policy to his means, he pursued an active diplomacy."

– *Leonard Thompson, from his book*
Survival In Two Worlds: Moshoeshoe Of Lesotho 1786-1870

would eventually leave, which they did in 1966.

Lesotho is far from a model democracy, we know. But it is an independent state with a culture and traditions all of its own, and of this the Sotho are justifiably proud. Shaka's Zulus get all the headlines for their martial skills, but their leaders lacked the political skill to avoid their eventual assimilation into the South African morass. It is because of Moshoeshoe that South Africa contains an entire country landlocked within its borders, one of only three instances in world where this occurs. (Bearing in mind that the other two, San Marino and the Vatican, are microstates and hardly count.)

A final thought: it was Moshoeshoe's humanity and diplomacy that endeared him to his people. He was, effectively, a CEO with a brilliantly strategic mind *and* good people skills. He welcomed small clans to his kingdom, even lending them cattle so that they might get a start in their adopted home – state loans to asylum seekers, in modern parlance. He helped recently defeated foes to their feet and struck deals with them to work together, as a modern company might merge with another. He attracted people, as opposed to co-opting them by force. There's probably a lesson in that for South Africa's current crop of leaders, none of whom are a patch on King Moshoeshoe I.

Elon Musk

b. 28 June 1971

Entrepreneur; risk taker; world shaker; the man behind Tesla, PayPal, SpaceX and Solar City; quite possibly the saviour of all humankind

THE YANKS CLAIM HIM, he has described himself as "nauseatingly pro-American" and, to interrupt the petty flag-waving for a moment, it's quite obvious that what he has achieved could not have been done here in South Africa. He's still ours, though, born and bred in Pretoria and educated at Pretoria Boys High. And though his name sounds something like a men's cologne, possibly invented on the set of *Anchorman*, he is well worth claiming because he has done much, and plans to do so much more. Elon Musk wants nothing less than to save the human race. And at the rate he's going – who knows? – he might just.

It was after school, in the late 1980s, that Musk realised he was set to face the fate of all white boys at the time: two years' compulsory service in the South African Defence Force. "I don't have a problem with serving in the military per se," he would later recount, "but serving in the South African army suppressing black people just didn't seem like a really good way to spend time." That's a classic Musk quote. Careful not to diss the army in the military-loving US, and equally careful to explain why it was the right thing to dodge the draft in South Africa. Thoughtful and self-aware. It's almost as if he knows he'll be quoted.

So, paying his own bills, the teenaged Musk moved to Canada, his mother's country, where he went to Queens University and then, by virtue of a scholarship, the University of Pennsylvania's Wharton School of Business. Here he studied, rather usefully as it happens, Economics and Physics. Musk was no intellectual slouch, but he was no predictable genius either. He was accepted to do a doctorate in high-energy physics at Stanford, but chose to drop out after two days with the intention of taking some time off to start a business – before probably going back. "I didn't really expect it to make any money," he explained later. "If I could make enough to cover the rent and buy some food that would be fine. As it turned out, it [was] quite valuable in the end."

It being 1995, and this being a tale of astonishing and astonishingly quick financial success, the company in question, Zip2, was an internet start-up. It had something to do with online publishing solutions – the details hardly seemed to matter during the internet boom – and of course Musk timed the selling of the company perfectly, just as Mark Shuttleworth would do in a few pages' time. *(See Mark Shuttleworth.)* In 1999 Alta Vista gobbled it up for something approaching $350 million but, unlike Shuttleworth, Musk only left with a few tens of millions of dollars. Shame. He hadn't hit it *really* big. So he went and co-founded a little thing called PayPal, which, as everyone with an internet connection knows, has taken the connected world by storm. If you don't spend any time on the internet (and perhaps shun electricity, too), PayPal is a company that allows payments to be made online from anywhere in the world. It's massive. So massive that when the dot.com bubble burst later that year it handled just fine. Indeed, PayPal, of which our boy from Pretoria owned 11 percent, was bought three years later, by eBay, for $1.5 billion. It was 2002 and Musk was 31.

Amazingly, he was still only warming up. Musk had three great interests when he left university: the internet, space and green technology. Time to try out number two.

Musk believes that space travel is a crucial step to preserving humanity. He put his philosophy into writing for *Esquire* magazine thus: "The next big moment will be life becoming multi-planetary, an unprecedented adventure that would dramatically enhance the richness and diversity of our collective consciousness. It would serve as a hedge against the myriad – and growing – threats to our survival. An asteroid or a super-volcano could certainly destroy us, but we also face risks the dinosaurs never saw: an engineered virus, nuclear war, the accidental creation of a micro black hole, or some as-yet-unknown technology could spell the end of us. Sooner or later, we must expand life beyond our little blue mud ball – or go extinct."

With that heart-warming vision of things to come, Musk started a company called Space Exploration Technologies, or SpaceX, in 2002. Its goal was to make cost-effective travel into space a reality. Given that the likes of Boeing and Lockheed Martin charged hundreds of millions of dollars to put payloads into orbit, this must rank as one of the most daunting business ventures ever undertaken. Making cheap, reliable and reusable rockets presented an array of technical problems too numerous to mention. Musk had no illusions: "We have to solve these problems and reduce the cost of human spaceflight by a factor of 100," he declared. And then, almost in the same breath: "I think the chances of success are tiny, but the goal [is] important enough to try."

Right, so here's a guy in his early thirties getting down to the business of putting things and eventually people into space – something that only a few decades earlier your average superpower struggled to do – and in so doing he's taking on some of the largest and most daunting aeronautical conglomerates in the world, and effectively the might of the American military-industrial complex, come to think of it. So what's a Pretoria boykie to do? How about start up a car company? But not just any old car company; one that revolutionises automotive technology and produces a sexy electric sports car, something that basically doesn't exist...

And so, the year after founding SpaceX (reminder: trying to make rockets to go into space), Musk launched Tesla, with the goal of making viable electric cars to challenge the world's great automakers. Once again, he knew he was in for an interesting ride. "Technology in any field takes a few versions to optimise before reaching a mass market, and in this case it is competing with 150 years and trillions of dollars spent on gasoline cars," he wrote at the time.

Suffice it to say that at this point in his career anyone who had ever doubted Elon Musk's ambition would have had to concede that the man wasn't scared of a challenge.

As it turns out, Tesla appears to have been the trickier of the two. In tackling his third interest – green technology (saving the world from a slightly different angle) – Musk sought to build a very fast electric sports car, the Tesla Roadster. The thinking was that, like new computer or mobile technology, it would be adopted by wealthy early adopters, allowing the firm to develop affordable mass-produced vehicles at a later stage. But to make the thing he had to defy automotive history and develop battery technology that could deliver genuine sports-car performance in a production electric car. Needless to say, with Musk at the wheel, this was achieved. The Roadster's performance was astounding, revolutionary even, and it shattered preconceptions about electric cars. But the car was – and is – very, very expensive, and Tesla has lost a great deal of money. Much of it, around $70 million by 2008, was Musk's. "There was a time when Tesla came very close to dying. I had to give it every last penny I had to keep it alive," Musk explained.

Though you suspect it wasn't quite his every last penny, things were definitely touch and go for the company; however, the technology eventually won the day, if not in the roaring success of the company then by putting the wind up some of the large American manufacturers. Bob Lutz, the vice chairman at General Motors, described in *Newsweek* as "The man who revived the electric car", cites the arrival of the upstarts at Tesla as direct inspiration for the successful Chevy Volt, one of the most fuel-efficient production cars in the world today. Eventually all the major players took notice.

"All the geniuses here at General Motors kept saying lithium-ion technology is ten years away, and Toyota agreed with us – and boom, along comes Tesla. So I said 'How come some tiny little Californian start-up, run by guys who know nothing about the car business, can do this, and we can't?'"

– Bob Lutz, former General Motors vice chairman.
The arrival of Tesla led directly to the development of the Chevy Volt

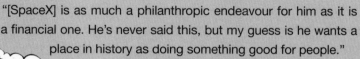

"[SpaceX] is as much a philanthropic endeavour for him as it is a financial one. He's never said this, but my guess is he wants a place in history as doing something good for people."
– Gwynne Shotwell, then a vice president at SpaceX, speaking in 2005

By securing state loans, and by cannily sharing intellectual property with the likes of Toyota, Lotus, Daimler and Panasonic, Tesla keeps on going. It has sold more than 2,500 Roadsters worldwide, at $100,000 a pop, and deliveries of the Model S, a mid-range executive car, began in June 2012. It's got a range of approximately 500 kilometres, does 0-100 in 5.7 seconds and is almost half the price of the Roadster. Next up is a hatchback. If Tesla does develop genuinely usable, day-to-day cars that happen to be electric, there's no reason the company won't fly. Musk, who now owns about a third of it, believes it will be profitable by 2013.

Either way, one of his strategic aims of shaking up the complacent auto industry has been achieved, and Musk has further advanced his green credentials by conceiving of and investing heavily in Solar City, now the biggest supplier of solar panels in the United States.

But it's the rockets that really get Musk into the news. Almost predictably, given his stellar ambitions, SpaceX made it into space, with no major mishap, in just six years. Given the incredible dangers, traditional expense and complexity of space flight, this was a remarkable achievement. In 2009 it became the first private company to launch a satellite into low-Earth orbit, on the back of a Falcon 1 rocket. The following year the bigger Falcon 9 had two successful launches, the second carrying aloft a Dragon space capsule, which orbited the Earth twice before splashing down in the Pacific Ocean. NASA was impressed. Having invested nearly $400 million in SpaceX in 2006, it awarded the company a contract worth at least $1.6 billion to make twelve cargo-delivery flights to the International Space Station (ISS). Like a galactic Mr Delivery.

D-Day came in May 2012 when the Dragon capsule was blasted off once more on a test flight to deliver supplies to the ISS, then returned to Earth with used equipment, experiment samples and other material. The first commercially contracted mission followed in October, and the next step will likely see SpaceX ferrying astronauts to the ISS as soon as possible; when that role is achieved the company will have filled the gap left by the Space Shuttle.

But, of course, Musk could never stop there. Speaking in 2011, he revealed his intention to get a man on Mars by 2025. Already Falcon Heavy is close to completion; when it is sent up, in 2013 or 2014, it will become the most powerful rocket since the Saturn V launchers that sent men to the moon. An eager NASA has started developing an unmanned mission concept called the Red Dragon that will use a SpaceX Dragon capsule and Falcon Heavy rocket for launch in 2018 to Mars for the purposes of looking for life of any sort. As a result of SpaceX's work on reducing costs, Red Dragon comes with a projected price tag of less than $425 million. By contrast, it cost $2.5 billion to put the *Curiosity* rover on Mars in August 2012.

Elon Musk is a hugely accomplished man and, in the way of the wildly successful, he rubs people up the wrong way. He laughs at his competitors' efforts and treats the media, especially the sceptical motoring media, with thinly veiled mistrust. But all great achievers have egos. It's not a crime. And for any individual, by the age of 40, to have pioneered important internet technologies, to have shaken up the global motor industry and to be flying to the International Space Station is pretty remarkable. The story of Elon Musk, the man *Esquire* calls "the most 21st-century entrepreneur on the planet", is one to watch.

A man on the red planet by 2025? Would you bet against Mr Musk?

"I would like to die on Mars. Just not on impact."

— *Elon Musk*

Mma Nthatisi

c.1781 – c.1836

Widely feared Tlokwa warrior-queen of the 19ᵗʰ century; diesel-electric attack submarine

WHEN SOMEONE IS THRUST UNEXPECTEDLY into a leadership position things tend to go one of two ways. They either perform admirably, or they fail miserably. When Edward VIII abdicated the English crown in 1936 so he could marry Wallis Simpson, his younger brother assumed the throne just as Britain was being sucked into a war with Nazi Germany. George VI, who famously stuttered, eventually became a much-loved and well-respected king, whose morale-boosting efforts in the war took years off his life. It made for good cinema.

Here in southern Africa, a similar event occurred around 1813 to a young woman known as Monyalue and then as Mma Nthathisi. She was married to Mokotjo, chief of the Tlokwa – or, depending on your tribal nomenclature, the BaTlokwa – a people living near the modern Harrismith district. But he died young, leaving the eldest of their four sons, Sekonyela, far too young to take the reins of power. Mma Nthathisi stood up to the challenge to rule the Tlokwa as regent until Sekonyela came of age, and she went on to become one of the most feared and respected leaders in the time of the Mfecane. Where Shaka's Zulus had displaced the Hlubi, it was the Hlubi who displaced the Tlokwa, forcing them to flee into the southern African interior. And they came intent on survival – "Manthatisi's Hordes", as European observers had it at the time, spreading fear before them as they made their way towards what would become Bechuanaland and then Botswana. At their head was their tall, attractive and – ahem – bare-breasted warrior queen.

Mma Nthathisi didn't have it easy. Her various in-laws wanted her out, and before she'd even been set upon by the Hlubi she had to see off her departed husband's relatives. She was herself of the Basia people, and had been married off to the nearby Tlokwa chief in a typical alliance-building process beloved of royal houses across the world. The scheming, feuding and eliminating of rivals that would come later was also typically regal.

As head of the Tlokwa, known as the Wild Cat People, Mma Nthathisi would eventually have an extraordinary time of it. In escaping Hlubi raiders – themselves displaced by Ngwane, who had been displaced by the Zulus – she moved her people west, where they ran into various roaming people, including Moshoeshoe's Sotho army, which she defeated at the Battle of the Pots.

It was important to keep moving. This was not a nimble cattle raid of old, but a procession of thousands that would lay waste to whatever and whomever came in their path in order to get to livestock and grain. Battle followed conflict followed battle, and Mma Nthatisi and her ever-growing following eventually knocked into the Fokeng people, forcing them north of the Vaal River. In 1823 her 40,000-strong following was to eventually meet its match in modern-day Botswana, where a wily Ngwaketsi chief held off her army. But she was smart enough to pull back and, as starvation threatened, and with wild animals and bandits picking off the stragglers, her people eventually made it to the Caledon area of the Free State in about 1833, where they settled. By this time legends abounded of the axe-wielding Mma Nthatisi and her "hordes". She was the "destroyer of nations", and men trembled at the sound of her name, while her people were no longer known as the Tlokwa; they were the Manthatisi.

Mma Nthathisi had guided her people as no-one else had, for nearly twenty years, cutting a swathe through the southern African wilderness as they sought to survive first Shaka's warring and then the hardships of the interior. She died aged 55 in 1836, having passed the crown to Sekonyela, and with the worst of the Mfecane now over. Despite everything, she had delivered her son a prosperous people living in

> "Numerous and strange reports had at intervals reached us, some indeed, of such a character as induced us to treat them of the reveries of a madman. It was said that a mighty woman, of the name Mantatee, was at the head of an invincible army, numerous as locusts, marching onwards towards the interior nations, carrying devastation and ruin wherever she went; that she nourished the army with her own milk, sent hornets before it and, in one word, was laying the world desolate."
>
> *– Robert Moffat, an English missionary and father-in-law of David Livingstone, who was stationed at Kuruman in the 1820s*

a time of peace. Sekonyela, however, displayed none of his mother's talents. His love of war and his rough treatment of both his own people and his neighbours led to the inevitable decline of the Tlokwa, which was matched only by the peace-loving Moshoeshoe's continued success and the growth of the Sotho kingdom. Constant raiding would eventually persuade Moshoeshoe to defeat Sekonyela in 1853, absorbing and scattering his people.

As an aside, it was cattle raided by Sekonyela belonging to the Zulus under Dingane that one Piet Retief was despatched to retrieve in 1837 in a doomed supposed land deal with the Zulu king. Retief duped the Tlokwa chief easily by offering him some "bracelets" that were actually handcuffs. Sekonyela really was a moron. *(See Dingane, 50 People Who Stuffed Up South Africa.)*

Today Sekonyela has been rightfully consigned to the dumpbin of historical failure, whereas the name of Mma Nthathisi lives on, now anglicised as Manthatisi, both as a unique warrior chieftainess and noble leader of men – and as one of the South African navy's modern diesel-electric attack submarines stationed at Simonstown, the SAS *Manthatisi*.

(See Moshoeshoe I.)

François Pienaar

b. 2 January 1967

Springbok rugby captain; World Cup winner; point man for Mandela's push to unite the country around the Boks; sound-bite king

TWENTY-NINE INTERNATIONAL CAPS. Three tries. Fifteen points. Not, one could rightly opine, a truly stellar rugby career. And no, he wasn't the greatest player, was he? Of course, to turn out for the Springboks just once is an achievement, and don't forget that he captained South Africa in every one of those 29 Tests. But let's be honest: when seen in the light of some amazing players, François Pienaar's numbers hardly leap off the page.

Consider briefly, for example, some of the global stars who have more than a hundred caps for their countries: David Campese, Richie McCaw, Philippe Sella, Brian O'Driscoll and, dare we mention him, George Gregan, who played for Australia an astonishing 139 times. Among the Boks themselves John Smit stands as a colossus of the game, with 111 caps, as does Percy Montgomery. Then there's the formidable partnership of Victor Matfield and Bakkies Botha, with 186 appearances between them. And what of Bryan Habana and his forty-something tries? And, delving into history, what of Danie Gerber, Naas Botha, Morné du Plessis and his namesakes, Carel and Michael? Or, even further back, there's Danie Craven, Hennie Muller, Mannetjies Roux and Frik du Preez... All legends who could get the call for a game played in rugby heaven.

And yet it is François Pienaar who we feature because fate was to bequeath to him something rather difficult: the responsibility of captaining an almost entirely white rugby team to represent an almost entirely black country just fourteen months after that majority had elected Nelson Mandela as the country's new president. At a Rugby World Cup, to be played in South Africa. And, as it happened, he did rather a good job.

Those of us who were around to read the papers and watch SABC news back then often forget how very tense South Africa was in those days. Sure, we complain today about our incompetent leaders and governmental corruption and all the nonsense that goes with it, but the idea of civil war doesn't feature much in our thinking. Back in 1995 it was just two years after the assassination of Chris Hani and only a year since the AWB had gone on a "*kaffirskiet piekniek*" in Bophuthatswana. Life was still tense, and life was also tense in the South African rugby team.

As an example, a black man who'd had the talent to beat a white system, Chester Williams, made the team on merit and, according to his biography, spent much of the time being called a "fucking kaffir", most notably by James Small. White rugby players were no different from white other people, and after years of being fed apartheid "truths" about the ANC, Mandela and black people in general, they were frightened about the future of the country, and their place in it. Performing well at the World Cup would be a major challenge for the young Springbok captain, especially with new Bok coach Kitch Christie having been appointed just nine months before.

And then, to his surprise, Pienaar was invited to tea at the Union Buildings by none other than Nelson Mandela, and the big man told him of a seemingly impossible plan he had in mind. Mandela, with Pienaar, was going to lure white South Africa into his New South Africa, and he was going to do it by getting the ANC to support his frankly unthinkable notion of supporting the Springboks. Unthinkable because back then the Springbok was hated, a symbol of proud Afrikanerdom and white domination, and a great many black South Africans supported just one rugby team – whomever the Boks were playing against. It was a huge ask, as Mandela would recall, and he first had to save the Springbok emblem itself from being consigned to history – as many wanted – before he could take the next step. "They booed me!" he told John Carlin, author of *Playing The Enemy: Nelson Mandela And The Game That Made A Nation*. "My own people – they booed me when I stood before them, urging them to support the Springboks!" But Mandela is nothing if not a great persuader – and so, naturally, he won out in the end.

A key element of this kooky nation-building plan was to get the new anthem right, something many of the players were rather clueless about. But Pienaar, with Bok manager Morné du Plessis, convinced his team of white Afrikaans men to learn the words of *Nkosi Sikelel' iAfrika* and they all attended singing lessons to get it right. The sight of a man-mountain like Kobus Wiese and even the reforming bad boy Small (who

> "I can say with some authority that none of the favoured teams came to the [1995 World Cup] with a more disrupted, less scientific build-up than the Springboks. It was clear that only a miracle could produce a World Cup-winning team from such disorganisation. But in coach Kitch Christie, in team manager Morné du Plessis and in captain François Pienaar, that team had the leadership to produce that miracle."
>
> – *Tim Noakes, Challenging Beliefs*

> "Any side with a captain such as Pienaar is bound to feel the positive effects of his presence. He was courageous to the point of endangering his health and ruthlessly combative... Pienaar is a man who in one moment managed to transcend the world of sport, creating an image alongside Mandela that will serve as a reminder for fans the world over of the changes for good that have occurred in the recent history of the game. As a player he was a defensive rock, as a captain a courageous leader and as a South African he became a legend."
>
> *— ESPN Scrum player profile*

cried when the team visited Robben Island) hammering it out with gusto, game after game, was quite something. People noticed. Slowly, Mandela's plot started to work. The *Sowetan*, of all organs, christened the team "Amabokoboko", and black South Africans, it is said, started to wonder if, indeed, these whites might want to play nicely in the new South Africa after all.

But Pienaar, aside from all of this political what-what and the classically South African fraught nature of just about everything, had another small task to complete. Because the plan would work so much better if South Africa could just go on and win the whole World Cup...

And, of course, we know how this story ends because we did exactly that, eventually beating New Zealand in a tense, uncompromising, far-from-pretty but utterly unforgettable final that we pulled off on little more than sheer guts and a brilliant drop goal. The Boks had won, Mandela wore the jersey, and the white crowd chanted his name. There were tears, there were celebrations in the streets, there were all-night parties. There was a brief, heady, drunken orgy of happy togetherness. It was awesome. And it remains one of the great feel-good stories to come from that era.

At every critical stage of the tournament Pienaar had been there: in convincing his team they could beat the defending champions, Australia, in the opening game; in marshalling the troops after the bloody Battle of Boet Erasmus Stadium; in the epic semifinal in atrocious conditions against the French; and in the final when he led from the front in defending every inch of the Ellis Park turf all the way until extra time was done, despite suffering a calf injury.

His two greatest moments, though, came right at the end, with television viewers around the world hanging on to his every word. First, and most memorably, he was asked by David van der Sandt what it was like to have 65,000 fans supporting him on the day, to which he replied, "David, we didn't have the support of 60,000 South Africans today [*sic*], we had the support of 43 million South Africans."

And then, perhaps more meaningful, was his response to Nelson Mandela as the great man handed the Webb Ellis trophy to him. "François, thank you for what you have done for our country," said Mandela. And Pienaar replied: "No, Mr President. Thank you for what you have done."

In 2010, when Clint Eastwood had turned John Carlin's book on this very story into the movie *Invictus* – a movie that had to take some poetic licence, it must be said – Pienaar found himself in front of the cameras again. He told *The Telegraph*, "June 1995 was the moment in time when the new South Africa took a long hard look in on itself and President Mandela showed the way towards reconciliation by putting his trust in the Springboks. It was a healing process."

After fifteen years he was still the captain.

In retrospect, François Pienaar was neither the best player in his World Cup squad (probably a shootout between Joost van der Westhuizen, André Joubert and Mark Andrews), nor even the best flank (Ruben Kruger). But if you had to pick the Springbok team for that World Cup final again, his would be the first name on the team sheet, without doubt. Because our victory would not have been possible without a little Madiba Magic and our inspirational captain.

And if this all sounds perhaps a bit misty-eyed and nostalgic, well, what's the bother? It's good to remind ourselves every now and then of those moments of joy in our past. A little moment that pictures that Stransky kick sailing over or Mandela and Pienaar in matching Bok jerseys, when we can think, ja, that was just great.

THE ROAD TO 1995 WORLD CUP VICTORY

Pool games:

25 May

South Africa v Australia *Newlands, Cape Town*
27-18

The game that kick-started it all, against the defending champions who were unbeaten in a year. Tries by Pieter Hendriks and Joel Stransky set up a relatively comfortable win in the end, sparking celebrations around the country and a new sense of belief in the team. Suddenly we were genuine contenders.

30 May

South Africa v Romania *Newlands, Cape Town*
21-8

The Boks came back to Earth with a scrappy and unconvincing victory over a team that Canada had beaten 34-3 a few days earlier. Admittedly, it was with a second-string team led by (another stalwart South African captain of the time) Adriaan Richter.

3 June

South Africa v Canada *Newlands, Cape Town*
20-0

A game that was first plunged into shadows by a power failure that delayed the start, then was entirely overshadowed by a mass brawl that involved nearly every player on the field. James Dalton and Pieter Hendriks were expelled from the competition as result, while Hennie le Roux was lucky not to follow suit.

Quarterfinal:

10 June

South Africa v Western Samoa *Ellis Park, Johannesburg*

42-14

A convincing performance saw Chester Williams returning to the team – replacing Hendriks in the squad – and scoring a record four tries in the process. But André Joubert suffered a critical hand injury that would require treatment in a decompression chamber.

Semifinal:

17 June

South Africa v France *Kings Park, Durban*

19-15

A game played after biblical rainfall had delayed the start saw the Boks swim to the tightest, tensest win. Had a contentious decision not to award a try to Abdel Benazzi gone against us, or had the game been cancelled entirely due to the weather – a possibility at one stage – we would not have made the final.

Final:

24 June

South Africa v New Zealand *Ellis Park, Johannesburg*

15-12

The greatest scoreline in South African rugby history was the culmination of the fiercest of battles. No tries were scored, it was hardly a celebration of running rugby, but it was entirely enthralling. The Boks were relentless in closing down the Jonah Lomu threat, almost fighting each other for the chance to tackle him, and it came down to the kicking skills of Andrew Mehrtens and Joel Stransky. Famously, Stransky got the winning drop goal in extra time. And that was that.

Oscar Pistorius

b. 22 November 1986

Double-amputee sprinter; the Blade Runner;
Paralympian; Olympian; multiple world-record
holder; incredible inspiration; incredibly nice guy

IN JULY 2011, in an event the importance of which would only truly be felt
a year or so later, something astonishing happened. A young man, a double
amputee, with the use of carbon prosthetics where once his lower legs had
been, ran 400 metres in 45.07 seconds.

Now that may seem like an arbitrary number, but the crucial point was
that it was within the International Association of Athletics Federation's

"A" standard time for the race. This meant that the man, Oscar Pistorius, could be legitimately selected to represent South Africa at the 2012 Olympics. Indeed, at the time, it made him the 15th fastest man over 400 metres in the world – legs or no legs.

That little fact is like a fine wine: worth sloshing about the mouth for a bit and enjoying. Because, really, what an achievement it was.

The thing is, Pistorius has been in the news for a few years now, having made a name for himself at the 2004 and 2008 Paralympics and competed at able-bodied athletics meetings since 2007, and indeed he has become so mainstream that we now tend to see him as just some regular guy on TV along with all the other athletes who pop up on model billboards or in SuperSport ads (as he no doubt would like us to see him). But yeah, familiar or not, the guy's got no legs and he's running against the fastest human beings in the whole world. Carry on sloshing. It's truly phenomenal.

And it hasn't been an easy road. He lost his mother at age 15 when she suffered an allergic reaction to malaria medicine. He's had to fight bloody hard to be accepted in able-bodied races, eventually taking his case to the Court of Arbitration for Sport. And, of course, there's the disability itself. Pistorius was born without fibulas, so his lower legs were amputated before he turned one.

But his parents just treated him as a normal kid and he's never felt sorry for himself in this regard. He wore rigid glass-fibre legs as a toddler, and played cricket, soccer and rugby like all the other kids. He even wrestled. In one rugby match in high school his leg came off in a tackle and he just carried on playing. Due to the weight of his prosthetics he never realised he had any aptitude for sprinting, but after suffering a severe knee injury playing rugby at the age of 16 he tried running as a form of rehabilitation. On the right legs he was a machine, and he was competing at the Athens Paralympics – and winning – within a year, and while still at school.

There's no value listing here everything the Blade Runner has won because he's won an awful lot. But, for the record, his highlights include six Paralympic gold medals, plus one silver and one bronze, and world records in the T44 category of the 100-, 200- and 400-metre sprints, and the 4x100 relay. Astonishingly, he won a silver medal in his first able-bodied World Championships, in Daegu in 2011, as a member of the 4x400 team – the first amputee to win a Championship track medal. (Though he didn't actually run in the final, a controversial decision, he had competed in the heats in which the South African team recorded a national record.)

And then the highlight: his competition in the London 2012 Olympics. Not Paralympics. Olympics.

Years before, when still trying to make his case to qualify for able-bodied competitions, Pistorius had explained his outlook in an interview with *The New York Times*. "These have always been my legs," he said. "I train harder than other guys, eat better, sleep better and wake up thinking about athletics. I think that's probably why I'm a bit of an exception." Indeed, he is an incredibly hard worker, and he lost 13 kilograms from Beijing to London to make his dream a reality. In the end he was eliminated in the semifinals, coming last in that race and finishing as the 16th fastest of 51 runners who qualified to run the 400 metres. In the process he became one of the most talked-about and most applauded athletes of the games. He had made his point.

"You're not disabled by the disabilities you have, you are able by the abilities you have," as he likes to say.

And what of the guy himself? Well, he's just the most decent, nicest oke you could find. Sure, there was that controversy when he complained about the length of a competitor's blades after coming – to the surprise of all watching – second in the Paralympic 200-metre final in 2012. But if anything that just proved he's human, after all. If you heard his apology afterwards you would have recognised it as a most genuine thing.

As for opting to keep tigers as your pet of choice, that's possibly a bit far out, but otherwise he's led a pretty blame-free life, always there with a ready smile and blessed with an obvious gift for relating to children, and inspiring them. ("I've got these cool legs because I lost mine, because I didn't eat my vegetables.")

Today Oscar Pistorius is a wealthy man. That smile and his looks, his astonishing achievements on the track and the way in which the Paralympics caught the public imagination like never before in London, have made him very attractive to sponsors such as Nike, Thierry Mugler and Oakley. All of which is thoroughly deserved, but it does leave us with the question as to what will happen now. He was 25 at London 2012 and it seems likely that gold medals and sprinting will not be the beginning and end of the Oscar Pistorius story. What will Oscar do next? It's unlikely to be accountancy.

> "He is one of the most recognisable sporting figures in the world. He does probably more for the Paralympic movement than anybody else because of the coverage he gets."
> – Roger Black, British former Olympic and world 400m silver medallist

Sol Plaatje

9 October 1876 – 19 June 1932

Founding member of the ANC; celebrated writer, translator, editor and man of letters and languages; first of the prominent black intellectuals

APARTHEID OFFICIALLY KICKED OFF IN 1948 when DF Malan's Nationalists came to power in place of the United Party under Jan Smuts. As far as turning points in a country's history go, this one is as embarrassing as it gets – voting out a revered international statesman in favour of a mean old Nazi sympathiser intent on racial segregation just isn't good for a nation's cred – and it's a key moment that we return to several times throughout this book. But of course apartheid had existed both here and around the world for hundreds of years, just in less official terms. Smuts, for one, was famously dismissive of native South Africans during his ascent to power in the early 1900s, claiming, among other things, that "these children of nature have not the inner toughness and persistence of the European". The fact that Smuts had numerous encounters with one Sol Plaatje over the years and was aware of the social capital he possessed makes this statement somewhat perplexing – for Plaatje was a man of great talent who showed immense mental toughness in a difficult time. But to dwell on the flaws of one great South African is to ignore the achievements of another. So, for now, on to Plaatje. *(See Jan Smuts.)*

Plaatje was born in Boshof in the Orange Free State in 1876. It is hardly overstating things to say these were interesting times in southern Africa. The Free State was an independent Boer republic under the presidency of Johannes Brand, while the Transvaal Republic to the east was also independent – for the time being, at least. In the other direction diamonds had been discovered five years earlier in the Cape Colony at Kimberley, not fifty kilometres from Boshof, and men of the calibre of Cecil John Rhodes and Barney Barnato were making names for themselves as the Big Hole sunk deeper into the earth. Back in the other direction again a gold rush was set to kick off on the Witwatersrand in 1886 when the city of Johannesburg would explode into existence, but not before the First Anglo-Boer War had seen the British embarrassed at Majuba Hill – and then, of course, the Second Anglo-Boer War would follow in 1899…

So, into this dynamic and quickly evolving state of affairs between recalcitrant Boer and predatory Brit came Solomon Tshekisho Plaatje, a young black kid with a gift for language. He received his education from missionaries in the town of Pniel on the banks of the Vaal River, and it was quickly clear that they were dealing with someone of special intelligence. By the age of 15 Plaatje was teaching his fellow pupils, but he was unable to complete his secondary studies due to a lack of funds. The diamond rush beckoned and he moved to Kimberley to take up a position as postman in 1894. By this stage he had learnt to speak English, Dutch, German, Tswana, Xhosa and Sotho, and he soon found himself as one of the very few genuine polyglots in South Africa. He would eventually speak at least eight languages, and after watching *Hamlet* and reading *The Merchant Of Venice* he developed a great appreciation for the works of Shakespeare.

As a young man establishing his career, Plaatje was mentored by Bud M'Belle, a man who was considered an "example of excellence" among those in Kimberley. The first African to pass the Cape Civil Service Examination, M'Belle was also a skilled interpreter, teacher, sportsman and singer. Plaatje's encounter with M'Belle was significant, not only because he would follow the disciplines of his mentor, but also because he ended up marrying one of M'Belle's daughters, Elizabeth.

In 1898 Plaatje left his new bride with his family in Pniel and moved north to the town of Mafeking to take up a post as a court interpreter – not the most romantic move but money was short and the simmering

English-Afrikaner conflict would soon turn to full-scale war, providing him with plenty of work. Between October 1899 and May 1900 Plaatje found himself diligently diarising the events of the Siege of Mafeking, the most prominent action of the Anglo-Boer War, while also providing his interpretive and typing services to foreign war correspondents. Though his diary would only be discovered and published forty years after his death, becoming an invaluable addition to the literature of the war, he began to realise that writing was "an effective platform to articulate views and advocate his ideals". Enter Plaatje the journalist.

The transition from civil servant to political journalist came naturally for Plaatje, as he took up editorship of the well-known but irregularly printed *Koranta Ea Becoana* (The Bechuana Gazette) in 1902. He had arranged himself a financier and now he needed an audience – which he found as far afield as Washington in the United States, distributed by means of exchange arrangements with foreign news outlets. Recognising the influence that came with the written medium, Plaatje didn't shirk the agenda that he had come to advocate so strongly: "the amelioration of the Native", as he put it.

"Above all Plaatje should be remembered as a great South African. A man of deeply conservative instinct, he drew inspiration from both African and European traditions, and was sustained throughout a life of ceaseless endeavour by a vision of what South Africa could be, given only the freedom to draw upon what he saw as the best of those traditions, created from South Africa's unique historical experience."
– *Brian Willan, Sol Plaatje: South African Nationalist, 1876-1932*

In the following years the newspaper's popularity and Plaatje's profile increased in parallel, thanks in no small part to his progressive perspectives on the issues affecting the African community. But the low rate of literacy within his target market meant that advertisers were not getting great returns on their investments, and as the CEO of any media

"I mention Sol Plaatje as an example of the ability to weave between the different languages and cultures, and to contribute through writing, literature and journalism, to the betterment of the lives of South Africans."

– Late Minister of Education, Professor Kader Asmal, speaking in October 2001

company knows, running an ailing newspaper is a fast track to financial ruin. Plaatje persevered with great passion and commitment to his cause but was forced to throw in the towel in 1909.

Plaatje's standing as an intellectual and a man of influence had increased considerably in his time at *Koranta Ea Becoana*, but financially he was broken. Realising that Mafeking held no further opportunity for him, he moved back to Kimberley to be with his family and start a new publication, *Tsala Ea Bechuana* (BaTswana's Friend). This new project was not to be without its own challenges, however, and again Plaatje found himself having to work extra jobs to supplement his income.

Of even greater concern to him was the Union of South Africa Act, which came into effect on 31 May 1910. This was the Act that finally brought together the former Boer and British republics as a dominion of the British Empire. It also stifled the rights of native South African citizens, a situation that was worsened with the passing of the Native Labour Regulation Act in 1911, which decreed that non-whites were prohibited from taking up certain occupations. Recognising that the situation had become dire for the everyday African, Plaatje answered Pixley ka Seme's call for the unity of African people, becoming the first General Secretary of the South African Native National Congress (SANNC) in January 1912. The multilingual Plaatje was the perfect candidate for this position; his interpretive abilities meant he could transcend language barriers, and his outspokenness on the issues of the time made him an invaluable asset to the party. Plaatje took it upon himself to draft the first constitution of the SANNC, though it would only be adopted in 1919.

"The white people of this country have formed what is known as the Union of South Africa – a union in which we have no voice in the making of laws and no part in their administration. We have called you therefore to this Conference so that we can together devise ways and means of forming our national union for the purpose of creating national unity and defending our rights and privileges."

– Sol Plaatje, speaking at the first meeting of the South African Native National Congress, later to become the ANC, in January 1912

The year 1913 was to be a testing one for Plaatje as a father, husband and leader. His youngest son died tragically at the age of sixteen months, and the pressure of Plaatje's political duties began to take their toll, so much so that he resigned as the scribe of the SANNC to be with his family. This was also the year that the Native Land Act was passed, threatening "the interests and wellbeing of virtually every section of the African population", as Plaatje put it. He travelled far and wide to document first-hand the effects that it had on those affected by it, and Sabata-mpho Mokae notes how in one instance, Plaatje observed "how one Kgobadi family had to bury their deceased child at night because they had nowhere legally to bury their son, except in the designated native areas, and so they had to use the roadside". The SANNC detested the draconian Act, and realising that their only recourse was to make an appeal to the more sympathetic British Crown, Plaatje and five other members departed for England in May 1914.

It was a trip that was supposed to take a few months but, with the first shots of World War I fired the following month in Sarajevo, it was to last all of three years. In this time Plaatje formed many lasting relationships with intellectuals, policy-makers and statesmen. He found solace in literature, consuming it voraciously and writing it religiously, and the fruit of Plaatje's dedication to the written word was his first published book in 1916, *Native Life In South Africa*. Upon his return home, he became despondent at the worsening situation, which saw his fellow

Africans being systematically reduced to second-class citizens. He left for England once again in 1919 in an attempt to publicise their struggle and lobby for their cause, and added to his itinerary the United States and Canada, where he met with influential advocates for the rights of the black populations in North America.

Plaatje's final return home in 1923 was marked by infighting between Pixley ka Seme and John Dube in the SANNC, which by then had been renamed the African National Congress. Plaatje was "embittered" that the ANC had not kept their promise of providing financially for his family; as a result, Elizabeth had had to sell the family printing press. Financially unstable, he turned once again to freelancing as a means of income, but some relief came in 1929 when the black community of Kimberley donated a house in Angel Street – now a national monument – to him and his family for the work he'd done for the community. The following year saw the release of his seminal novel, *Mhudi: An Epic Of South African Native Life A Hundred Years Ago.*

In publishing *Mhudi*, Plaatje made history by becoming one of the first African writers to produce an English novel. Reginald Dhlomo had already had his novella, *An African Tragedy*, published in 1928, but Plaatje's manuscript had been completed by 1919. After many years of diary keeping, journalism and translation – he had translated various Shakespearean works into Tswana, including *Othello, Julius Caesar, The Merchant of Venice, Comedy of Errors* and *Much Ado About Nothing* – this was the crowning achievement of his literary endeavours. The fact

"Plaatje was a diligent writer. He wrote under all circumstances, and almost every day of his life. While on board the vessel SS *Galway Castle*, coming back home from England, Plaatje spent his time translating Shakespeare's *Julius Caesar* into Setswana. The book was published later in 1937, five years after his death, as *Dintshontsho Tsa Juliuse Kesara.*"

– *Sabata-mpho Mokae, The Story Of Sol T. Plaatje*

that *Mhudi* was published a whole decade after its completion is a lesson in itself, as years of dogged pursuit finally saw it printed by the Lovedale Press in the Eastern Cape. He dedicated the novel to his daughter Olive, who had died in 1921 and was named for Olive Schreiner. (Plaatje had a habit of naming his children after his favourite writers and inventors, and so there is a story behind each of their names. Others included Frederick York St Leger, for the founder and editor of the *Cape Times*; Halley, named after Halley's Comet; and Johannes Gutenberg for, appropriately, the man who started the printing revolution in 15th-century Europe.)

While in Johannesburg submitting manuscripts during the winter of 1932, Plaatje contracted a bout of pneumonia from which he was never to recover. He died aged just 55. His commitment to delivering his manuscripts, despite his poor physical condition, alone spoke volumes about his dedication to the dissemination of ideas through the written word. In many ways, Plaatje was a literary forerunner for South Africa's intellectual giants and leaders. He was progressive in his thinking but also a moral beacon for those who found themselves disenfranchised. He had all of the "inner toughness and persistence" that Smuts spoke of, if not more.

Ian Player
& Magqubu Ntombela

Ian Player: b. 15 March 1927
Magqubu Ntombela: c.1900 – 21 October 1993

Pioneering conservationists who saved the white
rhino from extinction; wonderful men of the wild

It is an astonishing animal when you think about it. The white rhino. That magnificent beast like something out of *The Lost World* – not a thing we could begin to imagine were it not already here. And, of the southern variety, there were by some estimates twenty left. Just twenty, somehow eking out an existence in the remote "V" formed before the confluence of the White and Black Mfolozi rivers, the great hunting ground of one Shaka Zulu. That's how thin the thread was, the animals shot almost to extinction by poachers and big-game hunters.

This was the early 1900s, and on the entire African continent there were only 650 white rhino remaining, the others being (quite logically) the northern variety. Today there are close on 20,000 white rhino left in the wild, more than 90 percent in South Africa, all of them southern, and all of them roaming the Earth in their primal (if still somewhat tenuous) splendour because of the efforts of two men: Dr Ian Player and Magqubu Ntombela.*

Their story begins in 1952 when Player moved from Johannesburg to join the Natal Parks Board and met the man who would become his friend and mentor for life. Magqubu Ntombela was deeply connected to Africa, and filled with the traditional stories and lore of his particular place in it, specifically the area we now call the Hluhluwe-Mfolozi Park, the oldest protected park in the country.

At the time, the apartheid state was a mere four years old, and the esteemed South African government was far too busy setting out the legislative regime that would properly stuff up our country in the decades to come to worry about nature conservation. Rhinos, of which there were now several hundred in the area, were not particularly high on the agenda.

Wildlife conservation and the management of vast tracts of the South African wilderness was rather different back then to what it is now. Think of the bush today and the obvious name that pops up is the Kruger National Park, which was brought into existence in 1898 in its earliest form as a "*Goewernments Wildtuin*" by the then president of the Transvaal, Paul Kruger. To this day, it remains a fine national park, but if the picture you have in your head is that of a green Land Rover parked in a thicket

---

* By contrast, the northern white rhino has been eradicated from the wild, and as of early 2012 there were only seven individuals in existence. In 2009 four of them were moved from a zoo in the Czech Republic and placed in enclosures in an animal conservancy in Kenya in the hope that they will breed with each other and with southern white rhinos in the area. Meanwhile, the population of black rhinos fell dramatically in direct contrast to that of the white as uncontrolled poaching throughout Africa took its toll – from 65,000 in 1970 to about 3,400 in 1990. Black rhinos are more difficult to manage than whites and the rehabilitation of their numbers has been much slower as a result. Today there are fewer than 5,000 left.

of acacias next to a leopard, or a rimflow plunge-pool in front of a five-star chalet, then you're not thinking about Kruger proper, you're actually thinking about a private lodge in an adjacent reserve. The advent and rise in popularity of private game reserves since the 1970s has led to a massive influx of ecotourism money into the wildlife industry. It has become big business and as a result our animals are looked after far better than they used to be. In 1964 there were an estimated 575,000 head of game in South Africa; in 2007 there were 18.6 million. Today, a disease-free breeding buffalo can sell for up to R20 million. No-one could have contemplated such a ludicrous thought back in the first half of the 20th century when sheep and cows were the beasts of value – to the extent that game would be slaughtered en masse if they were believed to pose a health risk to farm animals. For this very reason more than 35,000 wild animals were killed in Zululand reserves in the two years from 1929 to 1931, which once again threatened the white rhinos, along with an increase in illegal poaching.

So it came to two people with a shared love for the veld, and the animals that roamed it, to see what they could do about the problem – this small problem, which no-one seemed particularly bothered about, of the potential extinction of the white rhinoceros.

The times being what they were, it would require Player's whiteness to get things done, but Ntombela's influence was central to success. Though illiterate and speaking no English, Magqubu Ntombela schooled Ian Player in Zulu culture, history and traditions, especially on the relationship between man and his environment. And Ntombela should have known – not only did he work in conservation from 1914 to 1993, he grew up in the hills of Zululand.

"The humility that comes from stumbling upon a pride of lions and the understanding of your place in the cosmos in the light of the countless galaxies illuminating the night sky are experiences that should be shared by every leader."

– Ian Player

> "You cannot lie there with an elephant or lion advancing on you, or a snake in your sleeping bag, without realising you are not omnipotent."
>
> – Ian Player

By the early 1960s, the two had initiated Operation Rhino, an anti-poaching campaign that saw them chasing down the hunters and setting up security networks to protect their animals. It was also a programme that would eventually see breeding colonies of white rhino sold to zoos, safari parks and game reserves far beyond the borders of Natal and South Africa. This was the vanguard of a new era in conservation, and they collaborated with the pioneering vet Toni Harthoorn to produce a wonder drug called M99, a synthesis of morphine that would render rhinos semi-incapacitated and easy to capture. They modified boma designs and worked to minimise animal stress during capture, when only years earlier dogs had been used to frighten game into snares and pits. It seems so sensible now, but this was revolutionary stuff back then; suddenly rhinos (and other animals) could be easily transported all around the globe.

In all, more than 3,500 white rhinos were moved to other areas, within their original range and all over the world and, as a result, the animal was eventually removed from the International Union for Conservation of Nature's Red List of threatened species. Player and Ntombela would ultimately succeed to the point that white rhinos have become a relatively common sight in some parks, and it is almost impossible to drive through the Hluhluwe-Mfolozi reserve without seeing them. It is sadly ironic that the success of Operation Rhino all those years ago is altogether evident in the scale of the slaughter that has taken place since wide-scale poaching returned in force in 2008; that South Africa can lose 450 rhinos in a year, as happened in 2011, and not actually be declining in overall numbers is testimony to their work.

Beyond their shared love of the wild, Player and Ntombela had something of a shared history too. Ntombela's father had fought with the *inGobamakhosi* – those Benders of the Kings – at Isandlwana on the same day that Player's grandfather, a Natal Hussar, was fighting at Inyezane.

In 1987 the two men, now both celebrated conservationists, took a pilgrimage to Brecon, Wales, headquarters of the Royal Welsh Regiment, the descendant of the 24th regiment of Foot that was slaughtered at Isandlwana. In a side chapel of the town's thousand-year-old cathedral hangs the queen's colour that had, in a simply gobsmacking story that requires a book in itself to be properly told, been extracted from the battlefield at Isandlwana at the cost of several lives. Kneeling down, Ntombela filled the cathedral with traditional Zulu poetry and prayer. It was, for all present, intensely moving.

Player and Ntombela went on from Operation Rhino to establish the Wilderness Leadership School, wherein a part of the Hluhluwe-Mfolozi Park was set aside for access only by foot. Player, in particular, was concerned that man had forgone life in his natural environment, the wild, and felt very strongly about encouraging city-dwellers to discover the power of the wilderness on the human soul. "You cannot stand or sleep in a wilderness area at night and not be humble," he explained.

Together with Ntombela, he took more than 3,000 people on walking trips into the wilderness areas of Hluhluwe-Mfolozi and Lake St Lucia game reserves. He was justifiably proud of their efforts and was always quick to credit his mentor's role in all they had achieved. "Through his patient instruction he introduced me to a new cosmology," Player wrote after Ntombela's death in 1993. "We worked together capturing

"To Magqubu, the hills and trees lived. The animals and birds were his brothers and sisters. His eyesight was phenomenal and his hearing so acute that he would wake from a deep sleep to the sound of a hyena or a leopard passing the camp. He had extra-sensory powers which enabled him to anticipate danger. He could not read or write, but he always smiled with teeth in perfect condition at the age of 93, and said, 'My lips are my pen, my ears my books'."

– Ian Player

rhino and on long patrols fighting poaching gangs... He always led with courage; following the rhino paths and stopping to explain the history of the landscape. For Magqubu the hills and trees lived."

But Player was not averse to criticising his friend's stubbornness: "Wherever he went he carried his little three-legged cooking pot that he had bought in 1925 for five shillings. To smart hotels or into the wilderness, the pot went with him. Once we were attacked by lions and he put his pot down as we were retreating. When he decided he was going back to fetch it we had a furious argument. I said his life was more valuable to me than the pot. He ignored me, braved a wounded lion and returned, smiling, with his pot."

What's also hilarious about this incident is the almost casual reference to being "attacked by lions". It was probably elephants the next day, perhaps buffalo the day after. It was a different and extraordinary time.

And it is an extraordinary legacy of conservation that both Ntombela and Player leave, a story that is not told often enough. The illiterate Ntombela, wise beyond teaching when it came to the wild, and Player who was a truly remarkable man – more remarkable and more likeable, we'd suggest, than his more famous brother Gary.

Not that Ian didn't do sport properly. On returning from active service in World War II where he fought in Italy as a teenager, he took up canoeing, and he eventually initiated, completed and won the inaugural Dusi Canoe Marathon, from Pietermaritzburg to Durban on the Msunduzi River. It was raced for the first time in 1951, and his victory came despite being bitten by a night adder during the event. He also won in 1953 and 1954. So stick that in your golf bag and smoke it.

Ian Player is old now, 85, but he is still a colossus of conservation, and very much involved with the current fight to save the rhino from the pathetic whims and affectations of Vietnamese party-goers and sad Chinese men whose penises don't work properly. And we take nothing from his great international standing when we say that he couldn't have done it without Magqubu Ntombela. Together, they have inspired future generations of new conservationists to ensure the rhino, and our wilderness, lives on.

Lucas Radebe

b. 12 April 1969

Football hero; captain of Bafana Bafana; African Cup of Nations winner; favourite son of Kaizer Chiefs and Leeds United; consummate sports ambassador; the type of guy missing from our current national soccer team

IT WOULD NOT BE OVERSTATING THINGS to observe that competitive sport, in general, holds a rather prominent position within the South African consciousness. In Kazakhstan, say, sport might take a back seat to yurt building, perhaps, or hot-plate dancing. In Armenia it's probably playing the duduk and herding goats. But in South Africa no Saturday afternoon is truly validated unless meat has been cooked over an open flame, ale has been consumed in the appropriate quantity, and one or more sporting codes have been viewed on a television screen, preferably a very large one. Whether it's the manifestation of a culture forged in endless warring or simply because we've got an outdoor climate and every kid likes to play with a ball in the garden, we love our sport. And, as a nation, we've become rather good at it.

On a global scale we punch miles above our weight, often despite great odds. We are one of only fourteen countries to have produced a Formula One Drivers' Champion. We're one of only four to have produced World Tour surf champions. We've won numerous tennis Grand Slams, both singles and doubles, and we regularly break athletics and swimming records. Our golfing history is almost unbelievable: we've won the fourth most majors of all countries, and we won two Masters and two Open Championships between 2008 and 2012 alone. Then there are the team sports. In rugby we're usually ranked in the top three, in cricket likewise, and in soccer… Damn. Soccer. Our one weakness. Our Achilles heel, if you will.

When it comes to soccer, South Africa is truly and monumentally crap. We say this with all the love and affection for Bafana Bafana that a home World Cup could ever engender – and that's *a lot*, as anyone who remembers Siphiwe Tshabalala's opening goal against Mexico in 2010 will recall. But a magic moment like that comes around once in a very blue moon for our boys these days. The rest of the time it's overpaid foreign coaches and overweight players and game after game of boring, gutless, losing soccer. Frequent have been the occasions in the last decade or so, as our international rankings have slipped towards the triple-figure mark, that our much-vexed supporters have thought that a gang of blind nuns in Batman outfits would stand a fighting a chance against our team. Or something similar.

Of course, it wasn't always so…

Once upon a time the name Bafana Bafana rolled with pride off the tongue. It was a team that inspired a nation. Indeed, it won the African Cup of Nations at its first attempt in 1996, a feat to rival the Springbok victory at the Rugby World Cup the year before. And it followed that up with very credible performances in further Afcon competitions and South Africa's first two Soccer World Cups. This was an era that included the likes of Doctor Khumalo, Neil Tovey, Mark "Feesh" Fish, Benni McCarthy, Mark Williams, Shoes Moshoeu – and, the greatest of them all, Lucas Valeriu Radebe.

Radebe's upbringing was, as is to be expected of a young black man coming of age in an apartheid-era township, humble and tough. The fourth of ten siblings living in a two-bedroomed house in Diepkloof, Soweto, he slept in the kitchen – so he was often up at 4am when the first kettle of the day was boiled. As a youngster he played soccer in the streets with a ball of rolled-up socks, and as a teen he ran with a vigilante group that "tried to do the right things but in the wrong way". Sometimes things turned ugly. It was the late 1980s and Soweto was in turmoil. Radebe's mother, who had "got us into soccer", recognised the dangers, as well as the talent of her son. He was sent to Zeerust in Bophuthatswana – following his eldest brother Abraham, also a talented footballer – to finish his schooling in a more settled environment. (He was playing goalie at this stage.) It was an inspired parenting decision, for he seldom looked back from that point on, and Radebe writes very fondly of his mother and father, Emily and Johannes. They certainly

"He had impressed the players, coaches and fans with his solid, no-nonsense style of play. He was quick, strong, he had vision, good anticipation and he was terrific both on the ground and in the air. He was, South African coaches all agreed, the country's most valuable player, the man they would want to anchor their side."
– Graeme Friedman, writing about Radebe's career in mid-1994 in Madiba's Boys

played their roles in shaping him into the fine representative he was to become for Kaizer Chiefs, Leeds United and South Africa. Perhaps that's what set him apart from so many other players out there.

Mostly, there are low expectations of international footballers. If a player doesn't do drugs, drive drunk or get caught with underage girls, he's generally considered a paragon of the finest behaviour. So it was never going to be that hard for Radebe to shine amidst the rabble, especially once he'd made the move to the English Premier League in 1996. But there are few sportsmen in the world, let alone soccer players, who have carried themselves as nobly as Radebe has throughout his playing career and beyond. He talks well, he dresses nicely, he conducts himself wonderfully in public. He is intelligent and thoughtful and speaks seven or eight languages (really). He gives both money and time to charity. He is a gentleman on and off a football field. In short, he is the perfect ambassador for the game and for South Africa, and it's no surprise that he is one of only nine active players to have been awarded the Fifa Fair Play Award.

Oh, and after all that, he wasn't half bad with a ball at his feet – or in the air. A solid, uncompromising centre back, Radebe was known as "The Chief" at Leeds because of his ties to Kaizer Chiefs and his commanding presence in defence. (Meanwhile, the rest of England knew him as Radibby.) He was so loved in his twelve seasons at Elland Road that the Kaiser Chiefs rock band named themselves in his previous team's honour (with a minor spelling evolution), and the club eventually called its mascot Lucas the Cop Kat. Of course he shone in national colours, too, and he was a natural choice to captain Bafana Bafana eventually, guiding the team to two World Cups, the second of which in 2002, saw us miss advancing to the second round on goal difference by a single, heart-breaking goal.

By the time Radebe retired in 2005, he had turned out seventy times for his country, more than 150 times for Chiefs and was a double centurion for Leeds.

And though the image of him is always one of sheer classy coolness, through it all there was often adversity. In 1991 he was shot through the back while driving to the shops, the bullet passing through his body without hitting any vital organs. A seemingly random incident, there was talk that it was retaliation for him signing for the "wrong club". Later, he struggled in the cold wet unfamiliarity of Leeds when he first arrived, and he almost quit after a year and a half – but he chose to stick it out, and less than a year later he was appointed captain. Then he went on to take his team to fourth and then third on the Premiership log in his first two seasons at the helm. Throughout his career, he suffered an endless array of near-career-ending injuries, but he showed tremendous courage – and earned huge respect from fans – when he repeatedly returned to action. His greatest setback, however, came with the death of his wife from cancer in 2008. As ever, he stood tall in tough times.

Earlier, we were harsh on the recent travails of Bafana Bafana. After all, soccer is easily the most popular sport in the world and we are but one team in a vast pool of competition. Even in the countries that aren't sporting mad, people love soccer. Hell, Armenia, for all our sniggering about the land of duduks and goat herders, actually has a reasonably successful team, and is currently ranked quite far above South Africa. (Kazakhstan, at least, is not.) But lo, there is hope for us, because as of July 2012 Lucas Radebe is back in the Bafana Bafana fold… Along with Doctor Khumalo and Fani Madida, Radebe has been brought in by new head coach Gordon Igesund as a key member of the technical team. Gone are the foreign coaches on their ludicrous salaries. (Igesund is on R400,000 a month; Joel Santana was on R1,400,000.) Now, finally, we have a man in charge with local knowledge and a particularly impressive CV, and three ex-South African stars to assist him in righting a ship that has, for too long, sailed in circles (when it hasn't been sinking). And one of those three is Lucas Radebe, The Chief. If he can't do it, then, well, at least the team will be classy for a while.

"This is my hero."
– Nelson Mandela, introducing Radebe to dignitaries in the UK.
Mandela referred to Radebe as Big Tree

Cyril Ramaphosa

b. 17 November 1952

Billionaire businessman; occasional politician; former General Secretary of the NUM and the ANC; peace negotiator; constitutional architect; BEE kingpin; possible saviour of the nation

WE'RE NOT GOING TO SPEND TOO LONG on Cyril Ramaphosa right now. He's here for one reason and one reason only: because he has "potential future South African president" written large on his forehead. Or, more accurately, because he has "potentially brilliant future South African president" embroidered on his business suit. This may be something of a reaching political prophesy, given the impossibility of trying to predict what will happen in South African politics tomorrow, let alone months or even years in the future – and, hey, if he does get into power he could turn into the next Mugabe for all we know – but we're rolling with it anyway because it just makes so much sense. Here's why.

First up, he has *genuine* struggle credentials. He was twice jailed as a student in the 1970s, spending a year and a half in prison, and he earned his reputation the following decade by building the National Union of Mineworkers (NUM) from nothing into the most formidable trade union in the country.

Fine, you might argue, but Joe Modise, Stella Sigcau, Jackie Selebi, Manto Tshabalala-Msimang, Ivy Matsepe-Casaburri, Bheki Cele, Gwede Mantashe and any number of corrupt, inept and/or useless senior government officials also had sterling struggle CVs. Not to mention Thabo Mbeki and Jacob Zuma, our wildly contrasting but equally ruinous presidents who have done their utmost to run South Africa a) as their personal fiefdoms and b) into the ground since the former came to power in 1999.

And yes, fair enough. All this really means is that Ramaphosa has the respect of the voting majority, which is non-negotiable for a genuine presidential candidate in South Africa.

What he also has, though, is brains, competence and integrity. No-one else mentioned above has all these qualities and several, including Zuma, have none. How smart is Ramaphosa? Smart enough to earn his own money without getting involved with the Schabir Shaiks of the world, that's for sure. Whatever your take on BEE may be, Ramaphosa has performed phenomenally as a businessman since stepping back from mainstream politics in 1997. He has stakes in MTN, SABMiller, Bidvest and Standard Bank, among others. The *Sunday Times* estimated his wealth at R2.22 billion in 2011, making him the 13th richest man in the country. And he's accumulated this fortune while maintaining an active, if quietly unassuming, political role within the ANC. More than this, though, when Cyril Ramaphosa speaks he doesn't sound like a pontificating old fart reciting ludicrously inappropriate Shakespearian quotes, or a giggling fool who doesn't understand the words coming out of his mouth. He is articulate and measured and his voice instils confidence in those listening.

As for competence and integrity, Ramaphosa was seen as a trusted negotiator; he and Roelf Meyer were the key players in the peace talks between the ANC and NP during the transition to democracy. In 1994 he assumed the critical role of chairperson of the Constitutional Assembly, which was tasked with creating a new South African constitution. The final product is still celebrated as a work of brilliance (when it's not under threat from the current government), having been signed into law by Nelson Mandela in 1996. Speaking of the big man, we need look no further than Mandela for further endorsement; Mandela supported Ramaphosa rather than Mbeki to succeed him as president of the ANC and thus South Africa in the early 1990s. For one, his stewardship of the NUM proved he was a great unifier, a trait that Mandela naturally valued. (Ramaphosa still considers the dissolution of tribalism on the mines "one of the great achievements of [the] union".) But Mbeki was

> "The man has X factor. He walks into a room, everyone stops and looks. It's really quite something."
>
> *— Stephen Grootes, 2012*

the superior political operator and beat him to the post, with the result that Ramaphosa retired honourably to a life in business. Not many modern contenders would do the same; see Zuma, Julius Malema and any number of African despots as evidence.

Ramaphosa has subsequently steered clear of the current rabble in charge whenever possible. Whether it's because he was too interested in raking in the cash or because he doesn't like the odour they emit is perhaps debatable, but he retains contact with the ANC and, as an added feather in his cap, he was chairman of the party's disciplinary appeals board that upheld Julius Malema's expulsion from the ANC in early 2012.

So that's all well and good, but Ramaphosa does have one small problem counting against him: he refuses to get back in the ring and compete for the top spot. "I have not engaged, nor sought to engage others on my behalf, in any campaign with respect to the presidency of the ANC, and have no interest in being a candidate," he said way back in July 2006 when there was already a strong movement to get him involved again. Whether it's a pride thing, or because he doesn't have Mbeki's stomach for political manoeuvring or Zuma's thick skin, or simply because he enjoys making money, is difficult to say. But, with Zuma having merrily steered the good ship South Africa further and further up shit creek during his time in charge, it's surely time Ramaphosa had a shot at real glory.

To be honest, we'll take Kgalema Motlanthe ahead of Zuma. Or even Tokyo Sexwale. Hell, we'll take the guy who sells boerie rolls at the rugby ahead of Zuma. But wouldn't President Cyril Ramaphosa make for exciting times? Ah, we can only dream.

Sixto Rodriguez

b. 10 July 1942

Folk-singer-cum-labourer; unwitting apartheid-busting superstar; resurrected mystery man of music; rare example of exceptional Saffer taste

HE'S A MEXICAN-AMERICAN, he first came to South Africa nearly three decades after producing his greatest work, and none of it was influenced by this country in any way. And yet if anyone deserves honorary South African citizenship it's Sixto Rodriguez. Sixto what-what?

If the name doesn't ring a bell, that's because in South Africa the man doesn't have a first name; he's just Rodriguez. And he's the Sugar Man. As in, the guy who needs to hurry because we're tired of these scenes.

If you're still confused, then clearly you never attended a party or social event with any vaguely liberal white people between the early 1970s and late 1990s. Certainly, there's no way you haven't heard a Rodriguez tune if you went to university during the Vorster or Botha eras and experimented with a bit of marijuana – otherwise known as sweet Mary Jane. And we're not even getting in to the silver magic ships, jumpers or coke here...

In short, Rodriguez was a word-of-mouth music phenomenon in South Africa for at least two decades, outselling Elvis, The Beatles and The Rolling Stones. His brilliant record *Cold Fact* somehow made it to our shores in the early '70s – no-one really knows how – and became, in time, one of the most beloved, and possibly most bootlegged, albums this country has ever known. He wrote folksy tunes about drugs, disillusionment, inner-city turmoil, the system and political apathy. He sang about crucifying your mind and he wondered how many times you'd had sex – and he seemed to speak directly to an entire generation of young white South Africans, both English and Afrikaans. During the oppressive apartheid years, his anti-establishment lyrics were exactly what they wanted to hear, and he directly influenced the Voëlvry Movement, which saw the likes of Johannes Kerkorrel, Koos Kombuis and Bernoldus Niemand upsetting the powers that be and creating "an unprecedented orgy of Afrikaner anarchy". On the border, troepies got high and listened to Rodriguez while they wondered what they were fighting for. At progressive universities students rallied to his music. The apartheid censors couldn't bear the licentious, drug-addled lyrics of this mixed-race American and official SABC copies of his records were scratched so that certain prohibited songs would not be played by mistake (or perhaps by a rebellious DJ). Even in the less political 1990s, the tremendous bands that would take the South African rock scene to new heights, such as the Springbok Nude Girls, Just Jinger and Sons of Trout, took inspiration from him.

Along with his second record – known here as *After The Fact* but originally titled *Coming From Reality* – Rodriguez has sold somewhere in the region of 500,000 albums in this country, an amazing figure given the small local market. The real kicker to this story, however, is that back home in America the singer was a complete failure; though *Cold Fact* was extremely well reviewed, both albums flopped and he was dropped from his record label in 1975. He had modest success in Australia, enough to warrant tours there in 1979 and 1981, but he was forced to return to a life of manual labour to pay the bills. Most incredibly, he had no inkling of his great success in South Africa until 1997, and it appears that the royalties he should have been earning over the years simply disappeared into the unscrupulous music-industry ether.

The failure of Rodriguez to make it big in America and worldwide is almost inexplicable. In the superb 2012 documentary *Searching For Sugar Man*, Swedish film-maker Malik Bendjelloul travels to the US to interview four of his early producers. To a man, they cannot explain it. These are proper music industry heavies, guys who have worked with the likes of Michael Jackson, Wu-Tang Clan, Bill Withers, Diana Ross

> "A man who lives his whole life in Detroit working as a construction worker, really hard manual labour, without knowing that at the very same time he's more famous than Elvis Presley in another part of the world. I thought it was the most beautiful story I've ever heard in my life."
>
> – *Malik Bendjelloul, director of Searching For Sugar Man*

and Jerry Lee Lewis, and yet they are all sincerely, a couple of them with a tear in the eye, at a loss to explain how such a talented songwriter never made it. He was an inner-city poet, a prophet, a wise man of music; a songwriter who should have been revered as a contemporary of Bob Dylan and Lou Reed – but he ended up making a living doing demolition work. They speculate that he was perhaps too shy for the stage because he sometimes played with his back to the audience. Elsewhere it is suggested that his record label, which later went under, let him down. Bendjelloul eventually tracks down the ageing Rodriguez and finds him living in a sad little house in snow-driven downtown Detroit, the same house that he's lived in for forty years.

At least he is alive, though. For many years his fans in South Africa thought Rodriguez had committed suicide, in some or other awesome fashion suitable to such a legend. "Thanks for your time and you can thank me for mine," he was said to have declared on stage, borrowing his own lyrics from *Forget It*, before blowing his brains out. Or setting himself on fire. Or, more prosaically, taking an overdose. He had become a cult-like figure and, in the absence of information in the censored apartheid state, it was simply assumed that the only way he wasn't as famous as Mick Jagger or Billy Joel was because he was dead.

Rodriguez was eventually resurrected by two South Africans, Craig Bartholomew and Stephen Segerman, who spent years trying to track down the musical genius the world had forgotten using clues in his lyrics, among other things. In the end, the internet found him: in 1997 one of his daughters responded to a website that Segerman had created called The Great Rodriguez Hunt, and suddenly years of rumour and speculation could be packed away and the real man revealed. Well, kind of. Because it turns out that even in person, when being interviewed face to face, Sixto Rodriguez is almost impossible to decode. Here he is describing where his optimism comes from in 2008: "Well, geez – you know what I mean. I hide my despondency well, like everybody else. I mean, look at Exxon-Mobil – they made so many billions. It's really rich against the poor – that's really true. And what keeps us separated is the military between us. The cops and the military. It's a tripod society. They talk about it in Greek times – Plato and Aristotle. The same kind of model there. In America, the multinationals got their cheap labour, and now they're hiking the prices. It's as clear as that. And the Iraq war – Cheney's people – it's so blatant, and there it is!"

There it is, indeed...

Turns out Rodriguez had earned himself a Philosophy degree in the early 1980s and run for mayor of Detroit a couple of times and even for senator – but, as with the music, his own people never really took him seriously. On one of the ballots they even spelt his name wrong. Given the narcotic preoccupations of some of his music, one suspects that perhaps he spelt his name wrong himself once or twice.

Amazingly, Rodriguez seems to feel no bitterness at the path his life has taken and doesn't even harbour resentment for the unidentified and seemingly un-prosecuted individuals who failed to pass on his (substantial) royalties from South Africa. Because of them, the following headline would later become a reality: "Sixto Rodriguez becomes

"We set up a tour of South Africa and I expected to see a bunch of disgruntled older people in the audience. But there were all these young faces, youngbloods. When I came out in Cape Town they all rushed the stage... I didn't believe it. I still don't. South Africa made me feel like more than a prince."

– Sixto Rodriguez

superstar, doesn't know for 30 years". But in 1998 he was brought out to South Africa for a long-overdue tour and played six sold-out concerts in Cape Town, Johannesburg and Durban. It was an almost inconceivable event and there were many who believed the whole thing to be a con of sorts. But it was real, and in a poignant, emotional entry to his first gig, he piped up, "Thanks for keeping me alive," to thousands of cheering Capetonians at the Bellville Velodrome. Then he sang *I Wonder* and they cheered even louder.

Rodriguez would return for four more tours in the following years, and even ended up with a South African grandchild for his efforts. Back home in Detroit his blue-collar friends couldn't believe the stories of him playing to tens of thousands of South Africans, but finally he started gaining a measure of the recognition he deserved, and the record companies got back on board. *Cold Fact* was rereleased internationally in 2008 and was once again well reviewed. *The Guardian* called it "a darkly funky Dylanesque gem"; the *Sydney Morning Herald* praised his "Dylanesque singing style and simple, sunny melodies". He started touring in the US. Now, with *Searching For Sugar Man* having won a number of awards at the Cannes Film Festival, Rodriguez's fame continues to grow. The North American tours are bigger and more numerous; his music is available on iTunes; he has played for David Letterman in front of an audience of millions.

Today Rodriguez is 70. He has weather-beaten skin and the veiny, muscular forearms that come from a life spent roofing and knocking through walls and hauling refrigerators down stairs single-handed. Even though he apparently gives the half-decent money he is now making to friends and family, he has at last found his rightful place as a recognised and celebrated musician. And it's all because of us. In what is perhaps the only ever example of white suburban South Africa revealing better taste than the entire rest of the world – barring some Australians, of course – we spotted the genius of Sixto Rodriguez and never let it go. Bob Dyl-whatever. We'll take Rodriguez any day.

Thanks for your time, man.

Ampie Roux

18 October 1914 – 22 April 1985

Apartheid-era nuclear physicist and rocket scientist; father of the South African atom bomb

BY SHEER VIRTUE OF HIS OCCUPATION Johannes Andries "Ampie" Roux was a brilliant man. Which is to say, he was a nuclear physicist. The only job that tops nuclear physics on the traditional intellectual-genius list is probably rocket science – but, to cover his bases, Roux dabbled with that too. So it's official: he was brilliant. But his position here is not (merely) for his intimate understanding of nuclear fission and rocket telemetry; it's because he was the most senior player in the development of South African nuclear technology and, as a result, became the father of our very own nuclear bomb. And though the possible ramifications of apartheid South Africa's clandestine development of nuclear weapons are just a little bit frightening to contemplate (translated: bloody frightening to contemplate), the feat itself was undeniably impressive. In fact, it's probably safe to say that Ampie Roux's secret project is quite possibly the pinnacle of the *boer-maak-'n-plan* ingenuity.

Many South Africans will be aware that the apartheid government possessed several atom bombs before abandoning its nuclear weapons programme in the early 1990s and dismantling them. They may even know that, in so doing, South Africa became the first and to date only country to willingly give up its nuclear stockpile. But further details of this remarkable achievement have been understandably overshadowed by other events of the time: the release of Nelson Mandela, the unbanning of the ANC, the transition to democracy and such and such.

Here are the basics, then.

In the 1950s and '60s, South Africa collaborated on nuclear research with a number of countries, most notably the United States. From the start, Ampie Roux, the brilliant and highly motivated member of the Council for Scientific and Industrial Research and The Atomic Energy Board, was the man in charge of South Africa's nuclear development plan. The US was rather partial to the apartheid government's vast uranium reserves, and in return for a steady supply it was happy to take in and train South African scientists and, in 1965, supply a complete nuclear reactor for research purposes. The reactor was dubbed Safari-1 and was situated at Pelindaba outside Pretoria. South Africa's first indigenously designed reactor, Safari-2, went online in 1967, and things were humming along just fine; everything was above board and the research had legitimate non-explosive applications.

So far so peaceful. But it's hard to believe there wasn't some kind of intent, some element of savvy Afrikaner forward-planning, right from the start. After all, Roux went on the record as early as 1960 to say that South Africa was "capable of producing a nuclear weapon if it was prepared to isolate the best brains in the country, and give them all the funds they needed".

By the early 1970s, this was indeed the case. Apartheid South Africa, sinking ever further into pariahdom, had been dropped by its primary arms suppliers, the US and UK, and its paranoid leaders were observing with alarm the flourishing influence of Soviet and Chinese communism through central and southern Africa. When the Portuguese decided enough was enough and fled Africa, it was panic stations: the *rooi gevaar* was approaching and something had to be done. In 1974 BJ Vorster, prime minister at the time, authorised the development of nuclear explosive capability and the construction of an underground testing site; then, three years later, he made the formal decision to acquire the nuclear deterrent.

And so, from the late 1970s and into the 1980s, South Africa produced definitely six, and possibly seven, working atom bombs. They were similar to "Little Boy", the American bomb dropped on Hiroshima in 1945, with a fairly rudimentary gun-type system that fired a projectile of uranium-235 into a larger target of uranium-235, and a comparable explosive power in the 10-18 kiloton range.* At a length of 1.8 metres and diameter of 65 centimetres, the bombs weighed in at about one ton each, with later models designed to be delivered by specially adapted Buccaneer strike aircraft.

Depending on when exactly Israel first acquired its bomb, South Africa was in all likelihood the eighth country in the world to possess nuclear weapons, following in the footsteps of the US, the USSR, the UK, France, China, Israel (probably) and India. Later, Pakistan and North Korea joined the club.

Simply comparing the economic capacity of these countries – North Korea, a very special case, notwithstanding – lends some understanding to the weight of the achievement. But even more revealing, perhaps, is the list of countries that have actively sought, or are seeking, nuclear weapons: Sweden, Switzerland, Brazil, Saudi Arabia, Taiwan, Egypt, Iran, Iraq and probably another twenty more. With a small band of scientists working on the project – estimated at under 1,000, with no more than 300 working on it at any one time, and possibly only six senior scientists under Roux – South Africa managed to outdo them all. To put those numbers in context, Saddam Hussein had around 20,000 people working (ultimately in vain) on the Iraqi bomb before the 1991 Gulf War, and the Manhattan Project, which produced the US's (and world's) first working bombs in the 1940s, employed upwards of 130,000 people, including some of the greatest scientific minds of the time.

Of course, the Manhattan Project was an urgent wartime research and development programme, one of the biggest and costliest scientific projects in history, with an end price tag of more than $25 billion in today's money. Our bomb was, in comparison, a backyard DIY number.

The budget was laughably small: in 1994 David Albright, then president of the Institute for Science and International Security, claimed

---

* In the case of Hiroshima, the explosion was equivalent to 15 or 16 kilotons of TNT and produced a circle of "severe destruction" with a diameter of more than three kilometres. Various death tolls range from 90,000 to 140,000.

> "The scientific zeal and drive of the AEC's Ampie Roux and Wally Grant to demonstrate South Africa could make a nuclear device established the technical foundation for the program. Yet their work was not done in isolation from the political leadership, the support of the military on military-to-military cooperation matters, and the technocrats for actual weapons production."
>
> *– A 1997 US Air Force Institute for National Security Studies paper*

the annual budget was R20-R25 million by the programme's end, up from R10 million a year in the early 1980s. The South Africans saved untold time and money simply by gathering critical information from public libraries and research centres around the world, including valuable declassified information from the Manhattan Project. And not only was the team small, but the personnel were limited for security reasons: only South Africans were chosen and candidates were excluded if they had dual citizenship. Roux himself was descended from Huguenots who arrived in South Africa in the 1680s and eventually settled in the Orange Free State.

Even the premises were something of a joke. Whereas the Americans developed their first bombs on twenty or so vast sites spread across the US and Canada, the South African team initially had to work out of a poky building on the premises of a military facility that manufactured propellants and explosives. Eventually, a secret complex of nondescript buildings was constructed at Pelindaba, well away from the main (and officially recognised) facility – but even then South African scientists were frequently compelled to use "creative" methods to solve otherwise insurmountable problems. For example, simple two-axis machine tools were adapted for the creation of complex three-dimensional shapes for the bombs.

The most prohibitive problem of all, and often the sticking point in a country's quest for nuclear weapons, was the difficulty of obtaining a sufficient quantity of highly enriched uranium. Roux and his similarly brilliant collaborator, Dr Wally Grant, played particularly crucial roles here, and they were jointly awarded the Hendrik Verwoerd Prize – rather more highly valued then than it is now – for their efforts in developing a new uranium-enrichment process. Nevertheless, it reportedly took eight years to make the first complete device as a result.

And if that were the complete story, it would be pretty damn impressive. But it's not – because somewhere along the line the Israelis got involved in the whole process.

Rewind to 1974 again, to a top-secret meeting in Geneva between Vorster, then Defence Minister PW Botha and Israel's head of state, Shimon Peres, and thus was born the Israel-South Africa Agreement (ISSA), a mutual defence pact between the two countries. A shady and deniable event if ever there was one, little is known of exactly what went on, but it seems that this was around the moment that South Africa took a fancy to the idea of developing nuclear-tipped intercontinental ballistic missiles (ICBMs)… If that sounds a) somewhat implausible and b) incredibly scary, well, then you'd be right on the latter count only. Because with the Israeli's on board, adding their Jericho missile technology to the mix, this is where it starts getting a bit unreal.

The original strategy behind South Africa's nuclear deterrent was political and quite clearly thought out: the very revelation of its existence – covertly at first, then publicly if necessary – would surely be enough to involve the Americans and the Western world if the commies started knocking down the door, went the thinking. The bombs that Roux and his team eventually produced were hardly the most practical in terms of delivery and there was the very real possibility of a nuclear-armed Buccaneer being shot down if it came up against, say, the superior Soviet-armed Angolan air force. So the political-statement approach made sense.

But if Vorster, and later Botha, could get his hands on an ICBM or two, the chance of interception would become almost minimal. And, with the range they offered, it would be possible to target major African cities, such as Luanda, Lusaka and Dar es Salaam, as well as – and this really was the plan apparently – ultimately Moscow. Bearing in mind that the USSR possessed around 45,000 warheads in the mid-1980s, one wonders if the apartheid overlords rubbed their hands in glee at the idea of bombing the Russians and thought, what a genius plan!

As it turns out, the ISSA pact was rather productive. In September 1979 an American Vela satellite detected a distinctive "double flash" of light in the southern Atlantic near the Prince Edward islands, South African territory. Though it remains a controversial incident, it is widely believed to have been a small nuclear explosion, in the 2-3 kiloton range, most likely a test of an Israeli-South African device, but possibly independently undertaken by either side. More than that, though, there was clear progress in the development of South African rockets, with three test launches from the Overberg Test Range near Arniston during 1989 and 1990, including two two-stage vehicles. Given another few years, or perhaps a more generous budget, it is genuinely possible that Ampie Roux and his merry band of rocket scientists, with a little help from their Israeli friends, could have had us aiming missiles at the Soviets. Yes, this is *Dr Strangelove* territory, and if you think too hard about it you may blow a brain gasket.

Happily, apartheid (and Soviet communism) fizzled out in the end, and with it our nutty plans for mutual annihilation. FW de Klerk took over from PW Botha in 1989 and quickly prioritised decommissioning our existing nuclear armoury and abandoning all further research. "A nuclear deterrent had become not only superfluous," he noted in 1993, once the South African nuclear programme had become public knowledge, "but in fact an obstacle to the development of South Africa's international relations."

We can only be grateful that the deranged apartheid regime never took it upon itself to drop the bomb, and the dismantling of the tremendous destructive power of our atomic arsenal in 1990 and 1991 in fact nicely parallels the dismantling of the destructive regime itself. But that's not to say we can't allow Ampie Roux and his select band of inventive and ingenious scientists acknowledgment – their moral convictions, whatever they were, notwithstanding – for an incredible, if potentially world-ending, achievement.

How lovely that it all worked out in the end.

Ryan Sandes

b. 10 March 1982

World-leading ultra-distance trail runner; first person to win all four 4 Desert Marathons; South Africa's top sportsman in terms of world ability

RYAN SANDES IS SOMETHING OF A SPORTING MIRACLE. In 2006, at the age of 24, he decided to run a marathon for the first time. In fact, he decided to run a half marathon because his mates were all doing it and it was going to be a fun weekend – but he couldn't get an entry. So he had to opt for the full race and he ended up running it in just under three-and-a-half hours.

It's difficult to quantify just how impressive a feat this was. For the uninitiated, a marathon is 42.2 kilometres long – about the distance from Sandton to Pretoria – and getting through one is, understandably, a helluva thing. Most social runners do very well to finish in under four hours. Five hours is respectable. But this was Sandes's *first* ever marathon and he'd trained for just six weeks; his longest practice runs, a couple of them, were not more than twenty kilometres. This was not an everyday achievement.

Then again, he finished nearly an hour behind the winner and he only just made it into the top 15 percent of the field. Had you met him on the day – having a few beers with mates at Crab's Creek, perhaps – it wouldn't have been unreasonable to write off his achievement as a guy with some decent base fitness having a blinder of a day. Well done, Ryan. Moving on.

But running the Knysna Marathon at a frighteningly quick pace for a first-timer isn't actually what makes Ryan Sandes a sporting miracle; it's what that race led to that does.

Up to that point, Sandes "was never into running". He played decent-level rugby and waterpolo at school, and he was a beach bum, like any good Hout Bay kid. Surfing was his thing. But he kind of liked his first marathon so he figured he'd try a bit of trail running around Cape Town. And he kind of liked that too, so after a while he figured he'd set himself a proper challenge. He had "always been competitive" and was young and fit – why not try something totally off the wall while he still could? Something like the Gobi March, a 250-kilometre week-long race through the unforgiving deserts of China…

The Gobi March, originally run in 2003, was the first race of what was to become the RacingThePlanet 4 Deserts endurance footrace series. Later, the Atacama Crossing in Chile, the Sahara Race in Egypt and The Last Desert in Antarctica were added to the list, and these quickly came to be seen as the Dakar Rallies of ultra-distance running. Long, hard and attracting some of the toughest, most grizzled athletes from around the world, they are generally run in six stages; the first four are around 40 kilometres each, the fifth a beastly 80 kilometres, and the last a 10-kilometre victory leg to prove you're still alive. Competitors carry their food and sleeping equipment, and are provided with water along the route and a campsite at night.

Sandes fronted up his R30,000 entry fee for the 2008 edition of the Gobi and knuckled down to some serious training. Given the cost, he wanted to give it a proper bash. His aim: to get a top 20 finish, hopefully a top 10. Then he could tick that box and get back to his happy life in Hout Bay as a freshly qualified quantity surveyor.

"And then," as he explains it, "on that first day, when I came into that last checkpoint, I was in second position and I thought, stuff it, let me go balls to the wall and try and get one win – and who cares if I come last in all the other stages, at least I've won one stage."

Four years later the modesty of his early ambitions appears quite

"I don't like to do things in moderation."

– *Ryan Sandes*

staggering. Of course he won that first stage – and the second. Then, on the third day, one of the world's better-known ultra-distance runners realised he would have to turn it up against this new kid from South Africa, and made a storming move to the front to muscle his way back into contention. Sandes sat on his tail and was told in no uncertain terms to bugger off and run his own race. So he "stuck by for another five minutes and decided 'stuff you' and took off". In winning that particular stage, he realised he could genuinely compete at this level, and he cleaned up the remaining three stages, and the race, after that. The ultra-running world was stunned.

The elation of his victory was understandably immense, and the comedown from the high – "this empty feeling inside you" – equally so. In his week of loping across the unforgiving deserts of the ancient Silk Road, Sandes had found his calling, and realised he couldn't stop there. Turns out marathons weren't actually his thing: ultra-distance trail running was.

His achievements since then are unprecedented. He entered the Sahara later in 2008 and, once again, won every stage. The guy who came second overall finished three hours behind him. In 2010 he won both Atacama and The Last Desert, becoming the first man to complete a 4 Deserts event in less than 24 hours and the first man to win all four.

In between, he found time to complete the Jungle Marathon, a 200-kilometre bash through the Brazilian Amazon in plus 30°C temperatures and close to 100 percent humidity, which included frequent encounters with deadly snakes and other wild animals. On arrival competitors completed a jungle survival course and took training runs with armed guards. "I was more relieved to get out of there alive than anything else," says Sandes. Naturally he won the thing in record time. (A relief, because he never has to return.)

Creepy-crawlies and extreme conditions are just a couple of the challenges of ultra trail running. Not getting lost is another, especially when you're invariably in the lead, and managing water, food and equipment supplies is also crucial. Sandes generally runs self-supported races with an 8-to-10-kilogram backpack – which usually means a week without a toothbrush and mattress, among other luxuries. Injuries are another prime concern; mountain single track and stony desert trails are far less predictable than tarmac, and Sandes spends virtually all his gym time building his core and thus his sense of balance. Even so, sprained ankles nearly cost him dearly in both the Jungle Marathon and RacingThePlanet Nepal in 2011.

Then there's the cost. Simply affording to compete full time is a problem. Sandes gave up the quantity surveying in early 2009 to pursue trail running professionally, and he spends long hours keeping his sponsors happy. Though the popularity of his sport is growing rapidly – following in the tracks of road cycling and mountain biking – competitive events aren't overflowing with money. The most Sandes has taken home for winning a race is R8,000 – for a local event, the 2011 Otter Trail Run on the Wild Coast – and often, as with the 4 Deserts, there is no prize money at all.

> "I don't know how someone hasn't died in the Jungle Marathon yet, because if you get bitten by a bushmaster snake you've got two hours to live, and it takes about 24 hours to get you to the nearest hospital – so if you do the maths…"
>
> – Ryan Sandes

The greatest challenge, though, is a mental one: simply coping with the hours and hours of pounding the trails with no-one to keep you entertained but you. And this, more than genetic running ability, is what sets the truly great ultra runners apart. Of course, Sandes is a brilliant natural runner; his odd "duck-like" running style is superbly efficient and allows him to cover vast distances while expending minimal energy. But running ability alone won't get you through 100 hours of training every month, or 250 kilometres in a week or 100 miles in one go.

As Tim Noakes, South Africa's premier sports scientist, explains it, "Ryan's success is not because he is an exceptionally gifted athlete

> "There is definitely that addiction to testing your boundaries and seeing how much you can take. That's when I think you're alive, when you're in that moment. You crave that."
>
> – *Ryan Sandes*

competing against other athletes who are not his physical equal. I suspect that there are many against whom he runs who are his biological equal. But none can match the power of his mind. That is his great strength and secret. He does not set mental limits for himself the way the rest of us do."

If you ask Sandes he'll tell you that he thinks about all sorts of things while out on the trail, especially when training – from "relationships to sports to finances". Just like your average jogger, then. But then he mentions that in slower runs "I kind of start to daydream" and suddenly an hour or two might slip by. Noakes believes that Sandes has the rare ability, observed in a handful of great endurance athletes, "to enter a trance-like state when he runs, and in that state he is able to do what no-one else can".

But Noakes acknowledges that sports scientists are a long way from gaining a full understanding of the success of extreme-endurance athletes, and Sandes is quick to note that his mind-set varies, depending on trail conditions, running speed and, of course, whether or not he's actually competing – in which case he can't doze off because he needs to be mindful of the race situation and keep tabs on his nutrition and hydration (and avoid snakes and animals and getting lost…).

Whatever it is that keeps Sandes plonking one foot in front of the other, it seems that a general focused motivation underscores his entire running attitude. He loves what he does but his goals have to constantly change to keep it that way. Individual events take months of preparation, and once a race has been run well he's generally not interested in doing it again; there are too many others out there and not enough time. For this reason, he has in the last few years swapped self-supported multi-stage races for single-stage ultras of up to 160 kilometres. It was not a straightforward switch, by any means, but his victory at the legendary Leadville 100-miler in Colorado in 2011 proved he could do it. And if he does fail, as when he "blew up" at The North Face 100 in Australia in 2011 and finished in a lowly 3rd, then he grits his teeth and does it again. He returned to the Blue Mountains outside Sydney in 2012 and won the 100-kilometre race in 9h22, running at a pace of 5.37 minutes per kilometre. That's basically two-and-a-half off-road marathons at sub four-hour pace…

As of late 2012 Ryan Sandes had competed in fourteen major international races, winning nine of them and breaking records in three. His worst finish was fourth. In South Africa, he dominates everything he enters, including shorter runs. To put it in perspective, Noakes is happy to compare his athletic feats with those of sprint legend Usain Bolt and 800 metre world-record holder David Rudisha: "In terms of how much better he is than the rest of the world, he is the equal of David and Usain. Their success, however, is built on a superior biology than any other runners in their events."

Sandes modestly refuses to claim the title of world's greatest ultra trail runner, and mentions the Spaniard Kilian Jornet as someone he admires for his ability to win both shorter and longer races at international level. But we don't need to be bashful on his behalf. The truth of it is that Sandes was so dominant in one aspect of his sport – multi-stage ultra marathons – that he won every important race there was to win, and then moved on to single-stage 100-milers simply because it offered a new challenge. Whatever he competes in, if he keeps wearing out running shoes at the same rate – at least one pair a month – this is a guy who will rewrite ultra history.

"I cannot think of another South African athlete who is so dominant in their sports on a global scale as is Ryan. Of course he is competing in an exotic sport in which there are not millions of competitors. Yet against the very best in the world, he is apparently in a class of his own."

– Tim Noakes

Jody Scheckter

b. 29 January 1950

Madman; Menace; South African Wild Man; Formula One Champion; businessman; farmer

PEOPLE SOMETIMES FORGET JUST HOW DANGEROUS Formula One used to be, but even the most cursory Googling of the ways in which the likes of Tom Pryce, Gilles Villeneuve, Roland Ratzenberger and Ayrton Senna lost their lives makes it pretty clear: until the sport was made safer in the wake of Senna's death at San Marino in 1994, it was incredibly dangerous. That didn't stop one young man with the hottest of heads and the vilest of tempers from departing his home town, East London, like some kind of whirling dervish and making a tremendous impact on motor racing – before going into, of all things, organic faming.

Jody Scheckter's racing career started in South Africa, where he raced motorbikes and saloon cars and, aged 20, won the local Formula Ford championship. With it came a ticket to the UK, where he set out to make a name for himself as a driver for the ages. And make a name he would.

Aggressive and pugnacious, short-tempered and covered with a mop of curly hair, Scheckter crashed and dashed his way through Formula Ford and Formula 3000 (then known as F2), impressing beyond measure with his car control, but making many wonder whether he'd ever live long enough to take his talent to the highest level. He did. After just eighteen months in Britain, Scheckter's unadulterated driving skill tempted McLaren to give him a spot on the team.

In his first Grand Prix in France 1973, Scheckter was quick enough to mix it with the frontrunners at the start, but he wasn't restrained enough to avoid a huge accident with world champion Emerson Fittipaldi. The great Fittipaldi was so angry that he delivered the harshest possible verdict to a novice driver: "This madman is a menace to himself and everybody else, and does not belong in Formula One."

But Scheckter was in fact just getting going. At the very next race, at Silverstone, he almost ended his career – not through injury, but because he caused such a monumental pile-up on the very first lap that the Grand Prix Drivers' Association demanded he be banned for life. Losing control of his McLaren at 150mph, he slammed into a wall and ended up sitting in the middle of the racing line as trailing cars smashed into him one by one – "a multiple shunt" as commentator Raymond Baxter described it with some understatement. It was a scene in which Scheckter stepped unharmed from his ruined car with utter bedlam taking place all around – cars cartwheeling through the air in all directions, smoke and fire everywhere and debris scattering the track like hundreds-and-thousands. Half the field was taken out in the accident and it was a miracle no-one was killed. It did, however, take an hour to clear the track before the race restart, and it ended the career of the Italian driver Andrea de Adamich who broke his ankle, amazingly the only serious injury of the day.*

Somehow McLaren managed to arrange a stay of execution for Scheckter by promising to rest their young hot-head. His return to the track in Canada wasn't exactly filled with glory though: he crashed into the Tyrrell of François Cevert. But this wasn't enough to stop him being offered the seat of the other Tyrrell driver, the ex-champion Jackie Stewart, who would retire at the end of the season. Stewart had been impressed with the increased pace of his teammate Cevert, and was happy to leave the sport, the idea being that Cevert would assume the position of team leader, with Scheckter his understudy. Tragically, this was not to be.

The following Grand Prix and final race of the season was at Watkins Glen in New York, where Cevert was involved in a truly horrific accident in qualifying that, to quote Stewart, left him "clearly dead". After losing control in an S-bend and hitting the barrier at high speed, the young

---

* There is wonderful footage of the crash on YouTube; it's worth watching if only to compare the health-and-safety regulations of the time with modern racing.

Frenchman was severed in two across his midriff. Scheckter, who had been driving behind him, was one of the first drivers on the scene and what he saw seemed to sober up his driving style for good. "From then on," he said, "all I was trying to do in Formula One was save my life."

Scheckter flourished at Tyrrell and used his good relationship with the team boss, Ken Tyrrell, to fix his technical errors, to master his emotions and to drive with the Championship in mind. In 1974 he won his first Grand Prix and came third overall, something he repeated two years later at the wheel of the extraordinary six-wheeled Tyrrell P34. (The iconic car had four dinky wheels at the front and two massive takkies on the back.) In between, he became the only South African to win the South African Grand Prix at Kyalami.

After a stint with the Wolf team that saw him as Championship runner-up in 1977, Scheckter was lured to Ferrari. By now a wiser driver, he was fixated on the top prize and was careful to never let slip a good position. In 1979 he made it all count, and our boy from Slummies went on to win the Championship, chased all the way by his teammate Gilles Villeneuve (who would die in a spectacular crash three years later). It was the last time a Ferrari would take the season-end top spot until some German guy called Schumacher claimed it for the Tifosi 21 years later.

Scheckter quit motor racing at the end of the 1980 season, by which time the driver once considered the "South African Wild Man" was hugely respected as fast and intelligent behind the wheel. Jeremy

"I was 13, and it was the first ever motor race I had been to. I remember being bored out of my mind listening to people talking about tyre pressures and oil changes, and I was only there for one reason – to see a crash. Jody caused the mother of all crashes, and I liked him for that. I started following his career through his time with Tyrrell, Wolf and then Ferrari. I was so thrilled with his win I vowed I would call my son Jody."

– Jeremy Clarkson, speaking in 2011

Clarkson has spoken of how much he loved to watch him race, and how, despite all the trouble it caused, his huge accident in 1973 inspired him.

And it would have been so easy for that to be that – you know, for Scheckter to shuffle off into a comfortable life of media and commentary, as with so many professional sportsmen. Or simply to retire, seeing as he'd made good money already.

But no, Scheckter – who "unlike anyone else in F1 [is] not completely thick", according to Clarkson – was rather more ambitious than that and decided that it was far more important to be *really* rich. So, after moving to Atlanta in the US, he went on to establish a company called Firearms Training Systems Inc, which used new computer technology to create weapons-training simulators for military and state agencies. He ran the company as he drove, "flat out", and he ended up making a packet.

In 1996 he sold up and moved back to England, where he completely reinvented himself once more – as a farmer. In a move no-one could have predicted in his driving wild days, Jody Scheckter has now become one of the UK's most successful and admired personalities in organic farming, and he has been at the forefront of the organic revolution.

Of course, there have been no half measures at Laverstoke Park Farm, a hundred kilometres west of London. Scheckter's mission is to "produce the best-tasting, healthiest food without compromise" and his operation is, not to put too fine a point on it, extraordinary. One estimate suggests he has sunk £30-40 million of his own into the venture, an amount that is reflected in a wonderful array of purchases. "The list of outgoings reads as follows," wrote *The Independent* in 2006. "Complete restoration of one grand 17th-century mansion; construction of one new farm shop, one dairy-processing unit, one abattoir and one compost-production unit; rearing of 27 pure native Aberdeen Angus cattle, 65 Jersey cows, 135 pure Herefords, 350 water buffalo, 750 'other breed' bovines, 2,000 sheep, assorted wild boar and rare-breed pigs; general upkeep of 2,500 acres and wages for 35 staff." And he doesn't just produce cuts of meat – there's wine from his vineyard, real ale and lagers, biltong (of course), buffalo dairy products including milk and mozzarella cheese, ice creams, pies, bacon, sausages and burgers. Oh, and he's planted 130,000 trees,

> "He is a fighter who does not burn himself up by coming on too strongly at the beginning, but measures himself fully and evenly throughout a race."
>
> – *Enzo Ferrari*

thirteen kilometres of hedgerow and what he calls a "mixed salad" of 31 different types of grasses for his herds to feed on.

Not that he'll be running into any financial difficulties soon; the *Sunday Times* Rich List reckons Farmer Scheckter still has £60 million in reserve. More to the point, though, the farm, after fifteen years of pedal-to-the-metal hard work, finally started turning a profit recently. Scheckter now supplies meat to no less than Heston Blumenthal, Raymond Blanc and Abel & Cole, among others. He even has a butcher's shop in Twickenham. It may be an odd business – his chickens are around four times more expensive than the battery-reared type – but it is, finally, a business that works.

Jody Scheckter, now in his sixties, has come a long way from his apprenticeship at his father's Renault dealership in East London. His incredible feats have perhaps gone, if not unsung, then more quietly sung in South Africa than they might have been, probably because Formula One didn't have the enormous television audience in the 1970s that it has today. In fact, most of his races weren't even screened in South Africa, with that wondrous modern invention only reaching our shores in 1976. But no-one just happens to win a Formula One race, let alone a World Drivers' Championship. His 1979 triumph was a magnificent crowning achievement to a wonderful and entertaining racing career in an era replete with danger, mayhem and the constant threat of a dramatic death. And that was before he even got into business.

Jody Scheckter, Formula One champ, the man who drove like a thing possessed, the man who survived an age of peril, the man who revolutionised firearm training, the man who revolutionised organic farming... we salute you.

Caster Semenya

b. 7 January 1991

800m runner; island of rare dignity amid corruption, racism and political opportunism

IN 2009 A YOUNG SOUTH AFRICAN GIRL called Caster Semenya won the 800 metres at the World Championships in Athletics in Berlin. This was, of course, fantastic news – and now, years after the fact, we know that it was a brilliant achievement and she had every right to be there. Our

Caster's still a world champ, let us not forget, one of only two South Africans to ever win individual World Championship track golds.*

Then again, she shouldn't really have run at Berlin. Athletics South Africa (ASA), headed by the repellant and deceitful Leonard Chuene, had known long before the race that there was a problem. In the previous year or so, Semenya's times had improved by 25 seconds over 1,500 metres and eight seconds over 800 metres, stunning results that had raised eyebrows in the athletics world – to the point that the International Association of Athletics Federations (IAAF) had requested ASA to administer gender tests on her to judge if she was competing fairly.

Chuene understood what was in store for Semenya, but he also understood that her race times put her in a good position to bring back gold from Berlin – and what a bonus that would be! So he sent his athlete to Pretoria for gender testing, ensuring in the process that she thought it was a fairly routine drugs test – except that, being a gender test, it involved procedures that aren't necessary in the administration of a drugs test. For Semenya the insult on her integrity, both bodily and personal, had begun.

When the results came back, ASA team doctor Harold Adams requested that Semenya be quietly withdrawn from the World Championships. Hers was quite clearly an exceptional case, and it would be some time before her situation could be resolved to the international athletic community's satisfaction. In other words, the good doctor was recommending discretion and the protection of Semenya's rights to personal privacy, all the more relevant given that she was a quiet 18-year-old with a poor rural background. Semenya is from the small village of Masehlong, north of Polokwane, and it is fair to say that she

---

* The other, at the same championship and in the same discipline, 800m, was Mbulaeni Mulaudzi, and we also have three world champs in field events: Marius Corbett (javelin, 1997), Hestrie Cloete (high jump, 2001 and 2003) and Jacques Freitag (high jump, 2003). Besides these achievements, South Africa pulled off the retrospective shock of the 2001 meeting in Edmonton, Canada, by winning the men's 4x100m relay four years after the race was run; the team of Morné Nagel, Corné du Plessis, Lee-Roy Newton and Matthew Quinn was promoted to first place when the Americans were disqualified in 2005 because of a doping conviction for Tim Montgomery.

> "I don't even know how they do this gender testing. I don't know what a chromosome is. This is all very painful for us, we live by simple rules in our culture. We do not intrude. This is not natural. To go through such an unusual thing must be very hard for Caster. I really have been concerned for her wellbeing."
>
> *– Jacob Semenya, Caster's father, speaking in 2009*

was somewhat naive about the ways of the world. But Chuene was having none of that. Vile man that he is, he packed her on the plane to Berlin knowing full well that he was sending her into the jaws of the international press utterly unprepared for what was about to hit her.

The wheels fell off for Chuene when the IAAF's own investigations were embarrassingly leaked, revealing to the world what ASA administrators already knew: that Semenya does have a rare and complicated medical condition. The results of further testing have never officially been made public, but she reportedly has what is known as "a disorder of sexual development" that has left her with internal testes rather than ovaries, unusually high levels of testosterone and the inability to bear children.

This, of course, was life-changing and shocking news for Semenya, and it's hard to imagine how she must have felt when it surfaced. Yes, she had suffered the indignity of being "checked" by opposition coaches in the toilets at school sporting events, but these test results – all news to her, remember – were suddenly making international headlines everywhere, with the press clamouring for a piece of her. It must have been beyond awful, and she was understandably angry.

But things got worse. Chuene did what weak people do when cornered: he lashed out defensively, in his case with an extraordinary rant about the "imperialist" IAAF. "Who are white people to question the make-up of an African girl?" he demanded. "I say this is racism, pure and simple. In Africa, as in any other country *[sic]*, parents look at new babies and can see straight away whether to raise them as a boy or a girl. We are now being told that it is not so simple. But the people who question these things have no idea how much shame such a slur can bring on a family."

Well, yes. Exactly. So nice of you to point that out, Mr Chuene.

What he didn't say on that particular occasion – the admission came later – was that he had repeatedly lied to the press to avoid implicating himself as the key player in the whole affair. Meanwhile political opportunists such as Winnie Madikizela-Mandela and Julius Malema leapt onto the race-bashing bandwagon, pawing at a mortified-looking Semenya upon her return from Berlin at a specially called and widely covered press conference. *The Independent* called it "a stage-managed political carnival"; *The New York Times* described it as "a choreographed welcome by political professionals". Whatever it was, it was disgraceful, and Semenya appeared hugely uncomfortable throughout.

But quietly, as is her way, Semenya was teaching all those about her – the heartless sports administrators, the self-serving politicians, the rabid press – how to conduct themselves in public and in private. It was a lesson in dignity for all those "dignitaries". Later she would tell an interviewer, "God made me the way I am, and I accept myself."

In the end, Chuene and his fellow ASA trough-guzzlers were found out. Naturally, beyond the appalling public behaviour, there were backdoor

"Caster Semenya became world 800m champion at 18. Rather than adulation and sponsorship deals, her victory led to a ban, invasive medical examinations and a flurry of media reports that she had both male and female sexual characteristics. Semenya unintentionally instigated an international and often ill-tempered debate on gender politics, feminism and race, becoming an inspiration to gender campaigners around the world. This summer, she returned to the track at a small meet in Finland and did what provoked the controversy in the first place – she won."

– Caster Semenya's entry in the New Statesman's
50 People That Matter list for 2010, headlined "Intersex symbol"

shenanigans aplenty: fraud, corruption, a bit of bribery and a Mercedes-Benz bought from the association for one rand. Chuene was stripped of his job and banished from sports administration for seven years.

And, of course, the IAAF went on to make the point that it had had no intention of leaking the results of Semenya's tests, and that it would have much preferred to keep things all under wraps. They were, at least, far more discrete about the follow-up testing and negotiations that kept Semenya from competing for eleven months. The details were never made public, but she was eventually cleared to run as a female – because, despite her condition, that's what she is.

Semenya's torrid few years at the hands of immoral and incompetent swine came full circle when, to a great cheer and smiling widely, she led the South African Olympic team out for the opening ceremony of the 2012 Olympics in London, our flag held aloft. Then she went on to win a silver medal in the 800 metres, the first black South African woman to win an Olympic medal. Gold would have been nice, but not to worry; she's only 21, and she has a great future in sport and beyond. And that's not only because Caster Semenya, a woman, can run like the wind. It's also because she carries herself with humility and dignity.

Many of the entries in this book are, justifiably, about the difficulties of overcoming prejudice and the fight to be seen as equal. The battle against colonialism and apartheid has been a huge challenge – *the* challenge – for this country. It is something that has come to define us. The story of Caster Semenya is similar in certain ways, but is possibly even more poignant because the very nature of her condition has her fighting her particular battle largely alone. There are no marches or rallies or leagues she can join. And it's precisely because she's shown such bravery to return and compete and win on an international stage that she is here.

The Caster Semenya affair has shown the best and worst of South Africa – how those in high places are content to step over the people in their supposed care for their own self-serving needs. And all the while it's the people, like Semenya, who are the real heroes. Watch and learn, is what we say to our sports administrators and politicians.

"More than the glorious gold from our swimmers, more than anything else, I wanted this controversial woman to win – even if it wasn't the final. I wanted her to win because she is a stupendously brave athlete, her journey to London cloaked in a gender scandal and political games that would have lesser men and women wilt and blanch in the face such extreme intrusion, mocking and interference. And when those powerful arms and legs propelled her past her opponents on Thursday night, she swept so many of our hearts with her across the finishing line. Caster Semenya is a true champion, and we should all be so very proud of her. Well done, Ms Semenya."

– Phylicia Oppelt, writing in the Sunday Times,
after Semenya had won her Olympic semifinal

(See **Leonard Chuene, 50 People Who Stuffed Up South Africa.**)

Shaka

c. 1787 – 22 September 1828

*King of the Zulus; military genius; nation-builder;
conqueror of people; subject of legacy tug-of-war*

SHAKA. IT'S A NAME THAT HAS RUNG THROUGH THE AGES. And today, as
when he was alive, it's well worth treating him, his story and legacy with
kid gloves, because the man who formed a martial nation in what we
now call KwaZulu-Natal is often as imagined as he is known.

Certainly, the idea of a brutal and bloodthirsty tyrant would have helped the cause of racists who wished to dismiss blacks as savages. Equally, the image of a benevolent king bringing together the disparate peoples of southern Africa with his harmonious and all-embracing leadership, only for this budding new nation to be crushed by foreign invaders, is of use to those who might like to demonise white colonisers. Shaka's alleged brutality and the Mfecane he was said to have instigated were merely alibis for the theft of this country's land from its original inhabitants, they have argued. And then there's a position that is, on the face of it, more sensible: that much of the revisionism concerning Shaka is misplaced political correctness; that white guilt regarding colonialism has resulted in a wilful misrepresentation of what one historian calls the "often appalling facts of life in many pre-literate societies".

You only have to read the history of, say medieval England, with its torture chambers and its red-hot pokers and its hanging and drawing and quartering, to know that it's not a race thing. Violence is violence, and it has dominated much of human history. As Thomas Hobbes, who took a dim view on human nature, explained it, life without the protection of responsible government was one of "continual fear, and danger of violent death; and the life of man, solitary, poor, nasty, brutish, and short". It was his famous *bellum omnium contra omnes* – the war of all against all.

It is surely fair to say that life under Shaka was much like that. He was, we know, capable of staggering cruelty – and that's why he featured prominently in *50 People Who Stuffed Up South Africa*. With the amount of blood on his hands, it was impossible not to include him there. But we'll tiptoe lightly around all that for now because this is a book about brilliance, not niceness, and Shaka was also a bit of a genius. And no-one can deny that genius and violence, when working well in tandem, can get a heck of a lot done. In Shaka's case it birthed a nation.

The first thing he did when he assumed power of the insignificant chiefdom of the Zulus, in around 1816, was create an army. Then he armed it like no army in the region had been armed before, and he gave it tactics that would prove themselves again and again.

The key, it seems, was his ability to harness a cultural phenomenon present throughout the region and militarise it. Age grades existed in society for all kinds of things – for the tending of cattle and for various rituals and so on. He turned such age grades into regiments, or *amabhuto*, each with their own insignia and coloured shields. He ensured this army was trained, was fit, and could cover a lot of ground fast. Boys as young as seven were organised as *udibi*, apprentice warriors, following the main impi with rations, weapons and equipment.

The change of weaponry was similarly important. While the traditional long-shafted throwing assegai remained in the arsenal, Shaka encouraged the use of the *iklwa*, a shorter, broader-bladed stabbing spear. It was named for the sound it made when extracted from a victim. Shields were made bigger and heavier.

Then came the tactics. Traditional battles involved longer-range engagements – essentially spear-throwing – and Shaka's insight was to realise that hand-to-hand combat could be devastating in such an environment. The *iklwa* came into its own when his warriors got in close. Shaka also introduced the now famous horns-of-the-buffalo formation: the head and chest of his army attacked directly, and the horns, left and right, encircled and trapped the enemy, leaving no room for escape. As Donald Morris wrote, Shaka "changed the nature of warfare in southern Africa" from "a ritualised exchange of taunts with minimal loss of life into a true method of subjugation by wholesale slaughter".

Shaka's military prowess was incomparable and his enemies had no answer. His army began absorbing clan after clan and the Zulus became more than an insignificant people; they were a mighty nation. Eventually this campaign of violent assimilation ignited the Mfecane and all that came with it, reengineering entire populations. Before he was murdered by his half-brothers in 1828, Shaka ruled over, depending on who you ask, up to 250,000 people and could call on a standing army of 50,000 soldiers. All this in twelve years.

That's hellish impressive, no matter how you look at it.

(See Shaka, 50 People Who Stuffed Up South Africa; see Ntshingwayo Khoza and Moshoehose I.)

Mark Shuttleworth

b. 18 September 1973

*South Africa's youngest self-made billionaire; first
African in space; possible Steve Jobs of the future*

MARK SHUTTLEWORTH WAS 26 WHEN HE HIT THE BIG TIME. In 1999
he sold his small start-up IT company for $575 million and, just like
that, he was a South African multibillionaire with the world at his feet.
It was an incredible leap from obscurity into the limelight, and he was
just getting started; three years later he became the first African and the
second private citizen to travel into space when he rode a Russian rocket
to the International Space Station. By the time Soyuz TM-33 touched

down in the Kazakhstan desert in May 2002, Shuttleworth was a local and international celebrity. It had been an astonishing few years.

An instant tall-poppy story like this generally attracts two kinds of responses. Mostly, people admired a young man's great financial success and were wowed by his space flight. But a more cynical take was that Shuttleworth's wealth was pretty much a fluke, materialising as it did at the peak of the dot.com bubble, and his space-tourist vanity project was little more than a PR coup to ensure his name in history. After all, it came with a $20-million price tag, and surely that money could have been put to more philanthropic uses? And besides, he emigrated to the UK as soon as he made his cash anyway...

This second opinion is, of course, simply mean-spirited and short-sighted, but the first is also unsatisfactory. Because there is more to Shuttleworth than this glossy surface impression. When the depth of his backstory is fleshed out, and when his subsequent lower-profile career is added to the tale, then he starts getting really interesting. As it turns out, Mark Shuttleworth was a brilliant boy who, almost predictably, became a brilliant and successful young man who could in older age, if luck continues to favour him, go on to revolutionise the computing world.

From the age of 13, Shuttleworth attended Diocesan College (Bishops), the oldest and one of the most prestigious private schools in the country. It allowed him access to a privileged world, but as a scholarship kid he eschewed any sense of entitlement; rather, he saw his time there as an opportunity to be embraced to the fullest. His achievements were immense. He was first in his standard every year and won a multitude of class prizes and national competitions. He was sent on international school exchange to the US and won a three-week trip to London for his performance at the National Science Olympiad. He earned awards for acting and gold medals for judo. At one point he won a computer and, without prompting, donated it to an underprivileged school. In matric he headed his school's three-man team for the national Gee-Whiz Mintek Science Quiz, which was televised in prime time; they won the entire competition easily with Shuttleworth answering the bulk of the questions. To no-one's great surprise he graduated with As in every subject in a time when such a feat was still remarkable.

Shuttleworth was eventually head boy of the school, a rare achievement for an "academic" who loved science and computers. He was well liked, earning the position by bringing drive and personality to his intellectual achievements. Perhaps the most illuminating element of his school career – at least for our purposes – came on his final day, in December 1991, when he delivered his leaving address to the school. It gave a glimpse into his future as he encouraged the boys to take advantage of their school and its facilities. He concluded by asking "two things of every boy here":

> Firstly, that you try to wake up each day with an idea, no matter how small, and do your utmost to put it into practice. Seize each day as an opportunity to achieve something; refuse point blank to allow yourself to drift with the crowd. Don't be afraid to stand out... Secondly, in your dreaming, think big. Go beyond the perimeter of the school. As South Africa and indeed the world warms to a new age of communication, there is no reason why [you] should not be at the forefront of the movement.

At this point Shuttleworth could have headed off to university, gained a first-class PhD in something or other then disappeared along the usual career path of the super-intelligent: a happy life in academia or perhaps something less exciting but more lucrative down the corporate road. But he lived by his leaving-address words and dreamt big, focusing on that "new age of communication".

In retrospect the rise of the internet was one of the most profound revolutions of the 21st century, comparable with the invention of the printing press or telephone, and ultimately something of an amalgamation of the two. But in the early 1990s it was a still a gimmick and an unknown. Shuttleworth was one of those who recognised its potential. He tracked its development closely and was involved in installing the first residential internet connection at the University of Cape Town, where he studied Finance and Information Technology. "I was very interested in how the internet was changing commerce and was determined to pursue it," he would later explain.

> "I am very conscious of the fact that life is very short. I feel like we are all on a short fuse so we should make the most of our time here. It is very dangerous to think that life is indefinite because then there is no urgency to get on and do anything. I think a good life is about getting out and doing things. You may live for another fifty years, but if you get on with it you're likely to enjoy it so much more."
>
> *– Mark Shuttleworth, 2010*

By 1995, he had identified a gap in the market: web security. Online shopping was the way of the future, he figured, but for it to flourish there had to be a readily available way to pass credit card details safely over the internet. He was specifically interested in the way web browsers verified the identity of a company, and he started looking into the creation of electronic identity documents known as digital certificates that would secure this process. Thus was born Thawte Consulting, operated from his parents' garage in Durbanville.

The angle was an inspired one and, though the technical challenge was far from simple, Shuttleworth nailed it. This is what success sounds like for a future-billionaire computer nerd: "The moment at 2am when my Python RSA implementation produced a digital signature that OpenSSL then would verify… That was quite a rush."

Translated, this was the first time that the algorithm he had created for a digital certificate had worked. He had programmed the code that would, literally and digitally, secure his future.

Both Netscape, then the world's leading web-browser maker, and Microsoft, the developer of Internet Explorer, bought into the new product. Thawte became "the first certificate authority to issue SSL certificates to public entities outside of the United States", and within four years it had offices in 22 countries and had cornered 40 percent of the world market. In 1999 VeriSign, which had the rest, offered Shuttleworth $100 million for his company. He turned them down. Several months later, with the dot.com bubble expanding at exponential rates, they made him an offer he couldn't refuse: $575 million, at the time R3.5 billion.

In his own words, Shuttleworth had simply been "willing to work on an obscure piece of technology when everyone else was pursuing normal careers", but this is a typically self-effacing take on things. The truth is his triumph fitted perfectly into Malcolm Gladwell's extreme-success formula: years of practice, the luck to find the perfect gap and the smarts to take it. In this case, he had spent thousands of hours on computers as a youngster, which meant he had all the knowledge and technical skills he would need; by virtue of his birth in 1973 he entered the job market just as the internet boom began in 1995; and he had the intelligence and business training to work himself into a niche that presented itself to someone willing to look. Without any of those factors he wouldn't have reached the heights he did (bearing in mind that by 1999 he was already successful and wealthy by normal standards). Only in this case, Shuttleworth's luck was in fact compounded: six weeks after signing over Thawte on 1 February 2000, the dot.com bubble peaked, and a month after that it had burst, bringing down the Nasdaq. At the end of February of that year VeriSign shares topped out on the exchange at $258.50; a year later they were trading below $30.

For Shuttleworth, that was neither here nor there. He took the money, gave his sixty employees million-rand bonuses – including the gardener – and once again dreamt big.

From South Africa's youngest billionaire to the world's first "Afronaut", the next step in the Shuttleworth journey was particularly well documented and earned him global celebrity. Following the lead of Dennis Tito, the first-ever space tourist, he arranged a $20 million trip to the International Space Station with the Russian Federal Space Agency. He underwent a tough cosmonaut-preparation regime that saw him closeted in Star City, Moscow, for the better part of a year, and included four hours of Russian lessons per day, ocean-survival training in case of a splashdown in the sea, torrid sessions in the "vomit chair" for space-sickness acclimatisation and, of course, reams and reams of technical space-travel know-how. On 25 April 2002 he was blasted into orbit from the Baikonur Cosmodrome in Kazakhstan on top of a Soyuz-U rocket. He spent eight days on the station, and returned to a hero's welcome and a ticker-tape parade through the streets of Cape Town.

Once again, the paragraph précis only tells half the tale. Conscious of his new status as a super-rich white South African in the world spotlight, Shuttleworth made sure to underscore his trip with a sense of moral responsibility. Yes, he was a young man fulfilling a kid's dream to go into space, but he was also someone in a position to do good and inspire others. It was a tricky line to walk without coming across as a self-promoting phoney – follow your dreams, you can reach your goals, I'm living proof! – but he somehow managed to pull it off. Besides maintaining a well-run connection to the South African public with his First African In Space team, he made a genuine effort to contribute to the trip as a scientist and flight engineer, not just a "space tourist". He conducted experiments, backed by various teams of South African scientists, on stem cells, HIV and the effects of microgravity on the human body.

Perhaps most tellingly, however, the whole process was incorporated into the launch, the year before his space flight, of the Shuttleworth Foundation, which was conceptualised to be a driving force for real social change, with investments in education and technology projects. The foundation's most widely recognised project is the ongoing HIP2B² initiative that encourages interest in maths, science and technology among South African schoolchildren. For all his success and efforts, Shuttleworth was awarded an Honorary Doctorate by UCT at the end of the year – at 29, he was the university's youngest ever recipient.

Fast forward a decade or so, and the Shuttleworth name occupies an

"I have done well with investing, but it has never felt very fulfilling. I fear getting to the end of my life and feeling you haven't actually built something. And to do something people thought was impossible is attractive."

– *Mark Shuttleworth, 2009*

understandably lower media profile compared to those heady times at the turn of the millennium. It still crops up in the business pages from time to time,* but the man himself is content to avoid the big headlines when possible and work away on his longer-term project, Ubuntu.

Named for the philosophy that Desmond Tutu made famous – *ubuntu*: a person is a person through other persons – Ubuntu is a free operating system for desktop computers and servers that has been developed and is regularly updated by open-source communities. Which is to say, it is a computer operating system like Microsoft Windows or Apple OS, with all the word-processing, spreadsheet, media player and other useful programs included, but it doesn't cost anything and none of the computer engineers who put it together are paid for their efforts. If it sounds like a weekend amateur job, well, it might have been without Shuttleworth's guiding hand. Members of the open-source community are generally very knowledgeable and extremely passionate about what they do, and they have produced many excellent products over the years. But they are almost indecipherable to normal human beings – see the Python RSA quote earlier – and it is impossible for such software to compete with massive corporate design teams and their billion-dollar budgets without some form of collective strategic guidance. And this is where Shuttleworth, once again, spotted the gap.

In 2004 he set up a team of developers and got them working on a brand-new system of the highest possible quality with the intention of drawing it out of the geeky open-source community and making it accessible to the average computer user. It was to differ from similar and earlier projects by being user-friendly and entirely free, and by being updated without fail every six months. At the same time Shuttleworth founded Canonical, a company to help steer the process and govern strategy, and ensure that Ubuntu meets specific performance criteria requirements.

---

* In 2011, for example, Visa purchased the mobile-banking-services company Fundamo for $110 million. Fundamo was partly funded through Shuttleworth's HBD Venture Capital, now overseen by Knife Capital.

Many updates later, Ubuntu has been widely acclaimed as a brilliant piece of software and is now the world's most popular open-source operating system for PCs. In 2013, "five percent of the world's PCs will ship with Ubuntu pre-installed", according to Shuttleworth, and it has excelled particularly in the area of cloud computing.

But there is a long, long way to go. Canonical, which makes its money by offering technical support for Ubuntu, runs at a loss while Microsoft and Apple continue to thunder along. There are many experts who believe open-source will never be able to outmuscle the big boys, and that Canonical will slowly bleed itself dry. Financially, Shuttleworth will be fine either way; in 2012 *Forbes* claimed he still had "a net worth north of $500 million". But that's not where his motivation lies. He seems to have moulded himself into the next generation's Steve Jobs – just a more moral and generally pleasanter version. Importantly, he believes in what he does.

"It's just a matter of time," he says. "This community is going to be producing the software the world runs – whether it's five years' time or ten years' time or twenty years' time, I don't really mind – the processes that we employ are going to win. They're better processes, I do believe that. If your people are better and your processes are better, the world adopts what you do."

"Look, I have a very privileged life, right? I am a billionaire, bachelor, ex-cosmonaut. Life couldn't easily be that much better. Being a Linux geek sort of brings balance to the force."
— *Mark Shuttleworth, 2009. He now has a live-in girlfriend*

Mark Shuttleworth had stunning success at an early age, but making Ubuntu the most popular operating system in the world will require far more patience and persistence than it takes to program a digital certificate or prepare for a trip into space. If half-a-billion dollars and a ride on a rocket was something, then this is a shot at the *really* big time.

Walter & Albertina Sisulu

Walter: 18 May 1912 – 5 May 2003
Albertina: 21 October 1918 – 2 June 2011

Iconic struggle couple whose endearing marriage
still serves as the finest moral compass even today;
"South Africa's greatest love story"

WHILE IT IS INARGUABLY TRUE that Nelson and Winnie Mandela claimed
the bulk of the attention during the fight against apartheid, and that the
Mandela name came to resonate with the most extraordinary symbolism
in this time, Nelson and Winnie are hardly the most celebrated of the
struggle couples. Individually they became icons but as a team they left

rather a lot to be desired, and after 38 years of marriage – 27 of those separated by prison bars, and the last four just separated, period – they were divorced in 1996. In fact, the dissolution of the marriage of our greatest South African goes to show a) that he was a mortal man with real flaws, and b) just how trying the attention of the apartheid state could be on personal relationships. So for the husband-and-wife partnerships that came to represent the moral backbone and endearing fortitude of the banned ANC during the long and difficult isolation years, we must look elsewhere – to the likes of Joe Slovo and Ruth First, Oliver and Adelaide Tambo, and of course Walter and Albertina Sisulu.

Without taking anything from the Slovos and the Tambos, and any number of other relationships that managed to survive years of police-state investigation, harassment, detention, exile, prison time and everything that came with it, the 59 years that Walter and Albertina were married are, in themselves, simply a phenomenal marker to shared love and human kindness. And yet it was not a marriage born of instant attraction. "At first I did not love him," Albertina admitted in an interview after Walter's death. "I didn't want any man, but Walter's sisters drilled me to accept their brother."

Albertina, born in Tsomo in the Transkei as Nontsikelelo Thethiwe, had suffered a broken and difficult family upbringing typical for a black South African at the time (and still not unfamiliar today). Her largely absent father worked on the mines a thousand kilometres away and would go on to die of silicosis; her sickly mother never recovered fully from the Spanish Flu and often relied on her eldest daughter to plough the fields and look after the family. But schooling was prioritised and Albertina won a scholarship to a Roman Catholic high school in Johannesburg. She was a convert by the time she graduated and originally intended to be a nun, eventually turning to nursing for the money it would provide – once again to help support her extended family.

Meanwhile, Walter Sisulu had endured a rather less typical, though not unheard of, South African upbringing, also in the Transkei. His father was one Victor Dickenson, a white railway foreman, and his mother was a domestic worker – a colour-barrier-defying union that was perhaps more common in the Western Cape of old, with its long history of slave-owning farmers finding a loving embrace down in the workers' quarters. Naturally, Dickenson and Alice Sisulu could never raise their coloured child together, and Walter took his mother's name and care. He had to leave school at the age of 15 and went through a variety of menial jobs, finding his way to Johannesburg in the process, as so many seeking their fortune did and still do.

It was there, in 1941, that the couple met, and it was that same year that, as regional leader of the ANC, Walter also met and took in a young lodger by the name of Nelson Mandela. Once Albertina had finally accepted Walter's marriage proposal – "It took me a long time," she would recall – it was that same Nelson Mandela who served as best man at their wedding in 1944. Despite Albertina's earlier reticence, and despite spending decades apart during Walter's imprisonment after the Rivonia Trial, theirs really was a romance for the ages. "We loved each other very much," Albertina once said. "We were like two chickens, one always walking behind the other."

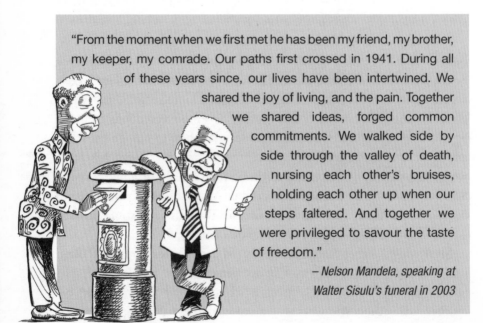

"From the moment when we first met he has been my friend, my brother, my keeper, my comrade. Our paths first crossed in 1941. During all of these years since, our lives have been intertwined. We shared the joy of living, and the pain. Together we shared ideas, forged common commitments. We walked side by side through the valley of death, nursing each other's bruises, holding each other up when our steps faltered. And together we were privileged to savour the taste of freedom."

– *Nelson Mandela, speaking at Walter Sisulu's funeral in 2003*

It was, of course, a relationship that was tested over and over. The year they were married, Walter formed the ANC Youth League with Mandela and Oliver Tambo (and others). In time, the three great comrades came to be the guiding lights of the anti-apartheid struggle. In its obituary of Walter, *The Guardian* described their combined efforts as such: "The closest of friends, their contributions were each subtly different, supplementing each other in a way which was perhaps crucial to the outcome of the struggle: Mandela, the dignified leader who led above all by example; Tambo, who took on the burden of the exile years, and the small and slightly dishevelled figure of Sisulu... [B]ut it was the calm, wise Sisulu in the background whom many came to regard as the outstanding thinker and organiser."

"She gave me unconditional love, she called me her son, I called her my mom and she was my second mother."
– *Dali Tambo, whose father Oliver was exiled from South Africa for three decades*

Walter was a gentle, humble man, a great unifier and an inspiration for those around him. Naturally, he steered Albertina into politics. Initially reluctant, she went on to become president of the ANC Women's League and was one of the organisers of a march to the Union Buildings, undertaken by 20,000 women, protesting the pass laws on 9 August 1956. The phrase "You strike a woman, you strike a rock" was derived from a song the marchers sang on the day, and in 1994 the date was enshrined on the South African calendar as a public holiday, Women's Day.

Unsurprisingly, the apartheid state's various agencies took a keen interest in both the Sisulus' work. Walter, who had become the ANC's first paid secretary general in 1949 (earning £5 a month) and was later heavily involved in the Defiance Campaign, was invariably banned, locked up or placed under house arrest during this time. In 1962 he was arrested on six separate occasions. And Albertina suffered too, assuming the honour of being the first woman imprisoned under the 90-day detention-without-trial law. She served two months in solitary confinement, and was banned for eighteen years, a South African record.

"It was the arrest of both of us, Walter and myself, which was the hardest time," Albertina would recall. "He was worse because he was taken to Robben Island. At least I was just in and out of jail here in Johannesburg. Whenever I had a meeting addressing the women, then I would go to jail for that. It was hard, when you have children. Fortunately for us we had real mothers who really looked after my children."

When she was arrested for the march on the Union Buildings, Nelson Mandela acted as her lawyer. She would return the favour upon his and Walter's imprisonment after the Rivonia treason trial in 1964, by going on to look after Mandela's children from his first marriage, along with five of her own, three more adopted children and various other orphans of the cause. (Three of the Sisulu children, Lindiwe, Max and Zwelakhe, became famous in their own rights.) In the 1980s she served as co-president of the United Democratic Front and was, once again, repeatedly jailed.

Walter was in his late seventies when he was freed, in 1989. (He arrived home, virtually unannounced, with one small suitcase.) Despite health issues, he was forced to fill a holding role as deputy president of the ANC for several years in the early 1990s while Mandela's potential successors elbowed each other about. On Thabo Mbeki's rise to the position, Walter retired to the same Soweto house he'd lived in sixty years before. Meanwhile, Albertina became a member of the ANC national executive and then, in 1994, a member of South Africa's first democratic Parliament.

During Walter's long imprisonment, Albertina had maintained the dignified bearing of a moral colossus. While Winnie Mandela looked for trouble and walked the most tenuous of ethical lines, to put it mildly, Albertina rose far above it all, and she is perhaps more deserving of the title Mother of the Nation. Most endearingly of all, she wrote constantly to her husband in jail, fanning the romance that would continue after his release until his death in 2003. When he died she wrote a note to him saying, "Walter, what do I do without you?" and signed it, "Your wife, Tienie." It's hard to escape the sense that, for all the time in jail they both faced, for all the upheavals and hardships, this was her saddest moment.

Without doubt both Walter and Albertina Sisulu were champions of the struggle in so many ways. But beyond that, they were good people who loved each other dearly and stayed committed to each other for six decades. They were – and still are – in the words of *The Star*, "South Africa's greatest love story". And they are a couple who you look at and reflect on and, on a purely personal level, only wish you can emulate.

"How can we speak about this great unifier to people without recognising and honouring that great unity in his own life: that of Walter and Albertina as a marital couple, a unity of such deep friendship and mutual respect, a personal and political partnership that transcended and survived all hardships, separations and persecution?"
    – *Nelson Mandela, at Walter Sisulu's funeral, 2003*

(See **Nelson Mandela** and **Winnie Madikizela-Mandela**.)

Jordy Smith

b. 11 February 1988

Surfer; styler; beach bum; rodeo-flipper; alley-oopser; Kelly Slater's heir apparent

IF YOU KNOW ANYTHING ABOUT the South African surf scene you'll know that Durbanites surf in boardies, Capetonians wear hoodies and J-Bay's ugly facebrick façade hides a reeling beast of a wave called Supertubes, which is regarded as the best right-hander there is. What you may not know is that Shaun Tomson was *Bustin' Down The Door* way back in the day taking SA surfing to the world and helping to bring professionalism and structure to the sport, and by standing on the shoulders of this giant, Jordy Smith chooned, "Hey, what kind?", backdoored a kiff shack, cranked off the bottom and, having sussed out the lip, klapped a rodeo-flip where everyone else would've come pipe.

Translated, this means there is an amazing surf break at Jeffreys Bay called Supertubes, which produces some of the best waves in the world, and that the original pioneer of SA surf and one-time world champ is a fellow by the name of Shaun Tomson. But if Tomson was knocking on the door of greatness in the 1970s, then times have a-changed because the new guy on the scene, Jordy Smith, has taken it off its hinges. He's got power, tricks, contest results and he *owns* J-Bay. He's also got the hottest rookie deal ever signed and one of the hottest girls in South Africa – and even though he only started hitting the big time in 2007 and he's still riding the wave, he's got future legend writ large.

Smith is a lanky kid with a swagger you only get if your natural element is the water – because once you've tamed the wild waves of serious surf, you draw the same confident lines on land. And if you catch him on a typical night out, wearing his backwards Red Bull cap and his red T-shirt and his sneakers, with his mates in tow, it's like stepping into a scene from *Entourage*.

The idiot bouncer waves a big fat finger in his face and shakes his head with a scowl, and although this kid isn't used to hearing no, he's unflappable, all shrugging shoulders and gurning with his mates, as happy as a litter of golden retriever puppies. Cue the hostess in her spray-on dress dropping her clipboard and throwing her little hands up and tottering over from behind the lectern, literally falling all over herself as she flicks her blonde hair. "So! So! Sorry!" she swoons. And the bouncer has to step back and allow into the sanctity of his precious nightclub not just this kid, but his whole motley crew as well. Because this is Jordy Smith, bru.

Ever since he hit the big time, the guy's been living it large. The parties, the Range Rover, the pad in Camps Bay. Not forgetting the harem of big-breasted, small-thonged girls who flock to the surf scene – not that he's interested any more, given that he's devoted to his girlfriend, lingerie model Lyndall Jarvis. Is it *Entourage* or is it *GQ*? Hard to tell.

As in any half-decent fairy tale or rap song, Smith's story came with a few speed bumps at the start. There are no tiny violins playing, though: he was born to an artisan father and schoolteacher mom in a neighbourhood he describes as "average". But if you drove through Umbilo in the late afternoon you'd probably be locking the car door with your elbow…

Growing up in Durban, Surf City, Smith cut his teeth on Durban's New Pier, a heavily localised scene with a pecking order that takes years to climb. Some used to think his size was a disadvantage – Smith is 6ft2 and weighs around ninety kilograms – but he's changed that mindset by

> "I look up to Martin Potter and Shaun Tomson, but my dad taught me everything and motivated me more than anyone else."
>
> – *Jordy Smith*

showing what's possible with a bit more weight over the board, tearing huge chunks out of the wave's face, throwing buckets of water and then shifting his rail and taking to the air with an intimidating repertoire of aerial manoeuvres. He's fast and loose, powerful and polished. Simply put, Jordy Smith is special. There are only a handful of surfers out there in this guy's league.

And like all truly gifted sportsmen, he had other options. Having been picked for South Africa at junior level and then been invited to a Manchester United training camp, Smith may well have end up playing top-league soccer if the sea hadn't come calling.

Still, there have been many great sportsmen – and surfers in particular – who were unable to turn on the goods when competing. In the modern parlance, they're the guys who've been unable to monetise their talent. Not Smith, who won his first national title in the under-8 division, claimed a pair of junior world champion titles, won a bunch of Billabong Junior Series and had bystanders tapping their noses and calling this freak the next Kelly Slater.

Then Smith went stickerless – he removed his sponsor's logo from his board – and the whole world went crazy. The surfing world, that is. Which, if you're in the surfing world, is the whole world. There was speculation, a bidding war, seven-figure salaries thrown around. Nike even went so far as to bring in Tiger Woods to convince the young surfer to sign with them. Smith eventually went with O'Neill, securing the highest-paying rookie deal ever heard of in surfing. In his first year in the big time, 2007, he shattered the World Qualifying Series all-time points record and won the competition with several events still to run, claiming the Triple Crown Rookie of the Year Award.

Instead of crumbling under the pressure of surfing in the World Championship Tour, he maintained the Jordy BMT, winning the Billabong Pro in Jeffreys Bay in 2010 (he'd do it again in 2011) and earning himself the position of top-ranked surfer in the world. Briefly. Kelly Slater put an end to Jordy's title dreams but, if it's any consolation, being second to Kelly Slater, eleven-time world champion in twenty years and the greatest surfer of all time, is no small feat.

Even though it's Smith's dream to get himself that world title, he's still having fun en route, whether that's free-surfing – watch Kai Neville's game-changing film, *Modern Collective*, or his new one, *Bending Colours*, for an idea of what it's all about – or recording a track with Goldfish, because, well, it was something that he wanted to do and the brilliant dance duo were only too happy to oblige.

But when you put aside the fun and games and girls and parties, surfing is Jordy Smith's thing and it's what the boy's all about. You're not special if you drive a fancy car and go hard at the jorl, but you are if you can pull a 360-degree flip off the lip on the critical bowl section of a wave, land facing in the wrong direction, spin right around in the blink of an eye and continue on your way. That's a rodeo flip if you didn't know, and it's nearly impossible.

Which, if we haven't mentioned it already, is to say this kid's a freak.

Kelly Slater is now in his forties so the time is fast approaching for a new surf king. And if you're one with the ocean and looking for sick signs for the future, here's a nice little coincidence: Slater and Smith share the same birthday. Perhaps the surf gods have this all planned out…

Jan Smuts

24 May 1870 – 11 September 1950

In short: genius; soldier; statesman
At length: Prime Minister of South Africa (twice);
Field Marshall of the British Army; member of
the Imperial War Cabinet during both World
Wars; revered Boer commando leader and East
African campaigner; founder of The League
of Nations and the United Nations; scientist;
botanist; inventor of holism; subject of pathetic
racially misdirected historical revisionism

AT THE TIME OF NELSON MANDELA's inauguration as the first truly democratic president of South Africa in 1994, South Africa's major airports were all named for famous politicians, inevitably white men of previous political power. So we had Jan Smuts International Airport in Johannesburg, DF Malan in Cape Town, Louis Botha in Durban, PW Botha in George, Ben Schoeman in East London, and the warmest and fuzziest of the lot, HF Verwoerd in Port Elizabeth. Seeing that all these bad bastards were little more than racist reminders of apartheid subjugation, one of the first symbolic gestures of the new dispensation was to do away with political names for airports. And, hey, fair enough.

Except that two of them weren't. Smuts and Louis Botha.

But because they both had Afrikaans-sounding names and were found to be hanging about with Malan and Verwoerd – if only as airports – there seemed to be a general feeling in many circles that they were cut from the same cloth. After all, what's the difference between Louis and PW when they're both Bothas? Quite a lot, as it happens.

Louis Botha we must (mostly) leave for another time – suffice it to say that he wasn't far from making the cut here – but Jan Smuts is a man who no amount of politically correct revisionist pandering could exclude from selection. In fact, if we had applied a seeding system instead of alphabetical ordering, he would probably rank a close second to Mandela. Really, that's how special he was.

Smuts's greatness can be analysed in many ways, and he must surely rank as one of the most studied and written-about of all South Africans, if not recently. For now there is space only to touch on three broad aspects of his life: his vast intellect, his soldiering skills, and of course his statesmanship. Though they are indelibly interwoven elements of his life, taken separately each one alone reflects brilliance.

Perhaps surprisingly, given all that he would go on to do, Jan Christiaan Smuts was not destined for greatness as a youngster. If tradition had had its way, he would have lived as a farmer in the Malmesbury district northeast of Cape Town, rearing sheep and cattle and most likely living a prosperous and peaceful life, as four generations of Smutses had done before him. It was customary for only the first-born son, in this case his elder brother Michiel, to attend school, and Jan's duty would have been to take over the farm when he came of age. But when Michiel died of typhoid it was decided that Jan should receive an education. This was, as it turned out, a solid parenting decision on behalf of Mr and Mrs Smuts.

Smuts first attended a village school in Riebeeck West at the age of 12; by age 16 he had been accepted to Victoria College, later to become Stellenbosch University, having covered the usual eleven years of schooling in just four. A native Afrikaans-speaker, he would become proficient in High Dutch and German, but "he was always at his best in English", according to one of his more recent biographers, Antony Lentin. On discovering that Greek was a mandatory subject, he confined himself to his room during a holiday and, as one does, learnt the entire language. In one week. He left Stellenbosch in 1891 with a joint First in Science and Literature – having also met his future wife, Isie – and headed to Cambridge University to take up a scholarship reading law. It was his first experience abroad, and it was quickly apparent that his brilliance would not be confined to his homeland; he performed so astoundingly and made such an impression that he left Christ's College with the reputation as one of its three greatest scholars in its 500-year history. The other two were John Milton and Charles Darwin.

Even while he was winning academic prizes and topping class lists, Smuts found time to write a book on the American poet Walt Whitman who, he later explained, had freed his mind from the "severely puritanical" thought of his Christian upbringing. As a boy he had developed a love of nature and the outdoors – later expressed in his great obsession with Table Mountain, his "cathedral" – but his time in Cambridge exposed him to all manner of worldly knowledge. And he supped deeply.

The Whitman book, published only in 1973, laid the seed for what would become Smuts's philosophy of holism, a term he defined in another book *Holism And Evolution*, released in 1926. It was, he wrote, "the tendency in nature to form wholes that are greater than the sum of the parts through creative evolution". Far from being the kooky musings of a politician who happened to have some time on his hands, holism has its roots in the works of Spinoza and Hegel, among others, and remains a seriously considered theory even today. It has applications in everything from medicine to geopolitics. Einstein, who believed that Smuts was one of the few people who actually understood his theory of relativity, was a fan. Smuts was also a distinguished botanist; he was made a Fellow of the Royal Society and was elected president of both the South African and British versions of the Association for the Advancement of Science, both notable achievements. Later he served as chancellor of the University of Cape Town and then Cambridge University.

Unsurprisingly for a man of such powerful thought and great academic achievement, Smuts was something of a loner at university, and he shunned sports. Nevertheless he turned out to be a superb leader of men and pretty handy on a horse, as his experience in the South African War would reveal.

Having been born in the Cape Colony, Smuts was technically a British subject, but in 1896 he denounced his British citizenship and moved to the Transvaal. He had returned to the Cape from his studies abroad, dabbled in law, journalism and politics, and then been appalled by the duplicity of Cecil John Rhodes for his role in the Jameson Raid of December 1895. Already a man of sophisticated political thinking, Smuts had a sense of what was to come and chose to side with his own people, the Boers. President Paul Kruger quickly noticed his talents, making him legal advisor to the government and developing a close bond with the younger man. Together they tried in vain to stave off war, but Lord Milner had his eye on the gold of the Witwatersrand and so war it would be. With it came Smuts the soldier, and in particular Smuts the guerrilla fighter.

The first stage of the South African War was a fairly predictable affair. Despite some early successes, the older Boer generals proved no match for the might of Imperial Britain; Pretoria was overrun after eight months of fighting, and with that the Boer republics were annexed as colonies of the Crown. But the relatively quick British victory proved an illusion when the Boer forces split up into independent commandoes of horsemen, each several hundred strong, to wander the land engaging in hit-and-run warfare as the opportunities arose.

The younger Boer leaders came to the fore, with Louis Botha taking overall command above Generals De Wet, De la Rey (of the song), Hertzog and Smuts. Smuts eventually spent eight months at the head of a commando on an odyssey through the Cape Colony that saw them covering nearly 3,500 kilometres. It was an incredible feat of resourceful leadership and hard living, as they harried a huge British force and helped keep the war alive. "Military life agrees wonderfully with me," he wrote to his wife, despite his many brushes with death (including, in one instance,

"His courage, flair and martial qualities won the devotion of his men, the respect of Afrikaners generally and the admiration of the British, who regarded Smuts and Botha as the finest of the Boer generals and Smuts as the most chivalrous to his captives."
— Antony Lentin, writing about Smuts's exploits during the South African War

having his horse shot dead underneath him). It was no understatement, and it proved to be the making of the man. Despite the futility of his efforts – Kitchener eventually had 400,000 men and a scorched-earth policy at his disposal – Smuts won the respect and admiration of his men, Afrikaners in general and the British.

A little more than a decade later, he would further his fighting reputation during World War I. Having helped put down a mutiny of Boer War veterans, he led an invasion force into German South-West Africa in March 1915, travelling a thousand kilometres on horseback across the Kalahari, and coordinating an attack with Botha to force a quick surrender. The following year he was tasked by the British to take command of a 45,000-strong Imperial army that was struggling to overcome German forces in German East Africa led by Paul von Lettow-Vorbeck, one of the most cunning German generals of the war. Though beset by disastrous tropical weather and disease – Smuts and many of his men contracted malaria – and though Von Lettow-Vorbeck would remain uncaptured during the war, Smuts turned the tide of the campaign, boxed in the Germans and assumed control of a huge area in less than a year. (Even in war Smuts was a perfect gentleman. At one point the Iron Cross that had been awarded to Von Lettow-Vorbeck for his sterling efforts found its way into Smuts's hands; he had it delivered to his adversary with his congratulations. After the war, the two became good friends.) He was then called to Britain in 1917 where he was received with great esteem and joined Lloyd George's Imperial War Cabinet, helping to found the Royal Air Force and proving a huge asset until the war's end in November the following year.

When World War II rolled around – as it so inevitably had to do, and as he had predicted with much despair at the signing of the Treaty of Versailles – Smuts advocated for South African involvement on the side of the Allies. It was a near-run thing, but he made it happen (and became Prime Minister of South Africa for a second time in the process). By this stage his strategic military thinking was so valued that Churchill didn't hesitate to invite him, once again, to be a part of the War Cabinet. Smuts accepted and in time became Churchill's "one indispensable man". In

> "My own case is a striking instance of how the enemy of today may be the friend and comrade of tomorrow."
>
> – *Jan Smuts*

1941 Smuts was made a Field Marshall of the British Army, the first and only South African to receive this honour. "My faith in Smuts is unbreakable," Churchill emphasised.

And then there's the statesmanship.

At an international level, Smuts was profoundly influential and well respected, and had the ear of the world's great leaders, from Woodrow Wilson to Churchill. Lloyd George wanted to make Smuts Foreign Secretary during World War I; Churchill wanted Smuts to take over as Prime Minister of Britain if anything happened to him during World War II. Smuts is the only person to have signed the peace treaties that ended both World Wars, and he's the only one to have signed the charters to both the League of Nations, in 1919, and the United Nations, in 1945. He was a founding father of the former and wrote the preamble to the charter of the latter.

And, of course, domestically he played an overwhelmingly dominant role in the history of our land for more than fifty years. Most notably he was Prime Minister of the Union twice, between 1919 and 1924 and between 1939 and 1948, and he held great influence under Louis Botha and JB Hertzog who he succeeded respectively. To say his name is woven into the legislation and trajectory of South Africa in the first half of the 20th century is, for better or worse, putting it lightly. Of course we are gunning for better, but there are those who would say worse – and so we return to the airports…

Any man who spends so long in the public eye, especially a politician and a leader, will face criticism at many levels, of his character and his actions. Smuts was no exception, and he came to be known quite early on by the stauncher, more recalcitrant Afrikaners of the Transvaal who didn't like his reforming (and honest) ways as *Slim Jannie* – Crafty Jan.

Later, when he sided with the Allies in the World Wars they viewed him as an outright traitor. He also engaged fiercely with Mahatma Gandhi on the "Asiatic question" *(see Mahatma Gandhi)*, and his reputation took a hammering on the back of the Rand Rebellion in 1922, when a general strike by semi-skilled Afrikaner miners turned very violent. It was something of a forerunner to Marikana, ninety years later, an episode that saw him become the first head of state to attack his own citizens from the air when the fledgling South African Air Force strafed and bombed rebels in Benoni; it also led to his first loss of power in the 1924 election.

But the real criticism of Smuts is the trump-card accusation of modern times: racism. As Lentin puts it, "Smuts's reputation today… is at a low ebb among historians who consider it their task to judge the past against current nostrums of 'equality' and 'diversity'. Stretched on this procrustean bed, weighed in these anachronistic and unhistorical scales, Smuts inevitably emerges as a 'racist' and 'imperialist'."

It really is time to get past this petty and weak-minded thinking. No-one is claiming Smuts was not flawed. And there is no denying that black South Africans suffered the life of second-class citizens while he held political sway.

But historical figures cannot be measured on the morals of today. If so, then the list of racist or misogynist or simply murderous – and thus "bad" – men of history would include nearly all the great names. George Washington? Benjamin Franklin? Thomas Jefferson? All slave-keepers. Virtually every European ruler of consequence before the mid-20th century? Imperial overlords. Gandhi? Racist and a bit nuts. *(See Mahatma Gandhi.)* Shaka? Totally nuts and a genocidal killer. *(See Shaka, 50 People Who Stuffed Up South Africa.)* And on and on.

The irony in Smuts's case is that he was, in his day, in fact a great reconciler of races – between the British and Afrikaner races, that is. He worked tirelessly to mend the battle wounds of the South African War, a war that had ended in the bitterest of ways. Admittedly, many Boers resented his efforts – and today there still remains among certain sections of the Afrikaner population a surprising level of enmity towards the British for the horrors of Kitchener's concentration camps.

Still, in 1905 he could write, "[The British] gave us back our country in everything but name. After four years. Has such a miracle of trust and magnanimity ever happened before?" The ultimate proof of his work came in the union of the country in 1910, when what was once two colonies and two republics could come together to form, as his ideals of holism suggested, a stronger whole.

And yet even in these times, long before the problems of colonial oppression, racism and Imperialism would be tackled throughout Africa, the Americas and elsewhere, Smuts was at least aware of the future dilemma to be overcome. In 1908 he wrote, "I sympathise profoundly with the native races of South Africa whose land it was long before we came here to force our policy of dispossession on them." He went on to explain that he believed "the ampler shoulders and stronger brains of the future" would have to fix this "sphinx problem".

A cop-out? Perhaps. Could he have fixed it himself? Unlikely, you'd have to think. In fact it's plausible to argue that his incremental approach to a change in black-white race relations was one of the key factors leading to the rise to power of the Nationalists. Malan and his party tapped into a core fear of the Afrikaner electorate, many of whom believed that Smuts was far too progressive in his handling of "the native question". To the surprise of many, including an ageing Smuts wearied by war, he was voted out in 1948.

What we do know for sure is that Smuts was a legend in many other fields, and is recognised by the rest of the world as such. For various reasons, he has been misplaced by many South Africans in the dumpbin of political history, along with other Afrikaners who used to have airports named after them. It's time we realised that the rest of the world has it right on this one.

> "Jan Smuts did not belong to any single state or nation. He fought for his own country, he fought for the whole world."
> — *Winston Churchill, speaking in 1952 after Smuts's death*

Irma Stern

b. 2 October 1894 – 23 August 1966

Visually expressive and inspiring Expressionist painter and ceramicist; creator of the most expensive art in South African history

ART IS, AS EVERYONE KNOWS, in the eye of the beholder. One guy's favourite artist is not necessarily the next guy's, and that's as it should be. But it's nice to think that there is, somewhere out there, an objective standard of "goodness" in art. Of something that qualifies, on an infallible and immutable scale, as aesthetically pleasing and inspirational to the soul and thus worthy of admiration.

Take the work of JMW Turner, the revered Romantic painter, for instance. Dramatic seascapes may not be your cup of tea, but it's simply not possible to stand in front of *The Fighting Temeraire Tugged To Her Last Berth To Be Broken Up, 1838* – on permanent display in the National Gallery in London, if you're interested – and not recognise the brilliance of what's in front of you. There's a good chance you'll draw breath sharply when you lay eyes on it; but if not, you'll at least agree that there is immense skill in its execution. It is, objectively, brilliant.

Then there's the award named for this fine painter, the Turner Prize, which year on year honours British artists for producing some of the most dumbfounding "artistic" creations imaginable. Such as, rather famously, a tiger shark pickled in formaldehyde by Damien Hirst, and an unmade bed by Tracey Emin. Really, an unmade bed. Which is, quite frankly, not art. It's an unmade bed. Or, if you prefer, bollocks.

The point here is that it's generally preferable that a country's preeminent artist leans more towards the JMW Turner side of things rather than the Tracey Emin side. And in Irma Stern South Africa is lucky to have produced an artist of the highest calibre whose work is instantly recognisable as wonderful to look at, whether you're an art critic with years of theoretical training or just some guy who happens to have wandered into an exhibition.

This being art, though, it wasn't always the case. Back in conservative 1920s and '30s Johannesburg, a young Stern was considered something of the Emin of her time, producing as she did graphic and colourful paintings that seemed to violate all the principles of traditional art. It didn't help either that she had a penchant for painting semi-naked black women. In the South Africa of today it's photographs of nude lesbian couples and pictures of the president's willy that get artists into trouble; back then it was a bared black breast that attracted the interest of the thought police. (Is it comforting to know that not too much has changed?) But Irma Stern was one of those unstoppable creative forces who lived a wonderful carefree life, laughing off criticism and simply powering on with her work, prolific artist that she was.

Born in the small town of Schweizer-Reneke, in what was then the Transvaal and is now North West, Stern would turn out to be anything but

Orchard, Ceres by Irma Stern, painted in 1933

> "She paints individuals separated by gulfs of culture and social status, by race and culture, and a vast disparity in achievement and opportunity. Yet the common humanity of all these types breaks through – not without a struggle which leaves its impress on the faces of her characters."
> – *Joseph Sachs, writing in his 1942 monograph of Stern's work*

a country bumpkin. After the South African War her wealthy German-Jewish parents returned with her to Germany, where she studied at the Weimar Academy, came under the influence of neo-Impressionism and then Expressionism and held her first exhibitions. Her work was well received in Europe and she won the Prix d'Honneur at the Bordeaux International Exhibition in 1927, so she wasn't short of confidence by the time she returned to South Africa permanently in the late 1920s. But the locals couldn't quite work out her extravagant European style. A *Sunday Times* review of an early exhibition was headlined "Irma Stern Chamber Of Horrors"; another one was titled "Art Of Miss Irma Stern – Ugliness As A Cult". The prevailing criticism was, in the words of Esmé Berman, "that she simply could not draw and [she] had no right to foist her graphic deformations on the public". It helped that there was family money because her sales weren't too flash at this point.

Stern travelled extensively throughout Europe and Africa, and made noteworthy trips to Zanzibar and the Congo that inspired some of her more renowned work. She painted portraits, still lifes and landscapes, using vivid colours and expressive brushstrokes, and often applying layers of thick paint with a palette knife so that the image almost leapt off the canvas. Her creative process was an art in itself: having conceptualised a painting well in advance, she would lock herself in her studio with a Do Not Disturb sign on the door, and chain smoke and drink vast quantities of coffee until it was finished, aiming to complete it in one sitting. When it was done it was done, with no tinkering required. She had a tremendous rate of production, setting up a hundred or more exhibitions in her lifetime, and she was in general a personality of tremendous energy and flamboyance. She often did her own framing, and many of her Zanzibar pieces were mounted using door frames taken from the island.

Unlike her work, Irma Stern herself was unfortunately not so lovely to look at. She was a lot of woman and she resembled, quite remarkably, Terry Jones of Monty Python fame. (Yes, a man, though specifically she looked like him as Brian Cohen's mother in *The Life Of Brian*.) But her paintings are astonishing in their way. Lively and vibrant and full of emotion, it is truly difficult to deny the ability on display. Emin she ain't. By the 1940s the tide of South African opinion had turned in Stern's favour, and she was established as a noteworthy painter and ceramicist.

Today her popularity has entered that rarefied atmosphere of art-scene insanity, with her paintings, as wonderful as they are, fetching obscene prices at local and international auctions. She first claimed the title of most expensive South African artwork in 1993, taking over from Gerard Sekoto when two of her paintings sold for R209,000 each. In today's terms that's a healthy R650,000 in terms of CPI inflation, or maybe R2 million if you compare it with stock market and property appreciation. And yet in 2011 she broke her own record for the umpteenth time when *Arabian Priest* was sold at auction in London for £3.044 million, now equivalent to around R40 million.* Other works have sold for more than R26 million, R21 million and R17 million.

Sure, this talk of pickled sharks, unmade beds and multimillion-rand paintings does tend to show up the more ridiculous side of the art world, but in Irma Stern we can at least say that we have a truly great South African artist. But maybe that's just our opinion.

---

* Hilariously the buyer, Qatar's Orientalist Museum, was then told they wouldn't be allowed to take delivery of the piece, as the South African Resource Heritage Agency initially refused to grant them a permanent export visa for the work.

Max Theiler

30 January 1899 – 11 August 1972

Doctor who developed the yellow-fever vaccine; winner of the Nobel Prize in Medicine; man responsible for the saving of millions of lives

THE 82-KILOMETRE-LONG PANAMA CANAL, which runs across the Isthmus of Panama and connects the Pacific and Atlantic oceans, was one of the largest and most troublesome engineering projects ever undertaken. A French-led effort began construction in 1881 under the guidance of the celebrated Ferdinand de Lesseps, but gave up after a decade's work. The French quitting is hardly a surprise, you might think, but De Lesseps was no pushover; he was the man behind the Suez Canal, which was twice as long and opened in 1869. Problem being that Panama was not northeastern Egypt: the terrain was trickier, there was inclement tropical weather and, worst of all, there was disease.

It is estimated that at least 20,000 canal labourers were killed by malaria and yellow fever during the French attempt, with many tens of thousands more incapacitated for long stretches. While malaria remains the plague of the modern world, it was yellow fever that was the deadliest of the two and the most problematic at the time. It derived its common name from the jaundice it often inflicts on sufferers, but its nastier symptoms are those that only a sickness borne of the tropical jungle can produce: in cases where it progressed to the toxic stage, victims would bleed from various orifices and often throw up bloodied vomit – hence the nickname *vomito negro*, "the black vomit". Of most concern to foreign workers was that epidemics of the disease were caused by their very arrival; local populations developed immunity over time but foreigners were virtually defenceless and were struck down in swathes. The canal would never be built without a solution to the yellow-fever problem.

It was only at the turn of the 20th century that the vectors, or delivery systems, of both malaria and yellow fever came to be recognised. Previously, doctors had believed infected humans simply passed them on to one another like flu, or that they spontaneously emerged from filth and garbage as "poisonous miasmas". Modern science eventually revealed that malaria is caused by a parasite and yellow fever by a virus, and that both are transmitted by the most annoying and, it just so happens, deadliest animal on the planet, the mosquito. (Specifically, malaria is carried by female *Anopheles* mosquitoes and yellow fever by female *Aedes* mosquitoes, which also carry dengue, Chikungunya and other tropical fevers. If ever the Lord's creations were intended for the Bug Zapper, it was these two little buggers.)

By 1904, the United States government, recognising the economic revolution that the Panama Canal could ignite for the country, had bought out the French and acquired the rights to continue construction. And so began the most expensive concentrated public-health campaign in history, to destroy resident mosquito populations throughout Panama and minimise the threats of disease. Through the use of house-by-house fumigation, the widespread introduction of fine-meshed window screens, and the eradication of mozzie breeding grounds, yellow fever was entirely eliminated from Panama by the end of 1905, and a relatively safe working environment created. ("Relatively" being the key word here, as a further 5,600 workers were to die, from disease and accidents, before the canal was completed in 1914. The total death count in the 33 years of construction was not far off 30,000.)

Today around 300 million tons of shipping passes through the Panama Canal each year, a staggering statistic that underscores the immense economic justification for its construction, a whole century after the fact. Given what was at stake, the enormous cost of the mosquito-eradication drive – in terms of both money and man power – was a necessary and viable course of action, but it would have all been so much easier had there just been a vaccine for yellow fever. After all,

"Once contracted, the virus incubates in the body for three to six days, followed by infection that can occur in one or two phases. The first, 'acute', phase usually causes fever, muscle pain with prominent backache, headache, shivers, loss of appetite, and nausea or vomiting. Most patients improve and their symptoms disappear after three to four days. However, 15 percent of patients enter a second, more toxic phase within 24 hours of the initial remission. High fever returns and several body systems are affected. The patient rapidly develops jaundice and complains of abdominal pain with vomiting. Bleeding can occur from the mouth, nose, eyes or stomach. Once this happens, blood appears in the vomit and faeces. Kidney function deteriorates. Half of the patients who enter the toxic phase die within ten to fourteen days, the rest recover without significant organ damage."

– Symptoms of yellow fever, as per the World Health Organization

this was a much-feared disease that had decimated populations across the world since the 16th century, with serious outbreaks occurring across North America and into Europe as well as in tropical climates where the disease felt more at home. It was only towards the middle of the 20th century that a South African by the name of Max Theiler almost single-handedly brought the scourge of yellow fever under control.

Born in Pretoria in 1899, at a time when Boers were fighting rooineks and the world still believed that yellow fever arose mysteriously from garbage dumps, Max was the son of the most famous veterinary surgeon South Africa has ever known, Sir Arnold Theiler. Arnold was Swiss, and no-one seems to know why he chose to move to the Transvaal in 1899, but move he did, and he brought with him a new field of expertise that was to bring South African farmers kicking and screaming into the 20th century. Veterinary science was a term that most of the Boers he first encountered would have struggled to pronounce, let alone understand, and there was much suspicion of his European-educated ways. But he slowly convinced them that feeding their horses gallons of linseed oil in the vain hope that it might protect them from horse sickness was pretty hopeless and that perhaps he could be of assistance. He founded the world-famous Onderstepoort Veterinary Research Institute, and his teams there performed pioneering work on such wonderful-sounding diseases – the likes you hear of regularly in Herman Charles Bosman stories – as *lamsiekte*, bluetongue, wireworm, East Coast Fever and rinderpest. The latter was particularly virulent, wiping out perhaps 90 percent of all the cattle in southern Africa in the 1890s and bringing with it widespread economic ruin. It came to Arnold Theiler to develop the vaccine that would save our cattle and our farmers, and eventually eradicate the disease in its entirety. In 2011, the Food and Agriculture Organization of the United Nations announced that rinderpest was the first animal disease, and second general disease after smallpox, to be entirely eliminated by man – a feat based on Theiler's work a century before. In a long and eventful career, which included losing his hand in a threshing machine in his twenties, he became renowned around the world and was hugely influential in South Africa, advising both Louis Botha and Jan Smuts.

The younger Theiler, by contrast, appears to have led a less event-filled and certainly less public life and, unlike his father, was never knighted. But, as it turns out, he had an even greater influence on world health, and went on to earn himself the Nobel Prize in Medicine for his efforts – the first Nobel awarded to a South African. While Max preferred human medicine to animal medicine, he chose to follow in his father's footsteps by specialising in tropical diseases, one of Arnold's interests. (Similarly, one of Arnold's daughters focused on zoology and became a world authority on ticks. The family dinner conversations must have been grand.)

On graduating from Rhodes University and then the University of Cape Town, he went abroad and studied at King's College London and the London School of Hygiene and Tropical Medicine. In 1922 he moved to Boston where he took a research position at Harvard University's School of Tropical Medicine, and if this is all getting a little tropically medicinal, at least we know where it's is going. Max had taken an interest in yellow fever in London already, but it was while working at the Rockefeller Foundation in New York that he eventually knuckled down to developing the vaccine.

The foundation's rather lofty ambition was "To promote the wellbeing of mankind throughout the world", and Theiler's efforts fulfilled them to a tee. Having dedicated more than a decade of his life to the disease – and having contracted it himself along the way – he presented the 17-D vaccine for yellow fever to the world in 1937. It was a live but weakened, or "attenuated", version of the virus that was easy to mass produce and would be manufactured in the hundreds of millions in the years to come. The modern yellow-fever vaccine that you would receive today if you were travelling to Tanzania, say, or South America is not much different to Theiler's original creation: a quick shot in the arm gives you – along with a possible case of mild flu-like symptoms – at least ten years of immunity against the disease, and possibly up to 35 years' protection. The disease itself remains incurable, and because of its prevalence in wild monkey populations in tropical jungles, and the easy transmission to humans entering these areas, it will likely always be around. But the vaccine has, in tandem with mosquito-eradication programmes, helped reduce the global effects of yellow fever, once one of the world's great epidemic diseases, to far less devastating levels. Today there are, according to the World Health Organization, an estimated 200,000 cases of yellow fever around the world per year, causing 30,000 deaths – the figures sound scary, but they put it way down the list of major diseases.

"The significance of Max Theiler's discovery must be considered to be very great from the practical point of view, as effective protection against yellow fever is one condition for the development of the tropical regions – an important problem in an overpopulated world."
– *Professor Hilding Bergstrand, Chair of the Nobel Committee, 1951*

Though it was of less concern in Panama at the turn of the 20th century, malaria is now the far greater killer. There are more than 200 million cases each year, causing up to a million fatalities, including a quarter of all child deaths in sub-Saharan Africa. In contrast to yellow fever, there is no vaccine, only treatments, many of which are cumbersome and increasingly ineffective to drug-resistant strains of the disease. But in August 2012 researchers at the University of Cape Town announced that they believed they had discovered a single-dose cure for malaria. There are still years to go before trials can be concluded, but the news appears really rather promising. Wouldn't it be something if we could add the men and women behind the cure for malaria to these pages in a future edition?

Charlize Theron

b. 7 August 1975

Oscar-wining superstar; superb actress; stunner;
overcomer of tragic circumstances; cool chick

IF, AS A RELATIVELY SMALL and culturally insignificant country, you could choose to lay claim to one Hollywood star of the current generation, it really is hard to think of anyone you'd rather take over Charlize Theron. Here is a woman who is undeniably talented, titanically gorgeous, smart, funny, likeable and just damn fantastic. Using the Academy Award for

Best Actress as a filter, she's competing with, maybe, Natalie Portman and Marion Cotillard for the honour. Which, let it be said, is not bad company. Simply put, it doesn't get much better than our Charlize, the girl from Benoni done good.

Just about the only vague complaint a South African might have of South Africa's most famous actress ever is the fact that she speaks, in private, with an American accent. But even this isn't an issue. Theron's first language is Afrikaans, and though she learnt English as she grew up, she did the majority of that learning and only became fluent in the United States, where she was taught by Americans. She may praat the taal when she's at home with her mom, but that American-English accent of hers is the only one she's ever really had. So that's cleared that up, then. With the result, we can now see, that she's basically faultless.

What is more, she's got a terrific, if traumatic, backstory. Theron was brought up on a plot outside Benoni. Her dad Charles was an alcoholic who had taken to abusing Theron's mother Gerda, and things came to a head one night when, during a drunken fight, Gerda Theron shot and killed him. As it was self-defence, no charges were laid. Charlize, who was in her room when it happened, was 15 years old at the time and for years she told interviewers that her father had died in a car accident.

Soon after, Theron moved to Milan to take up a modelling contract, but she was always clear about her aim to be a dancer: having studied ballet, that was her ultimate goal. "I saw modelling like waitressing – it was a way to pay for another career, and that career was dance," she said. But that, too, would end in disaster. Moving to New York to study further at the Joffery Ballet School, it became clear that her knees couldn't handle the strain. Short of money and living in a friend's basement, she realised her dancing days were over. "I went into a major depression. My mom came over from South Africa and said, 'Either you figure out what to do next or you come home, because you can sulk in South Africa.'"

And so, in the footsteps of many young dreamers, Theron booked a one-way flight to Hollywood. "When I arrived in California," she remembers, "I got in the cab and said, 'Take me to Hollywood.'" She was 19 and it was 1994.

And then came the hard yards: dispiriting auditions in which her heavily accented English played against her. As did her looks – after all, leggy blondes aren't in short supply in Hollywood. It was tough. But then fame famously came knocking when a bank teller refused to cash a cheque that her mother had sent to help pay the rent. Her ensuing outburst caught the eye of an agent waiting in line behind her, he gave her his card, and suddenly things started looking up.

Theron's first role was a beaut: an uncredited appearance in *Children Of The Corn III: Urban Harvest*. But then there was a speaking part in *2 Days In The Valley*, a decent enough film with a good cast. She played an assassin, looked great and got star billing – with a massive billboard on Sunset Strip to boot. She followed this with films starring Tom Hanks, Edward James Olmos and Michael Richards of *Seinfeld* fame.

Then, her breakthrough performance. Theron tested on no less than three occasions for a part in *The Devil's Advocate*, with Keanu Reeves and Al Pacino. Why three screen tests? They thought she was too pretty… As director Taylor Hackford explained, "She read and knocked me out, but was blonde and tall and sexy, so I wasn't sure she was right." "When he told me that," Theron retorted, "I went back in with no make-up and dirty hair. I fucking won this part fair and square."

It was a memorable role, to say the least – her character is, among other things, raped by the devil – and it set up Theron as a serious Hollywood star-in-the-making. Woody Allen wanted her in his next film (*Celebrity*), she started landing roles in big-budget flicks (*Mighty Joe Young*) and Oscar winners (*The Cider House Rules*), and she was suddenly on magazine covers everywhere – including *Playboy*, who managed to dig up some pre-fame nude photos of her, a sure sign of Hollywood success. By 2003 she was a regular A-lister, with the remake

> "If they ever do my life story, whoever plays me needs lots of hair colour and high heels."
>
> – *Charlize Theron*

of *The Italian Job* having recently dominated the entertainment news, but she hadn't yet delivered a movie that was really special. Then, bang – along came *Monster*.

Having seen Theron's darker side in *The Devil's Advocate*, director Patty Jenkins wrote a part with her in mind – the role of Aileen Wuornos, a bottom-rung sex-worker-turned-serial-killer. And what a role it was. Wuornos's (true) story is as depressing as it gets: she was sexually abused as a child, she sold sex for cigarettes at age 11, and she ended up murdering seven men, for which she was executed by lethal injection in 2002. Heavy doesn't begin to describe it. And yet Theron – the gorgeous, long-legged ex-model, a star of comedies and action flicks – transformed herself into a haggard lesbian serial-killer and was simply spellbinding. It was one of the great movie performances of recent years.

"There's the uncanny sensation that Theron has forgotten the camera and the script and is directly channeling her ideas about Aileen Wuornos. She has made herself the instrument of this character," raved veteran movie buff Robert Ebert.

And while we all know that she won an Academy Award for her efforts – the first South African to get an acting Oscar – what so many people don't know about *Monster*, was that Theron also produced it. Nobody else wanted to stump up the cash. Not a bad career move.

These days Theron is made, a bankable Oscar-winning star verging on Hollywood royalty – but, notably, without the sex tapes and the DUI arrests and sideshow scandal. Just one, long relationship with actor Stuart Townsend, now finished, and one adopted baby boy. Nothing too shocking in all of that. She admits that she no longer needs to work if she doesn't want to, so she gets to pick and choose her movies these days – which means less chance of duds like *Reindeer Games* and *Sweet November*. Instead there's been another Oscar nomination (*North Country*), two Golden Globe nominations (*North Country, Young Adult*), and some pretty spectacular box-office successes (*Hancock, Prometheus, Snow White And The Huntsman*).

The end result is a brilliant career with so much potential for more brilliance to come. Man, our girl from Benoni has done us proud.

Desmond Tutu

b. 7 October 1931

Man of the cloth; persistent thorn in the side of apartheid goons; persistent thorn in the side of goons in general; Nobel Prize winner; chair of the TRC; South Africa's moral conscience

DESMOND TUTU ALWAYS SAID that his activities in opposing apartheid were not political, but religious. Apartheid was not God's will and therefore it would fail. That was his persistent message, and it was a brilliant one, suffused always with an incredible sense of forgiveness.

Tutu originally didn't want to be a priest. His first choice, doctor, was beyond financial reach. And the second, teacher (like his father), also wouldn't fly in the end. He gave it a bash, but in 1953 the government passed the Bantu Education Act, a vile crime against the black people of this country the consequences of which we are still far from fixing. (And let it be said that recent efforts have been shoddy, to say the least.) As a result, Tutu felt unable to continue in teaching.

And so off he went to the church because it occurred to him that "the profession of priest could be a good way of serving my people". In 1960, at the age of 29, he was ordained as an Anglican priest in Rosettenville, the same suburb of Johannesburg in which the English cleric Trevor Huddlestone worked. Huddlestone – who would gain fame for his protests against the destruction of Sophiatown and for giving Hugh Masekela his first trumpet, among other things – was a rare white man who treated working-class blacks as equals. His example inspired Tutu as a boy, and later as a man of the cloth.

In the next fifteen years, as the situation in South Africa declined, Tutu spent time in London, earning an MA in Theology; back in South Africa, where he was made chaplain of the University of Fort Hare, that hotbed of revolutionary thought; in Lesotho as a lecturer; then once more in London as vice-director of the Theological Education Fund. In 1975 he returned to South Africa as the first black dean of Johannesburg – and it was in 1976 that the chaos of the Soweto Uprising horrified and motivated him. Now being a man of some standing, his public criticisms began to sting, and they were reaching a wider and whiter audience.

In 1978 he became the first black Secretary General of the South African Council of Churches, and his criticism of apartheid intensified. Had he been a mere ANC activist, he could have been dealt with accordingly – with a beating or a banning or worse if he'd persisted. But he wasn't. He was a man of God, supposedly the same God of the apartheid jackboots, and a man of increasing international standing. So the government had to grin and bear it, especially given the religious terms in which he couched his criticism. One can only imagine to what wonderful extents it must have irritated the Nats.

And, gosh, could he, as one biography has it, rabble rouse for peace. It's easy to forget, in his declining years, what an outstanding orator Tutu used to be; how he used to fire up the fury of oppressed people and then direct that fury in a cause for peace and nonviolence.

It's been noted in other entries already that arguably the closest this country came to all-out race war was on the death of Chris Hani in 1993. But it was Tutu, addressing 120,000 mourners at Hani's funeral, who managed to get a largely black crowd to chant over and over again, "We will be free! All of us! Black and white together!" And on he went: "We are the rainbow people of God! We are unstoppable! Nobody can stop us on our march to victory! No-one, no guns, nothing! Nothing will stop us, for we are moving to freedom! We are moving to freedom and nobody can stop us! For God is on our side!"

It was inspiring stuff where another kind of rouser might have precipitated disaster. And Tutu was more than a man of the downtrodden. He had the gift of being able to engage with any audience he interacted with, be it the poor and distressed attendees at Hani's funeral or privileged white school children in a church sermon or world leaders in the corridors of power.

In 1984, he was awarded the Nobel Peace Prize, the second of our four laureates, and the bridge between Luthuli and Mandela/De Klerk. How did Tutu celebrate? Did he punch the air? Did he laugh or cry? According to one biography, he sat down and quietly read Psalm 139: "For there is not a word on my tongue, But behold, O Lord, You know it altogether."

Tutu was elected Archbishop of Cape Town in 1986. Once again, the infuriation this must have caused PW Botha and co is marvellous

"The contribution [Tutu] has made, and is still making, represents a hope for the future, for the country's white minority as well as the black majority. Desmond Tutu is an exponent of the only form for conflict solving which is worthy of civilised nations."

– Nobel Peace Prize presentation speech, made by Egil Aarvik, 1984

to imagine. And finally, when it came, Tutu naturally welcomed the unbanning of the ANC and the eventual election of another moral icon, Nelson Mandela, as the country's first legitimate president. Decades of his work had been validated – but of course he was not done.

Mandela ended up asking Tutu to chair the Truth and Reconciliation Commission (TRC), a brutally trying and heartbreaking affair in which, in the main, white apartheid functionaries cowardly tried to save their asses without admitting too much, bar the odd notable exception, and black victims poured out their pain and grief at what they had suffered. Tutu was "appalled at the evil we have uncovered". It reduced him to tears on occasions, and no doubt it required a man of such towering faith to pull it off without being reduced to a gibbering wreck. In the end the TRC was a contentious and somewhat controversial undertaking; there are many who believe it didn't go far enough. But its importance cannot be underestimated, and Tutu was one of the few people, perhaps the only one, with the moral authority to shepherd the process.

But, ye gods, Tutu wasn't done, because his faith drives him to keep on going, to keep on calling out injustice at home or abroad, and to use his international standing to embarrass the powerful. And so, in no particular order, he has given the ANC hell for corruption and

> "To forgive is not just to be altruistic. It is the best form of self-interest."
> — *Desmond Tutu*

incompetence. He has lambasted Jacob Zuma as an embarrassment with "moral failings". He has infuriated Thabo Mbeki and the BEE elite that gets ever richer. ("What is black empowerment when it seems to benefit not the vast majority but an elite that tends to be recycled?")

But he hadn't simply morphed into Tony Leon; indeed, as recently as 2011 Tutu was still advocating for a wealth tax for white South Africans. "You all benefited from apartheid. Your children went to fancy schools, you lived in posh suburbs," he told white people, a great many of whom didn't enjoy being reminded of the past. At the same time he appealed to Zuma's cabinet all to sell their extravagant ministerial cars.

Tutu has hounded George Bush and Tony Blair for their roles in the Iraq War; in 2012 he sneakily waited until the last minute to withdraw from the Discovery Invest Leadership Summit in Sandton in protest at Blair's participation. He has called for boycotts of the Beijing Olympics in support of the Tibetan cause. He has eviscerated African leaders for their silence on Mugabe's depredations in Zimbabwe. "What more has to happen before we who are leaders, religious and political, of our mother Africa are moved to cry out 'Enough is enough?'" he said, before going on to call Mugabe "a cartoon figure of an archetypal African dictator".

He has hammered Israeli treatment of people in Gaza. He has railed against the Anglican church for its obsession with homosexuality. "God is weeping," he said, adding that the Church was "quite rightly" seen as irrelevant on the issue of poverty.

He just never stops. Or never used to. But now, at the age of 81, he has, much like Mandela, "withdrawn from public life". And, you know, doesn't it seem quiet? Not in a good way, that is. An unfailingly determined voice has softened. And though apartheid is gone, the causes remain. Will we ever again have as authoritative a moral conscience as the Arch? Given our current state of affairs, we can only hope so.

Pieter-Dirk Uys

b. 28 September 1945

Satirist; actor; author; playwright; giant of South African theatre; tireless activist; the man (or woman) most likely to call you "skattie"

SATIRE IS HARD. That's why, when people get it right, it goes down in legend; why those behind the explosion of British satire in the early 1960s went on to become global stars, and shows such as *That Was The Week That Was* and *Beyond The Fringe* became so well known. Names such as Richard Ingrams, Christopher Booker, Peter Cook, David Frost and Dudley Moore were made not in comedy, but in satire – on radio, on screen and in print. *Private Eye*, founded by Ingrams and Booker, is still, after all these years, a needle in the side of the famous and the influential. Later, *Monty Python's Flying Circus* and Rowan Atkinson's *Not The Nine O'Clock News* helped to evolve modern satire. Contemporary American shows that thrive on it include some of the most successful in television history: *The Simpsons*, *South Park*, *The Daily Show*.

Existing on the other end of the humour scale from slapstick and toilet humour, satire requires a far cleverer and more nuanced approach – a reverse-engineering process that subtly, or sometimes not so subtly, undercuts the big-headed or the wrong. Speaking truth to power is one thing, but making people laugh at the powerful is in itself a hugely powerful thing. And while it was conservative and pompous politicians who felt the wrath of the British satire boom, here in South Africa in the 1980s a matronly lady by the name of Evita Bezuidenhout set about apartheid's apparatchiks and the *verkrampte* citizens who supported it.

Evita Bezuidenhout is, of course, Pieter-Dirk Uys's most famous creation – based, it won't surprise anyone to know, on Dame Edna Everage, and like Dame Edna, a creation that has taken on a life of her own. As Evita's website claims, "Her ten years as the South African Ambassador in the Independent Black Homeland Republic of Bapetikosweti left an indelible mark on the blueprint of change, and today her recipe for bobotie is internationally regarded as the basis for reconciliation." In 2000 Evita even received the Living Legacy Award from The Women's International Center in San Diego; other (real) recipients include Mother Teresa, Hillary Clinton and Maya Angelou.

But there is more to Uys than Evita. The sheer quantity of what he has done is staggering. He's written twenty-odd plays, all of them timely and clever; he's written novels and cookbooks and memoirs, often on behalf of Evita or her troubled sister Bambi Kellerman; he's written TV shows and movies. And of course he acts and directs and produces and even makes Evita's dresses. Just the names of his work are inspirational: *You ANC Nothing Yet, Live From Boerassic Park, Never Too Naked, Macbeki,*

Elections And Erections, Just A Small Prick! He's even persuaded the likes of Nelson Mandela and Thabo Mbeki that going on national TV to be interviewed by Evita was a good idea. And, of course, Mandela and Mbeki, along with PW and Pik Botha, BJ Vorster, Piet Koornhof, Winnie Mandela, Jacob Zuma and friends, have felt the sting of his satire.

Throughout his career he has had South Africans "laughing at their own prejudices", as his honorary degree citation from Wits has it, and he has been widely acclaimed in many quarters as a result. Which all sounds jolly exciting and rather wonderful. And it is; it's always nice to admire a successful multitalented artist. But we shouldn't forget that in the deeply un-nice context of apartheid, what Uys was doing was actually incredibly brave. He naturally attracted the attentions of the powers that were, and a lot of what he wrote in the 1970s was banned from being performed. "The truth is that the censor board became my publicity department and helped make me known," he would later explain.

Evita, in fact, emerged in the late 1970s in a weekly column Uys was writing for the *Sunday Express* as a rather cunning way to sidestep the censors. She was his insider gossip from whose mouth scandalous "rumours/facts" of state impropriety "dripped like warm honey" – and those in power could never quite get their head around her. It was three years before she emerged in the flesh in 1982 in Uys's one-man show *Adapt Or Dye*, from where she would take on a life of her own.

"We now accept the cross-dressing performer with ease in our society but when Uys begun to construct his performance identity he did so in a very different country at a very different time; breaking new and controversial ground," says the Wits citation. "In these terms his theatrical creations were avant-garde and exceptional."

And it's true. An Afrikaner man dressing up as a woman and ridiculing the Nats was hugely controversial – almost unbelievable. Uys even had to hide his homosexuality lest it became something his enemies might use against him.

Like all true heroes of the struggle, Uys's struggle continues. He was mortified by the disastrous Aids policies of the Mbeki administration, and now takes a roadshow to schools across the country to talk to kids about HIV and sex on their terms. "You can't talk about 'the birds and the bees'," he explained when he started. "How does a bird fuck a bee? Get to the point and speak a language that children understand."

Whether he's on tour enlightening children or making people laugh or doing his thing at Evita se Perron in Darling, he just never seems to stop. Uys – along with Evita – is timeless and always on the money, and he has opinions on everything. As his website explains, "He is delighted to still have a government that on a daily basis writes his best material!" How, for example, should South Africans react to *The Spear* painting shambles? "Every South African should walk around with a large banana hanging out of their pants."

Of course they should.

Officially a "Living Treasure", according to the estimations of the Human Sciences Research Council, Pieter-Dirk Uys is without doubt our skattie-in-chief. Doesn't it say something about this country we call home that it takes a cross-dressing koeksister-eating sex-educating satirist to make sense of it all?

PIETER-DIRK UYS...

On Afrikaners:

"All an Afrikaner man has to do to drive his peers crazy is put on a dress."

On the Battle of Blood River:

"It wasn't a battle. That was Nationalist propaganda. It was really a braaivleis."

On politicians:

"Politicians are like monkeys: the higher they climb the pole of ambition, the more of their arses you can see."

On Zuma:

"In spite of every possible hurdle, he has hijacked the venerable old party from under the noses of the ancient regime, and turned it into his own bridal shower."

On Evita:

(As Evita) "I am the most famous white woman in South Africa who comes from a past that no-one remembers and goes into a future that no-one will forget."

(As Evita) "If Trevor Manuel can act like a black man and think like a white, I can act like a woman and think like a man."

(As Uys) "She always managed to tango where angels fear to tread."

On masturbation:

"If wanking really made boys blind, I would've had a white stick at 25!"

On PW Botha:

"After 26 years of impersonating him, I can truly say: yes, he was my bread and Botha."

On political intercourse:

"Hypocrisy is the Vaseline of political intercourse."

On South Africa:

"It is the most beautiful country in the world and we who live in it are without doubt the craziest, most absurd, most generous and most perplexing people ever plonked together on a rainbow foefie slide to the future."

Bibliography

BOOKS: *Apprenticeship Of A Mahatma: A Biography Of MK Gandhi 1869-1914 by Fatima Meer* (Mahatma Gandhi Institute, 1994) • *The Boer War* by Thomas Pakenham (Avon, 1992) • *Brewer Dictionary Of Phrase And Fable* (Chambers, 2007) • *Bridled Ambition: Why Countries Constrain Their Nuclear Capabilities* by Mitchell Reiss (Woodrow Wilson Centre Press, 1995) • *Challenging Beliefs: Memoirs Of A Career* by Tim Noakes and Michael Vlismas (Zebra Press, 2012) • *Commando* by Deneys Reitz (Faber & Faber, 1943) • *Defining Moments* by Marius Barnard (Zebra Press, 2011) • *Diamonds, Gold And War* by Martin Meredith (Jonathan Ball Publishers, 2007) • *Disgrace* by JM Coetzee (Secker & Warburg, 1999) • *Gandhi: The Man, His People, And The Empire* by Rajmohan Gandhi (University of California Press, 2008) • *Great Lives: A Century In Obituaries* from The Times (Times Books, 2007) • *Great South African Inventions* by Mike Bruton (Cambridge University Press, 2010) • *The Grove: Spanning Three Centuries* by Alixe Lowenherz (The Grove Primary School, 2012) • *How South Africa Built Six Atom Bombs: And Then Abandoned Its Nuclear Weapons Program* by Al J Venter (Ashanti Publishing, 2008) • *Jan Smuts: Man Of Courage And Vision* by Antony Lentin (Jonathan Ball Publishers, 2010) • *Just My Type: A Book About Fonts* by Simon Garfield (Profile Books, 2010) • *Let My People Go* by Albert Luthuli (Tafelberg Publishers, 2006) • *Life And Soul* by Karina Turok (Double Storey Books, 2006) • *Madiba's Boys: The Stories Of Lucas Radebe And Mark Fish* by Graeme Friedman (New Africa Books, 2001) • *The Midnight Sky: Familiar Notes On The Stars And Planets* by Edwin Dunkin (The Religious Tract Society, c.1869) • *New History Of South Africa* by Hermann Giliomee and Bernard Mbenga (Tafelberg, 2008) • *Painting In South Africa* by Esmé Berman (Southern Book Publishers, 1993) • *Part Of My Soul Went With Him* by Winnie Mandela (WW Norton And Co, 1985) • *Peaceable Warrior* by Maureen Rall (Sol Plaatje Educational Trust, 2003) • *The Penguin Dictionary Of South African Quotations* by Jennifer Crwys-Williams (Penguin Books, 2008) • *The Proteas: 20 Years, 20 Landmark Matches* by Neil Manthorp (Mercury, 2011) • *The Scramble For Africa* by Thomas Pakenham (Avon, 1992) • *The Selected: The 25 Greatest South African Cricketers Of All Time* by Michael Owen-Smith and Neil Manthorp (Don Nelson, 2007) • *Sol Plaatje: Selected Writings* edited by Brian Willan (Witwatersrand University Press, 2001) • *Sol Plaatje: South African Nationalist, 1876-1932* by Brian Willan (University of California Press, 1984) • *South Africa's Brave New World* by RW Johnson (Penguin Books, 2010) • *Starwatching: A Southern Hemisphere Guide To The Galaxy* by Anthony Fairall (Struik Publishers, 2002) • *Steve Biko* by Lindy Wilson (Jacana Media, 2011) • *The Story of Sol T. Plaatje* by Sabata-mpho Mokae (Sol Plaatje Educational Trust, 2010) • *They Came To South Africa* by Fay Jaff (online edition available at archive.org) • *The Washing Of The Spears* by Donald R Morris (Simon and Schuster, 1965) • *Winston Churchill: The Making Of A Hero In The South African War* by Eric Bolsman (Galago, 2008) • *Zulu Wilderness: Shadow And Soul* by Ian Player (David Philip Publishers, 1997)

INTERVIEWS: Johnny Clegg • Waddy Jones • Ryan Sandes • Jordy Smith

FILM AND AUDIO: *Searching For Sugar Man*, written and directed by Malik Bendjelloul (Red Box Films, Passion Pictures and The Documentary Company, 2012) • Much of the Anglo-Zulu War information was gleaned from the collected Zulu oral history as recounted by David Rattray. A tiny fraction of this is saved for posterity and is available for sale as a recording called *The Day Of The Dead Moon*, written and narrated by David Rattray.

MAGAZINES: *Archimedes*, Volume 44, No 2, July 2002, published by the Foundation For Education, Science And Technology • *The Diocesan College Magazine*, Vol LXXIV, No 4, December 1990; Vol LXXVI, No 1, March 1992; Vol LXXVI, No 4, December 1992 • *Rolling Stone* South Africa, Issue 4, March 2012 • *The Spectator*, 28 July 2012

PAPERS, ARTICLES AND TALKS: "Beyond *Black and White*: Rethinking Irma Stern" by Claudia Braude, Helen Suzman Foundation, 2011 • "Charles Darwin at the Cape: notes on his sociological observations" by Wilmot James, South African Journal of Science 105, November/December 2009 • "Evil Under The Sun: The Death Of Steve Biko" by Sydney Kentridge, Steve Biko Memorial Lecture, 2011, from www.uct.ac.za • Institute For Science And International Security (ISIS) Reports (August 1999) • "Jan Smuts, brilliant scholar and statesman, should not be cast from history" by Beverley Roos-Muller, Cape Times, 2 August 2012 • "The Mosquito Of High Crimes: The campaign against yellow fever during the American construction of the Panama Canal, 1904-1905" by Alexandra H Freeman, Historia Medicinae, Volume 2, Issue 1, E19 • "Wilding the farm or farming the wild? The evolution of scientific game ranching in South Africa from the 1960s to the present" by Jane Carruthers, Department of History, UNISA, from www.sawma.co.za, 2008 • "South Africa's Nuclear Weaponization Efforts: Success on a Small-Scale" by David Albright and Corey Hinderstein (13 September 2001) • "South Africa's Secret Nuclear Weapons" by David Albright (1 May 1994)

WEBSITES: archiver.rootsweb.ancestry.com • basildoliveira.com • designmuseum.org • heritage. thetimes.co.za • in.finance.yahoo.com • isis-online.org • jordysmith.com • larecord.com • ocp.hul. harvard.edu • memeburn.com • pdu.co.za • radiology.rsna.org • ryansandes.com • sportsillustrated. cnn.com • sports.yahoo.com • www.4deserts.com • www.adobe.com • www.africaninspace.com • www.airspacemag.com • www.anc.org.za • www.aspworldtour.com • www.books.google.com • www.britannica.com • www.citizen.co.za • www.citypress.co.za • www.cnn.com • www.cricinfo.com • www.dieantwoord.com • www.dwaf.gov.za • www.egs.edu • www.espnscrum.com • www.etana. co.za • www.evita.co.za • www.ewn.co.za • www.fao.org • www.fastcodesign.com • www.financialmail. co.za • www.forbes.com • www.formula1.com • www.globalsecurity.org • www.guardian.co.uk • www.herschel.org.za • www.independent.co.uk • www.info.gov.za • www.internetnews.com • www. iol.co.za • www.irmastern.co.za • www.londolozi.com • www.markshuttleworth.com • www.mg.co.za • www.music.org.za • www.news24.com • www.newstatesman.com • www.nobelprize.org • www.nytimes. com • www.oneill.com • www.politicsweb.co.za • www.raf.mod.uk • www.rock.co.za • www.roux.co.za • www.sahistory.org.za • www.savingrhinos.org • www.shmoop.com • www.shuttleworthfoundation.org • www.ska.ac.za • www.smh.com.au • www.spacex.com • www.spectator.co.uk • www.telegraph.co.uk • www.thedailymaverick.co.za • www.time.com • www.timeslive.co.za • www.tolstoyfarm.com • www. uct.ac.za • www.warbirdforum.com • www.watkykjy.co.za • www.who.int • www.whoswhosa.co.za • www.wikipedia.com • www.winstonchurchill.org • www.wits.ac.za • www.youtube.com • www.zulu.org.za